LIMP FORWARD

LIMP
FORWARD

A Memoir of Disability, Perseverance, and Success

LIBO  MEYERS

LIONCREST
PUBLISHING

LIMP FORWARD

A Memoir of Disability, Perseverance, and Success

FIRST EDITION

ISBN 978-1-5445-2853-3 Hardcover
      978-1-5445-2852-6 Paperback
      978-1-5445-2851-9 Ebook
      978-1-5445-4297-3 Audiobook

To those who are underprivileged and invisible,
yet still giving everything to reach their full potential,
with dreams and goals.

To those who have been wronged and undervalued,
yet still chasing relentlessly for what is right
and fair, with faith and confidence.

To those who feel desperate and hopeless, yet still fighting
against all the odds with even a slim chance of
winning, with courage and perseverance.

To those who are fighters and dreamers, believing
someday you may reach the impossible.

May this book give you the strength and inspiration
to limp forward during your darkest moments.

Love and Strength,
Libo Cao Meyers

CONTENTS

INTRODUCTION

On my desk beside me as I write this book are two items: a ten-year anniversary award from Apple, and my branch of the family book that holds the last five hundred years of the names of Cao ancestors. Those two items define where I am professionally at present and where I came from personally, rooted hundreds of years ago.

The Apple award reads:

Your 10-year award is made from the same 6000 series aluminum that we use to make our products. Remnants from the production process are collected and reformulated to create a 100 percent recycled, custom alloy. The alloy is cast into long ingots, then each ingot is sliced into blocks that are machined to finished size. The surface is fine blasted and the edges are diamond-cut. The block is then anodized to seal the finish and create a protective layer. Finally, a stainless steel Apple logo is set into the center.

This special metal block reminds me of my current professional mission —to build the most excellent products that enrich people's lives, in one of the best companies in the technology world. The company culture of innovation, thinking differently, taking risks, and executing with determination has influenced me deeply and aligns with my personal values.

But this book is not about my career or technology, and it doesn't contain any stories about Apple. Those stories are not *mine* to tell. This legendary company headquartered in Silicon Valley is the platform I choose to work for. It's a place where I have the privilege to work with many brilliant people who are also obsessed with details, seeking perfection, pushing limits, and proudly shipping products to people's hands to bring joy to their lives. I remind myself daily to deserve and add value to it.

The cover of the Cao family book proudly displays the emblem for our branch, which includes dragons and symbols for balance, harmony, and the fierce spirit. That's used as the icon for my maiden name, Cao, on the front cover of this book. That book is not just "another book," and that emblem is not just for aesthetics. I have fought for a lot of things in my life, and I've done so with the values reflected in that emblem. It is a way of being, a reminder that during challenging times in our lives, we can draw strength from our roots, from the faith and values that have sustained generations before us.

The first page of the Cao family book reads as follows:

Ancestors to human beings are like water has its source, and wood has its origin.

Since the Cao family surname was given, there were two ancestry trees. One was given to ancient Chinese states in Xia Dynasty, who started the ancestry tree for all Miao descendants. The second was given to everyone in a country started by Cao, (Shu) ZhenDuo.[1]

The first ancestor of our tree branch, Zhijia Cao, was the 71st generation of the Cao family. During the JiaJing period of the Ming Dynasty (1522–1566), he moved to 18 miles southwest of Liangbao Temple and started a village called the Cao Village. His descendants have been living there since then. Our family ancestry book has recorded the last 20 generations for nearly 500 years (from 71st generation to 91st generation). Last revision on March 26, 2016.[2]

The book I got only contains my dad's branch of ancestors. He is the eighty-sixth generation of the Cao family, and I am the eighty-seventh generation. Sometimes I read the names in the book, run my fingers across the letters, and think about how they lived their lives in the last five hundred years. Many people left Cao village, including Dad, yet they kept writing back to the village to ensure their names and their descendants' names were recorded in the family book. This book reminds me of my roots and who I really am.

Who *am* I though? For the first thirty years of my life, I never asked myself that question. I was born in 1976, the year of the dragon. I've got fire in me, and that fire burns me to persevere in chasing bright lights in my life.

---

[1] Cao, (Shu) ZhenDuo (曹叔振铎 ?–?) was the sixth son of King "Wen of Zhou" (周文王), who reigned from about 1041 BC to 1016 BC, and the second brother of King "Wu of Zhou" (周武王).

[2] Translated into English here from ancient Chinese language.

Where is that perseverance coming from? I didn't know for a long time; I just knew that I had it, and with that, nothing could beat me in life. Still, I kept looking for answers. Dad told me that I got it from my blood, which comes with that unyielding nature. But I think it's also through the heritage, the stories I have been told, and what I've learned and observed from my parents. Their perseverance is clear—but where does *that* come from? I believe the answer is *previous generations of stories and the characters of our ancestors*. If I look back to Chinese mythologies, there are stories passed down to all generations of Chinese that reveal a perseverance and unyielding nature that is built in us.

"The Foolish Old Man Removes the Mountains" (愚公移山) is a well-known fable from Chinese mythology about the virtues of perseverance and willpower. In it, a ninety-year-old man is annoyed by the obstruction caused by the mountains. As a remedy, he seeks to dig through the mountains with hoes and baskets, one round trip at a time. The foolish old man believes that even though he may not finish this task in his lifetime, through the hard work of himself, his children, and their children—and so on through the many generations—someday the mountains will be removed if he perseveres.

"Jingwei Fills the Sea" (精卫填海) tells a story of a girl who drowns in the sea and is resurrected into a bird. She is determined to fill up the sea so no one else suffers the same fate. To do this, she continuously carries a pebble or twig in her mouth and drops it into the sea, one at a time. The sea scoffs at her, saying that she won't be able to fill it up even in a million years. She retorts that she will spend ten million years, even one hundred million years...whatever it takes to fill up the sea so that others will not have to perish as she did.

Those are just two stories in Chinese mythology that are passed down from thousands of years ago. Leaving the plot aside, the core of the stories is clear: resistance and perseverance. The stories from my parents showed me *their* resistance and perseverance. My mom fought for her right to education relentlessly—starting at eleven and finishing at forty-five with her college degree and continued education—regardless of the hardships she faced along the way, including poverty and, at times, near starvation. For my Dad, ever since he was a young boy, he actively pursued opportunities for personal growth and development, even in the face of wars, famine, and political turmoil. He remained resolute in his quest for a better life, continuously striving to create a more prosperous environment for future generations to thrive in. My best friend growing up, Dongmei, also embodied these qualities. Before she passed away at age eleven from a lung disease and complications of poverty, she still smiled and said, "As long as I can keep breathing, I can keep writing."

As written in the *Tao Te Ching*, an ancient Chinese classic text from around 400 BC, "Heaven and the Earth are not benevolent; they see all creatures as mere straw dogs." (天地不仁，以万物为刍狗) This means that the universe itself is not benevolent, treating everything equally. To survive, you must rely on yourself, not others.

Looking back on my life, that resistance and perseverance were shown in every step of my own. I believe that I can lose, but I can't give in. I've got a stubborn spirit of unyielding. I fight the fight I believe in, and I keep limping forward on the road I've chosen to be on, no matter how many bruises and scars I am left with. When I am told "no," I make my own "yes."

No, you won't be admitted to college or study the major you want. Those are for "complete" talents, and you are disabled with polio.

So I went to college and completed a four-year degree in three years, aiming for more advanced education.

No, you can't go abroad due to your disability. You need to be taken care of and stay where you belong.

So I went to the other side of the globe, a totally different country, limping forward to stand on my own.

No, you can't possibly complete a PhD in one major and a master's degree in a totally different area! Nobody has ever done that, and you will fail in both.

So I pursued a PhD in chemometrics and a master's degree in computer science, completing both in three and a half years.

No, you can't participate in sports or be an athlete, because of your polio leg!

So I completed a one-hundred-mile bike ride, racing against 50 mph wind for eleven and a half hours with the strength of one leg.

No, you can't find your dream man to marry. You need to lower your expectations and settle for what you can get.

So I developed a scientific approach with machine-learning models for dating, found the man of my dreams after the eighty-second attempt, and married him... without lowering any of my expectations.

No, you can't excel in Silicon Valley. It's a man's world.

So I became a high-tech executive at Apple, and I kept learning, growing, and leaping forward to my next set of goals...

The list goes on.

I heard from people what I *couldn't* do, I limped forward and did all those things anyway, and I am not done yet. Those Nos and Can'ts may come from people who don't believe in us—due to discrimination and/ or biases—but they can also come from people who love and care for us... those who want to protect us from the cruel world. They want to warn us about the hard roads we are about to choose.

However, what really matters is how *you* want to live *your* life and deal with any consequences that come with those risky attempts. I choose to not select the easy routes. I choose to leap forward in a direction that allows me to control all my own destiny. I use all my strength to remove any obstacles in my way and keep going.

The Cao family history showed resilience over five hundred years. The high-tech award reminds me of over a decade of my own resilience. Looking back on all the lonely days and nights of fighting for something—for small progress or a big mission, even if others can't see it—I can see that those moments are when resilience was forged.

In this book, I want to *tell you stories* of that resilience. Stories of my own, of my parents, and of my ancestors. I want to take you on a journey with me. We will travel in time, from several thousand years ago to modern times. We will travel to places across the globe, from a frigid forest tent in the northernmost point of China to a sunny boardroom in Silicon Valley, California. We will travel through different emotions: fear and bravery; sadness and joy; remorse and love; despair and pride.

I want to *bring different perspectives* that may impact how you see or understand this world, as many other people's stories have changed mine. Our histories undoubtedly look different, as do our futures. But once we have walked this stretch of path together, my hope is that those memories and experiences can offer you the different perspectives you need to feel relieved, get unstuck, and build the courage to keep moving again. If you ever feel like you are limping through life, you are not alone.

I also hope to *build communication bridges* through my points of view. For some bridges, I can only stand on one side with my own identities: Asian; disabled; woman; wife; high-tech professional… For other bridges, I belong to both sides: Chinese and American; mother and daughter; ancient and modern; poor and wealthy; defeated and successful… Through my own identities and the diverse life I've lived, I hope to remove some discrimination and biases in this world. You should see in me—like you may see in others—that we are all the same beings, grappling with human nature's complexities. The more we explore those complexities, the more we can see each other for who we really are.

Now if you are ready, let's start my story from the very beginning.

1.

POLIO
AND CHILDHOOD
(1976–1983)

Though with the history and faith of your ancestors
pulsing in your veins, sometimes you'll still
feel alone in this life. We all do.

Polio made me feel alone and different from everyone around me.
It brought so much pain, agony, frustration, and
all those negative feelings that made me
forget to cherish what I do have.

Life will throw challenges your way, just like mine.

When that happens, you might feel alone, invisible,
or any other emotions that can drain your soul.
In those dark moments, remember the power within you
and the support around you.

Those challenges you are facing are merely a part of your story.
They do not control the whole thing.
You can change your own story, just like those who came
before you, and just like those who will come after.

The pen is in your hands.

1.1. THE FEVER THAT CHANGED EVERYTHING
(JULY 1977)

"Libo caught polio. Come immediately!"

When I was eleven months old, my parents received this terrifying telegram from the "third grandma" who was taking care of me at that time. With a high fever, I was initially paralyzed from the neck down. Nobody knew why, and my parents were over a thousand miles away.

I was born at the end of China's Cultural Revolution, in August 1976. The preceding decade had brought poverty and hunger, political instability, and a lack of educational and economic opportunities. As a newborn, I traveled everywhere with my parents, who were among the fortunate few with secure government jobs. Dad majored in geological survey and mapping technology at Wuhan University, working as a technical lead for the survey team, and Mom was an apprentice to the engineers at that time. They explored deep within the forested mountains—in the northernmost province in China—to make the first survey maps and look for new rare-metal mines. After my birth, the three of us lived in a wind-battered tent—heated by a small stove—but at least we were safe from the political unrest and violence. My parents had to leave me in the tent while they both worked long hours. During the day, Mom would rush back and forth between the tent and the field so she could feed me while working. It sounds cruel that I was in the tent by myself most of the day, but it was the warmest, safest spot for me while my parents tried to keep our family together and make a meager living.

As the months passed, Mom realized that as I grew older, this life would become more impractical and even dangerous for me. Once I started walking and could no longer be kept in the tent, it would have been a nightmare. Keeping me safe while my parents had to work would become nearly impossible. The weather was also a significant concern as the winters in North China were freezing and unpredictable. Without proper protection, people who exposed their skin outside during the winter could lose their limbs or body parts in a short time. If I accidentally escaped from the tent when nobody was watching, I could have frozen to death within an hour. For example, one of my parents' colleagues went out in a storm once without covering his ears. After he returned to the tent—instead of gradually warming up the tissue by rubbing snow on his ears to circulate the blood first—he held his frozen ears next to the hot stove and lost them permanently. Seriously. It was no place for a baby.

My parents had two options: send me to live with relatives, or have Mom quit her job to take care of me full time.

Many families, not just my parents, struggled in dire poverty—working demanding jobs and long hours to provide as best as they could for their children. My parents couldn't afford the loss of Mom's income, and it was nearly impossible back then to switch jobs. The job Mom got came from her dad, my maternal grandpa, after his years of traveling on bare feet during famine times in the 1960s, looking for the means to survive. This once-in-a-lifetime job opportunity was not to be given up for anything. In the 1970s in China, jobs were mostly assigned by the government. My parents couldn't simply post their resumes to a bunch of job sites and find something better suited to our family's needs. It was a necessity and common practice for extended families to pull together in raising the children. With heavy hearts, my parents sent me to live with my relatives when I was only ten months old. After that, they went back into the mountains to provide for me.

The relative my parents asked to take care of me was called "third grandma" from Dad's side. On that day, once they realized that I'd gotten a fever and had stopped moving any of my limbs, they rushed me to the hospital. Nobody knew what was wrong with me, but I wasn't the only one at the hospital with these mysterious symptoms. Suddenly, more than eighty children had fallen ill in the same way. All had a fever to start with, but some could still move their limbs, while others were fully paralyzed. I had been a healthy, cheerful baby when they'd left me in the third grandma's care, and now I was paralyzed and had a high fever, just a month after departing from my parents. Finally, the diagnosis was announced: I had polio. And so did the other children at the same village hospital. That's when the horrifying telegram was sent to my parents far away in the mountains.

By 1977, most of the world was vaccinated against polio, and I should have been too. An oversight by a very young nurse left us all vulnerable, and many of us ended up infected with polio. So many children and their families' lives were altered forever, simply because someone forgot to give the polio vaccination ("sugar pill" as we called it) to the kids in our village. Most families focused on working all day to keep their kids fed. Parents weren't closely tracking their kids' vaccinations and didn't realize the oversight until it was too late. When you live in such harsh circumstances, there isn't much mental energy left to spend on vaccinations. There was no malice, no intent, just human error...just an oversight that left more than eighty children fighting to move and breathe.

Mom said that after they got the telegram of me having "polio," she raced to the doctor in their field clinic. With trembling hands holding the telegram, she asked, "What is polio, and will that kill her?" The doctor told her that polio likely wouldn't kill me, but instead, it could paralyze some of my limbs or my entire body. Mom remembers feeling relieved at that news.

"As long as she can live, I will spend the rest of my life taking care of her, no matter what happens," she said.

My parents then rushed on the train and raced to the village hospital I was left at.

The doctors in the village had no hope for my recovery and told my parents that there was nothing else that could be done. With that devastating prognosis, I was sent home with my parents. Scared and overwhelmed, they took leave from their jobs to figure out their next steps. They would not give up on me, regardless of the seemingly hopeless circumstance.

They spent the little money they had on desperate attempts to help me recover: acupuncture, massage, physical therapy, even pointless surgeries —anything with even a remote chance of helping me regain function and movement. Finally, after some time, I slowly made progress: first my upper body, then my left leg. I was lucky enough to eventually stand up and be able to walk with a limp. My parents were educated and had good jobs with incomes, so I was afforded many treatments other children didn't have access to. I don't know what exactly happened afterward to the rest of those kids with polio, but I heard that some never recovered and that the disease forced them to lie in bed until they died.

We didn't have the courage to ever go back to that village and visit the other kids who also got polio at the same time. After what happened to me, my third grandma cried for months from guilt. The fact that the illness had caused so much lifelong damage to my body before I was even one year old—and that it had happened while she was caring for me—was something she couldn't bear. Her frequent tears were so strong and consistent that she destroyed her eyesight for life.

I don't know how polio survivors recover differently, but I ended up with a limp for life due to this disease. Growing up, I tried to understand polio better by seeking as much information as possible, but I found very little research done on this disappearing disease. To me, that means it's worth describing how polio impacted *my* body and what *I* learned through the years. I hope to provide that little bit of information about myself that could be valuable to others like me.

Polio impacted the right side of my body, including my right leg, hip, and part of my right chest, all of which are smaller and weaker than my left side. My right leg is around two inches shorter than the left and doesn't have much muscle development. It looks more like a stick than a leg. Depending on how I want to move my right leg, I have about 0–5 percent of the strength compared to my left side. I can stand on my right leg for a brief second, but I can't stand and bend the right knee at the same time without falling. This means if I have the slightest slip on my left foot—which holds up my body most of the time—it's certain that I'll slip and fall. I've broken my tailbone multiple times due to that weakness.

Jumping or climbing stairs with my right leg is impossible. Certain moves are more difficult than others. For example, I can lift the polio leg backwards with the strength of a toddler, but I can't turn the right foot even a bit to the left side.

Since my right side is not as developed as the left, my spine has become twisted due to years of walking in an unbalanced way. In my late thirties, I started to experience symptoms of post-polio syndrome (PPS), where acute weakness with pain and fatigue affected my daily life. I recovered from those symptoms within two years. The exact reason is unknown, but it was likely due to proper workout routines and weight control.

In 2022, I started seeking exoskeleton-type devices to help me stay physically active so that I could fight like a black-belt martial artist. With help from the modern technology that was used to help many veterans, I was finally able to do things I could never do before. My story started with polio that constrained me, but it turns out to be the blessing that unleashed so much of my potential later in my life.

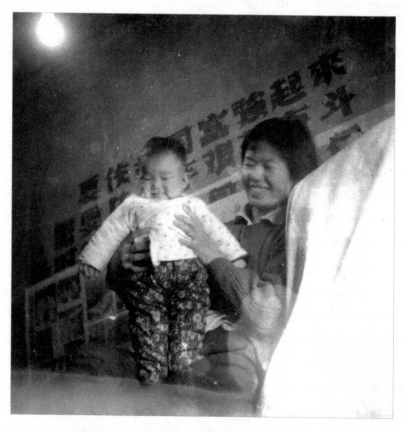

Libo as a ten-month-old with Mom before she was sent away to live with relatives (May 1977). They must have moved into another temporary housing, where on the back wall was written: "To make the motherland prosperous and strong, we need to persevere in hard work."

1.2. FIRST SURGERY (1982)

In July 1977, Mom was five months pregnant with my younger brother while taking care of me, a child with polio. My parents made a plan together: Dad needed to go back to his field work immediately so that our family had enough income to support our daily lives, as well as future medical care I might need; Mom would stay at their base city, a small town in North China, to maintain my physical therapy, give birth to my brother, then attempt to raise us both while also holding down a full-time job.

My brother was born in December 1977. When he was a baby, I was able to help Mom by keeping him in the bed and pulling him back when he got close to the edge. If you could hover from our ceiling, looking down onto our giant platform bed that took up half of the room, what you would see is a live "clock"—consisting of me in the center, holding on to my brother with my arms, and him crawling around me like a circle the whole day. The system worked well... until he started to walk. Then, Mom had to take care of two toddlers and maintain a full-time job, and she needed help. At that time, Dad's elder brother had a seventeen-year-old son, who became a local troublemaker. He'd dropped out of school already and often got into fights with other boys in the neighborhood. To help each other, Dad took that cousin to our house so that he could stay out of trouble, and also help take care of me and my brother. You can imagine what could go wrong when putting a seventeen-year-old rebellious kid in charge during the day for two young toddlers, but we had no other options at that time. Mom would take care of us once she got off work at night, and Dad would visit us a few times throughout the year during his breaks from the field work. It was a means to an end: they needed to make all the money they possibly could so that they could afford all the potential opportunities to cure my polio.

Those were tough times for us all. By the time I was four years old, that model had fallen apart.

During the day, our cousin would fall asleep a lot due to boredom, and I would see an opportunity to crawl out of the front door with my brother from the hole we cut out for the dog—which you may call a doggy door, but it was just a giant hole on the door made out of thin wood boards. You would see a four-year-old leading a three-year-old, trolling around town. Even though I have a polio leg that doesn't have much strength, my other limbs developed a lot more strength to tackle this world. I loved doing outdoor explorative activities: climbing trees to find bird nests while my brother cheered for me from the ground, or scaling the roofs and brick walls around the neighborhood, especially in yards that had fruit trees. Once, I climbed into a peach farm that had security wires in place to make stealing the sweet fruit even more challenging. After I climbed in carefully through those metal wires, I tried to reach peaches on one of the trees but heard a dog barking at me. I panicked and immediately climbed back through those wires, my skin scratched and clothes ripped in the process. Our young cousin, of course, didn't say anything to Mom about what happened during the day, but neighbors started noticing all those dangerous and naughty things I did with my brother. They started coming to our house and telling Mom that they'd noticed us around town doing things that were too dangerous. Mom would punish both of us by having us kneel in front of our invisible ancestor plates—we didn't have them put up, so we needed to use our imagination. It's like the time-out punishment in the Western countries, but ours was more serious—because we had to seek forgiveness from our ancestors, who we'd shamed with our wrongdoings. If Dad was around, my brother would be at risk of being spanked. It didn't matter what trouble I had caused, though, because my butt was always safe. I didn't understand why at that age, but Dad explained his reasoning after I'd grown older. I'd suffered so much from the sickness that they were just happy I could simply be a naughty kid when I was not in pain.

Then, in early 1980, Mom was called to work in the field again along with Dad. They had no choice but to send us away again to stay with relatives. I was sent to Dad's second brother's family, and my brother was sent to Dad's oldest brother.

My parents set a goal to save all the money they could make to afford surgeries for me, so that I could be cured. At that time, little was known about polio, or at least with the resources we could obtain. There were claims from some hospitals that through surgery, polio could be cured. Dad's salary was 70 yuan a month, and Mom's was 60 yuan a month. With a total of 130 yuan (about eighteen dollars) as their combined monthly income, they put more than half of that away—80 yuan a month as my surgery fund. With that rate, each year, they could accumulate about 1,000 yuan, and each surgery would cost several thousand yuan. They calculated that by the time I was five or six, we would be able to afford my first surgery. That's exactly how they executed in the following years until my first surgery at age six.

When that moment finally arrived, my parents found a hospital that claimed to be able to cure polio, and they scheduled the surgery for me. Everything was ready to go. But due to their work in the field, they could only afford to have Dad make the trip to the second uncle's house I was in. He took me to the hospital to prepare for the surgery, then he had to leave the next day. Luckily, I had my rebellious teenage cousin to stay with me for the surgery until Dad picked us up later.

Since I was only six years old, I don't remember any of the pain associated with that surgery. I only remember the fun *before* the surgeries started, since I could still move around without a cast on me.

I was very eager to learn how to read at a young age, but nobody could teach me. So, I used every opportunity to nag people in the hospital to read me stories and teach me to read and write. I remembered that some doctors and nurses started to like me enough to bring me books, and some were even willing to stay and read with me. Having the capability of offering random kindness is human nature; I've strongly believed that from a very young age, and I've benefited from so many acts of random kindness people have offered to me.

I loved "Bunny Time," which is a game in the hospital I created for all the kids who were mostly waiting for surgeries or recovering from them. The hospital wasn't like a modern hospital today, where you must stay in your room and have little contact with other patients. Instead, when I wasn't in surgery, I was trolling around rallying the other kids. I would organize rabbit hop races—hence the name "Bunny Time"—up and down the stairs of the hospital. Many kids had polio or other physical limitations, but almost all of us were still able to move in some way. We'd line up at the bottom of the stairs, and then we'd hop up one stair at a time and back down to see who was the fastest. I usually won . . . because I only raced against the kids who I thought had no chance of winning, and I created a rule: only one leg could be used in the game. Looking back, I see that my need to win came from being told in so many ways that I was inadequate. I always felt I had to prove myself.

However, being around other kids dealing with similar disabilities and feeling the same despair also allowed us to see each other's humanity more fully. One of the kids next to me was my age and also had polio. Her family didn't have much money, and her wish was to taste sugary sweet peaches canned in syrup. Can you imagine anyone asking the Make-A-Wish Foundation for some canned peaches? However, in 1982 China, canned fruit could be a luxury to many families, especially those who had to save everything to pay for medical bills. Before Dad left me, he overheard the little girl's request and came back the next day with canned peaches for me. Dad pretended that he accidentally bought too much and asked the girl to help us finish the food. She was so overwhelmed by receiving this delicacy that she refused to eat it immediately. Instead, she sniffed the metal can. Throughout the day, she'd go off to play and come back to smell the imaginary sugary aroma through the lid. Finally, at the end of the day, she decided to open it. Maybe she was too excited, but before she could taste the peaches, she accidentally dropped the can and spilled the fruit all over the floor. An entire day's worth of anticipation vanished in a split second.

I held out my half-eaten can.

"Don't worry. I can't finish this one myself. You have it!"

This was a rare treat in our daily diet of potatoes and beans. I can't tell you how tired I got of potatoes and beans, potatoes and beans, over and over. I would sneak out with my bowl and dump the slop, then tell my cousin I ate all my food. I could take the pain of surgery but not the boredom of eating the same food every single day. While I was bored with the food, I learned to entertain myself during those many hours spent alone in hospital beds. Because I couldn't experience the outside world, I made my inner world that much more colorful. I dreamed of my life as a grown-up, the places I'd visit, the adventures I'd have. I learned to be content in my own company and value my own thoughts and ideas.

Though I can't remember how painful my first surgery was, I remember the months I spent in bed with a full-body cast on. My whole right leg, hip, and up to my chest were wrapped in a cast for several months until it was ready to be taken off. For a six-year-old, lying in bed for months mostly alone can be cruel—note that it was a world without TV, iPad, or any modern electronics or entertainment. Luckily, I had somehow learned to read by then. Also, during his short time staying with me, Dad taught me how to use a dictionary to look up characters I didn't recognize. My bed was next to a window, and I could see a tree in the yard. I remember reading "The Last Leaf" by O. Henry, in which the sick young girl has taken the thought into her head that she would die when the last leaf falls, only to find out later that a kind artist has painted the last leaf there to give her hope. I spent many hours a day looking at the tree outside of my window, hoping that someone had also painted a leaf for me that could provide me with company. I was very sad to see all the leaves of that tree drop throughout the winter.

I started reading complicated books at a very early age, though I can't recall how I learned so fast. Still, by the time I was eight, my parents found that I had already completed all four of the famous Chinese classic novels and many Western books. Although many stories I couldn't fully under-stand or digest, I was so fascinated by the world in all those books. One of my favorites was *Jane Eyre*, so much so that I used Jane as my social name when I needed one later in my life. During those lonely times, at least I had my books, and those characters in the books became my imaginary friends.

After so much time in a cast, your skin begins to itch. Because of that, one of the activities I used to do was to scratch my skin at the edge of the cast, peeling off either dead skin or scabs. One of the four Chinese classics is *Journey to the West* (西游记), in which the Monkey King has a power to pull any of his hair out, blowing it into the air to create anything he wants. I would peel a piece of dead skin off, make a wish, and blow it into the air. Magic never happened. I started to invent games for myself: Which day would I peel off the deadest skin the most? Could I line up the scabs to form an army? Could I make a face out of them? Those days recovering in bed were long and lonely, and imagination was my only friend.

I remember feeling hopeful that once the cast was removed, I would recover from polio. Months later, when my cast was removed, I looked down: my polio foot was now not only weak and useless but had become distorted and tilted to the right instead of forward facing. I wondered if the doctor thought that would make me drag it forward easier.

I concluded that all my surgeries were failures up to that point, but I was still hopeful that the next one could "fix" me.

Libo the three-year-old trolling the town, the expression looked like I owned this town (1979).

1.3. STRUGGLING TO BELONG,
WITHOUT PARENTS (1979–1983)

After I grew older, I tried many times to talk to Mom about what exactly happened in those early years before I had memories: my polio diagnosis, treatments, and recoveries. But every time, Mom was so overcome by her emotion that the tears made it difficult for her to speak. She felt guilty. She wondered if any of this would have happened if they had kept me with them instead of leaving me with our relatives before I was even one year old. As a mother myself, I understand why Mom felt that way. We always want to protect our children, and seeing them hurt and in pain is unbearable. I don't fault my parents for what they had to do to provide for me. They had no other options. They loved me so much, and they did what was necessary to ensure I had food, clothes, shelter, and later, an education.

Mom took me back for a few years when my brother and I were toddlers. But she had to send both of us to relatives again when I reached four years old, when both of my parents were called to the field for work. Also, I was causing trouble doing dangerous activities when nobody was watching. From 1980 to 1984, my brother lived with one uncle, and I lived with another. All of my childhood memories before I was eight involved either living with relatives or living in hospitals.

Dad's brothers had many children of their own; the big uncle had five kids, and the second uncle had four. My brother was sent to the big uncle, and I was sent to the second uncle. Even though our uncles lived in the same town, my brother and I barely saw each other for the many years we lived there. My parents now had to provide for two children. Additionally, they were determined to make as much money as possible, to afford the surgeries that might cure me fully. Later, I learned from Dad's writing that he spent those years leading his team to gain extra income by securing business outside of the government. In an agreement with his organization, he was able to sign contracts with external companies that allowed profit sharing. He was able to use that extra income for his organization to buy more equipment, boosting productivity and therefore salaries. In short, Dad brought capitalism to Communist China before 1980—by creating "capitalist surplus value," something I later learned about in school. He made this effort not only so that his team could make more money, but also to save more for my surgeries. Our family was apart, but our parents worked hard for us, fighting for a better future so that we could all be together someday.

Our uncles lived in a rural area of Fushun, in Liaoning Province. You may call it a town or village. Both of my uncles worked as coal miners. Among the three brothers in the family, only one could afford to continue his education. The two elder brothers decided to give Dad that opportunity, and they both started earning income at a very young age to support Dad throughout his college. Every day, my uncle would go to work, and my aunt would stay with all the kids at home. There, she cared for us, the household, and the small farm. She fed chickens, pumped water from a well, washed our clothes with bare hands, cooked on a stove that required making your own fire with wood, and so on. I never saw her rest.

Though life was surely hard for the adults, it was somehow heaven to me. When my aunt was busy spinning like a top around the house, all of us children were left to our own devices most of the day. As soon as a child could walk and didn't need to be carried anymore, they stayed in the village with all the other kids during the day. We kept ourselves entertained and explored the area together. When the adults came home from work and the whole family sat together to eat dinner, oftentimes, they found their kids with ripped clothes, dirty faces and hands, and some bruises or even blood. All said and done, though, as long as we were still alive, punishments were usually just a gesture.

The houses in the village were small one-room brick structures with a big family bed, called a Chinese kang, in the middle. The kang consisted of a brick platform with a hollow area to make a fire underneath the bed. We would start the fire in the morning to heat the house and the bed, and that warmth would last for the rest of the day. Though we had nothing, my memories are full of warmth and love. My favorite times are the coldest winter holidays. The entire family would gather on the warm kang, and my aunt would rock me and tell me stories of our family.

We didn't have running water or refrigerators, but we did have electricity for lights. In the winter, we simply stored food outside as the temperature was nearly the same as the inside of a modern refrigerator. In the summer, we stored perishable food in an outside underground vault, referred to in the US as a root cellar. A vault is an impressive term, but it was just a large hole in the ground with a heavy lid. It was not vacuum sealed, and the circulating air kept the stored vegetables cool.

One day, on an exploratory mission, I crawled into the vault and pulled the lid shut over me. It seemed like a great idea until I realized I couldn't reopen the lid to get out. I sat in that underground vault for the entire day, until late in the evening when the adults came home. They searched for me, finally finding me stuck in that hole in the ground. I was only five or six years old then, but I remembered that moment: sitting alone in the darkness, first trying to call for help, then giving up quickly because I realized that nobody would hear me. I started to assess my situation. *It was good that I could breathe through the crack in the lid that covered the vault, there were cabbages and carrots in the vault that I could eat if I was hungry, and eventually someone would notice that I was missing and would find me.* I then decided to just preserve my energy, wait patiently by staring through the sunshine coming through the lid, and observe shadows or sounds that may pass through for my opportunity to come out. I was very proud of myself. I had done a whole-day adventure alone, without panicking and breaking down.

Because I was smaller and slowed down by my limp, I was sometimes bullied as a child. Strangely, the bullying didn't make me hide from the other kids. Instead, it taught me to protect myself at an early age. I don't remember feeling sad about being ridiculed during my early childhood. What I do remember is my determination to exact revenge on the kid who humiliated me again and again.

The ringleader in the group of bullies, an older boy who was much bigger and stronger than me, would run up to me and push me down. They knew I'd have a difficult time getting back up. Sometimes they'd pile on top of me, pinning me to the ground and hurling insults at me. I knew I was outnumbered and outmatched physically, but that would not deter me from getting back at my tormentor.

Instead of diapers, children in rural China wear *kai dang ku*, which are pants with an open crotch. Kids can squat to do their business, then grab some leaves or paper to wipe themselves and go on their way. We didn't have bathrooms or running water, so it was a practical way to live.

Even though everyone was stronger than me, we were all exposed and vulnerable in the same way. I hatched a plan for payback. The next time the bully pushed me down, I looked up and grabbed his pants. Spreading the clothes open, I took a big bite—of his butt! I bit him so hard that I drew blood and left teeth marks as he started wailing in pain and running away from me, crying.

Later that night, his family visited my uncle to complain about my behavior. I stared at them, without any fear.

"He kept pushing me down! What did you expect me to do? He got what he deserved!"

The boy never dared to touch me again.

Decades later, I was reminded of this incident when I picked up my own son from daycare. The teacher told me that my son got into a fight with a bigger kid, so I checked in with him on the way home. My son informed me nonchalantly that his best friend was soon to return from vacation, and with his friend's help, he'd take care of the situation. "I got it, Mom. Don't worry about it." I see myself in both my father and my son. Sometimes I wonder if it's in our Cao blood. Dad and I would not be messed with, and neither will my son. Of course, I had to do what a mother should do, telling him violence is never the solution. In that moment, though, flashbacks of my own fights as a kid made me understand how he would handle his situation that way.

Sticking up for myself gave me some street credibility in the town, and I was often the leader who came up with a new game or decided what we were going to do. We didn't have toys in the traditional sense. What we did have was a pile of dirt and a big stick. First, I commanded all the boys to pee on the pile of dirt and then safely dug the stick right in the middle. For an entire day, we played a game where each kid had to remove a set amount of dirt without causing the stick to fall over. If the stick toppled, you lost. Yes, I conceptually invented Jenga.

While we weren't poor enough to starve, we had no luxury food items, like fruit. Or bubblegum. Bubblegum! It looked so magical and mysterious. I watched other lucky kids from afar, chewing those colorful, stretchy blobs and blowing giant bubbles covering half their faces. I couldn't ask for a piece of gum though. My parents worked so hard, living far away, to put food on the table where I stayed in the village. Asking for something that wasn't a necessity felt like an insult to their efforts, especially after all they were doing to pay my medical bills. Though I understood the sacrifice my parents were making and was grateful for the kindness of my uncle and his family for taking me in, I never felt like I belonged there. Instead, I felt abandoned and struggled with feelings of worthlessness. Gum may seem small, but it felt like a luxury I didn't deserve to ask for.

But I was still a kid and I really wanted to know what bubblegum tasted like. One day, I stealthily watched a boy as he chewed a piece, my mouth watering. Once he was done chewing it, he took it out of his mouth and played with it before smearing it onto a tree. I stood there, staring at the dirty gum stuck to the tree, until everyone had left. Looking around cautiously to make sure nobody could see what I was about to do, I walked toward the tree. I tried to fight the urge to take that gum. I really did. But the pull of that unknown delicacy was more than I could handle.

I peeled the cold, hard gum off the tree and popped it into my mouth, convinced I was about to experience one of the best moments of my young life. I can still feel the rigid wad in my mouth as I unsuccessfully tried to manipulate it with my tongue and teeth to blow a bubble. It didn't even taste sweet! What was the big deal? This was disgusting. For the life of me, I couldn't understand why all the other kids couldn't stop raving about these rubbery, tasteless globs. *Well*, I thought, *at least I can tell everyone that I've tasted bubble gum and it's not a big deal.*

The cookies, however, were a different story.

I had never seen, let alone tasted, a cookie in my entire life. I was hopeful that would change when my uncle's family was given a small box of cookies by my parents, who visited me once or twice a year. It was such a special treat that my uncle decided to store them above the highest cabinet where no kid could reach. A luxury item like this had to be rationed. They promised that once a week, we'd each get a piece of cookie.

The trouble was that the adults didn't understand how much I wanted those cookies and that I wouldn't stop at anything to get them! My oldest cousin had a cognitive impairment. A big, tall boy, he loved to be helpful. I would call him to my side and beg him to turn me into a giant by putting me on his shoulders. He'd agree, happy to make me smile, and once I was on his shoulders, I'd steer him toward the hidden cookies. I'd eat a cookie and give him a tiny piece, making him promise to keep our secret. I feel terrible about exploiting my cousin now, but back then I was solely focused on getting what I wanted by any means necessary. Those moments savoring the forbidden cookies were pure joy, and I looked forward to the buttery sweetness on my tongue all day.

My uncle never figured out my magical disappearing act, and I've never had another cookie as delicious as that first one.

During those years, I rarely got the chance to see my parents because they worked so much and so far away, but Mom would come for an occasional visit. During the last one of those visits, when I was six or seven years old, I broke Mom's heart. I had asked my aunt if I could call her "Mom" because I missed my mom desperately. But when she came to visit, she seemed almost like a stranger to me. I peeked out from behind the door, both scared and wishing so badly I could run up to her and throw myself into her arms. After every visit, she would have to leave again, and I would be alone. I didn't understand why. During that last visit, all day I refused to speak a single word to her. I wouldn't let her touch me and ran away to hide instead.

I now look back and realize that I was acting out because I resented my parents for leaving me to live with another family instead of taking care of me themselves. But more importantly, I loved and missed my parents so much that I couldn't bear spending a day in Mom's loving embrace, catching up and talking, only to be left again. It was easier to shut down and disengage. I was sure that at the end of that visit, she'd leave me again, and it would be months or even years before I saw her next. So, I hid. I wouldn't even hug her goodbye. Mom took a picture of that moment: I was very upset and very hostile to her. You could see all those emotions in the photo of me standing next to the wall by myself, staring at Mom like a total stranger.

It was the last straw for her. Devastated, she traveled back to my father and told him, "This is it; I can't do it anymore." Around 1984, when I was almost eight years old, Mom found an opportunity to stay in a base city instead of going to the wild field again, so she could take care of me and my brother. The three of us would finally live together, and Dad would visit us as often as he could, when he didn't have to do field work. We would see Dad a few times a year, and the rest of time, Mom would take care of us while keeping up with a full-time job and her continued education. We would be a family again. After I heard that Mom was going to pick me up and I would live with her afterward, I couldn't believe it. I could finally be with my own parents under the same roof. I practiced calling "Mama" and "Baba" in private many times before the day arrived.

Finally, my brother and I were able to unite with Mom. Our second family photo was taken during one of Dad's visits. Smiles came back to our faces—life couldn't have been better when being with my whole family.

Before departing with Mom to live with Dad's brothers (1980)

When Mom dropped my brother and me off with relatives,
we didn't know it would be four years before we would unite again.

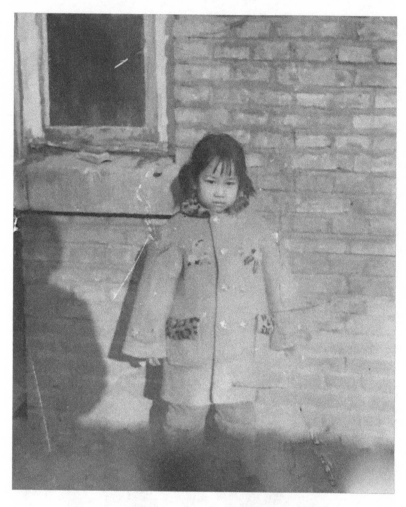

*The last time Mom visited me while I was staying at a
relative's house, I stared at her like a stranger.*

2.

LIFE APART AND
ON THE MOVE
(1984–1988)

Author William Faulkner famously wrote,
"Always dream and shoot higher than you know you can do.
Do not bother just to be better than your contemporaries
or predecessors. Try to be better than yourself."

To me, this is what it means to strive for your full potential.

Potential is something we are all born with.
Whether we reach it or not depends on a combination
of our circumstances and our character.

When I think of potential, I think of Mom's drive
to finish her education on top of all the obstacles in front of her.
I think of my best childhood friend, Dongmei, and her wish
to write despite her inability to even breathe.

Both stories have very different outcomes, but
they are born of the same desire: to strive for greatness,
whatever that means to us.

2.1. A MOTHER WITH TWO KIDS, CHICKENS, DUCKS, GEESE, AND A DOG

I could feel the presence of someone or something else right next to me. My eyes wide open, I saw nothing in the deep darkness. I held my breath and didn't make a sound.

Initially, Mom was in Longjiang (Dragon River) County under the jurisdiction of Qiqihar City in the west of Heilongjiang (Black Dragon River) Province. It was a very rural place adjacent to a city. Our new home was a one-room house without running water, though we did have a well around the block from which we could pump water out of the ground. Of course, that also meant no plumbing. Our toilet was a small shed in the yard with a hole in the ground. Imagine being a little kid having to poop in the middle of the night. Heading out into our pitch-black yard in the below-zero temperatures, I had to find the hole by memory and feel. When I squatted down to do my business, I sensed that I wasn't alone. My heart beating into my throat, I held perfectly still but kept pooping because mother nature can't be stopped! I felt fur beneath me and heard a smacking noise. With horror, I realized something was in the shed with me—and worse, it was eating my poop! In a panic, I bolted out of the shed and into the house, waking up Mom to tell her I would never again use the bathroom in the middle of the night.

Only in the light of morning did I understand that I had not been stalked by a wild animal in the middle of the night. It was just our dog, "The Big Yellow," following me into the shed for a little midnight snack.

Settling in to start our family's next chapter was a difficult undertaking for my parents. My brother and I lived with Mom in that tiny one-room house. Dad continued working long hours in the mountains—living in a tent and weathering the harsh environment—day in and day out. He could only visit on the weekends for some months, making the long trip via train to spend a single day with us. Sometimes, he had to work in the field or mountains for over nine months, and we couldn't see him for longer stretches. Mom worked a local job and took care of us without any modern conveniences. Being a single mom is hard enough when you have a refrigerator full of food, a house with heat and air conditioning, a washer and dryer, and a car. Mom didn't have any of those. To wash our clothes, she had to pump water out of the well, heat it over the fire during winter or use it cold in frozen weather, then scrub our clothes by hand. During winter, our yard itself was the refrigerator, where we had stacks of cabbages, tofu blocks, and sticky red-bean-rice buns to consume for the whole winter. In the summer, we soaked fresh vegetables and fruit with water from the well. This worked because the water we pumped from the underground well was always cold, even in the summer.

Mom was extremely frugal and resourceful. She made that tiny yard in front of the house a little heaven for us. We had multiple garden beds where she grew vegetables that she tended and harvested. We collected eggs every day from our chickens. We had one rooster and about a dozen hens. Every morning the rooster would act more like a sheepdog and herd all his hens out of the yard to forage for food. At the end of the day, he'd lead them back home. I watched him jump on a big rock and count his hens. Often, he'd have to go back out, find a missing hen, and coax her back into our yard. We raised ducks and geese at the same time, and Mom would marinate their eggs to send them to neighbors as gifts.

Mom had an awesome tomato plant one year, and it grew one giant yellow tomato that was so juicy and looked delicious. My brother and I wanted so much to pick it and taste it, but Mom said we couldn't touch that tomato because it was the best one. The best one, she said, had to be saved to be used for seeds for the following year. So, every day for weeks, my brother and I passed that juicy, giant yellow tomato and resisted the temptation to pick it. Instead, we could only imagine what it would taste like. Then, one day, our elderly neighbor visited us. After chatting with Mom, he walked through the yard, and…picked off that special tomato we'd tried to protect the whole season. He ate it with a big bite. All three of us just stared at him, eating our precious tomato, walking out of our yard. I have never forgotten that moment and the life lesson it taught me. After that day, my brother and I protected our food very carefully. He would even spit on his so I wouldn't take it—anything to keep it safe.

Every morning during the summer, Mom would leave for work and lock us in the house. She needed to make money, and there was no other option but to leave us at home during the workday. I was eight at the time, and my little brother was seven. When there was no school, we had to entertain ourselves while Mom was at work. Of course, we didn't want to stay in the house and be bored the entire day. As soon as Mom left, we squeezed through the dog door into freedom and spent the whole day exploring. Those are happy memories for me, spending time with my brother, roaming free without a care in the world and no chores to complete. For snacks, we'd sneak onto somebody's farm, dig out a few carrots, wipe them off on our shirts, and eat them right there. It was a naughty thing to do, and we frequently got chased by angry dogs. We carried rocks in our pockets to scare them off if they got too close, but it didn't always work. Once I got bit badly on my leg, which is why I'm still scared of dogs to this day.

Often, the temptation of a delicious treat, like a piece of ripe fruit, was too much for us to withstand. When my brother and I spotted some golden peaches, we had to have them. We'd had that type of adventure when I was only four years old, but at that point, we'd grown and become masters. There was a big fence around the farm with chicken wire on top. My brother gave me a boost. Once I had climbed the fence, I pulled him up. We crawled through the chicken wire and jumped down into the yard. As we were stealing the peaches off the tree, the dogs came running. Back up the fence and through the chicken wire we scrambled and then ran all the way home, squishing the peaches in our pockets and dragging ourselves through the dog door into the house.

When Mom returned shortly after, her face was priceless, her eyebrows pulled-up arches, mouth gaping open: "What in the world happened to you two?"

Our clothes were completely shredded, our pants ripped from the chicken wire, hair matted and faces sweaty. I can't believe I lied my way out of that one, innocently exclaiming that I had just been playing with my brother.

There are times I couldn't get out of trouble because often I was the one leading the pack of kids doing naughty or dangerous things. The flats of houses we lived in were very close to each other, and often there were little sheds attached to them. I created another game for the kids to jump through houses and sheds (nowadays it's called parkour). Though I had a limp, nothing prevented me from using the other three limbs to climb up and jump with one leg. I did that for a long time with the other kids, often winning, until one night a neighbor dropped by our house. She told Mom that I was leading the kids to jump through the roofs of houses. Mom warned me to set an example for my brother: no jumping from the top of roofs allowed. The fun was over, and it was always the neighbors who ruined my adventures.

My brother and I tried to help Mom when we could. One day, we decided to help Mom wash all the clothes while she was gone for work. We gathered all the clothes around the house, not understanding what materials they were or what color they were. We piled them all up in the middle of the yard, and we pulled out the big bucket Mom used to wash clothes. I pumped one bucket of clean water out of the well and began dunking clothes into water, rubbing them with the washboard just like Mom did. Then, I asked my brother to hang them up to dry on the clotheslines. We did that for hours, racing to get them all done before Mom came home to cook us lunch. We were thrilled by how surprised we thought she'd be when she came home and saw how much we'd helped. She was surprised indeed! Poor Mom was supposed to just cook lunch for us before going back to work, but instead, she found a yard full of clothes. Some were laying on the ground and some were hanging on the clothesline. They all seemed as dirty as the bucket of water we were using. She sighed, thanked us, cooked us lunch, then started to clean up by rewashing those clothes, after which she had to return to work for the afternoon duty. Of course, Mom didn't have time to have her own lunch that day.

In September 1984, it was time for us to start school. There, we got an education but also a way to keep us occupied and out of trouble while Mom worked. Our elementary school ran all day from 7:00 a.m. to 6:00 p.m. We ate all our meals at school, too. Every day, I brought two bento boxes full of food and lined them up with everyone else's on a metal cart. At mealtime, the kids who served as daily staff took all the metal boxes and heated them up in an enormous stove. There was no refrigerator at school, and all our food was sitting out at room temperature. It's surprising we didn't have more incidents of food poisoning—or maybe the high heat killed off most of the bacteria during cooking.

In North China where we lived, the winter days were icy cold with snow piled knee high. Well, waist high on my brother and me. From the start of winter—sometime in October until nearly the end of March—every morning, Mom had to drag us through the snow for miles and miles so we could go to school. Mom was determined that we shouldn't miss any days of school. No winter storm would get in her way. Once spring melted the snow into puddles, we rode a bike to school. The bike was a hand-me-down and way too big for my small mother, who looked like she could barely keep it upright. But she would not be deterred. I asked Mom why she didn't pick a bike that was easier for her to maneuver. She just laughed: "You think we have the luxury of picking a bike? That was the bike passed down from your grandpa. It's the only one that's available to us. You take whatever you've got in life!"

It wasn't easy for a tiny woman who was five foot three to ride an old twenty-eight-inch bike, carrying two kids (seven and eight years old) at the same time. In order to accomplish the task, she would first find higher ground, put me in the front of the bike, then hop on it and pedal downhill. Then, my poor brother needed to start chasing the bike and jump into the back seat while Mom was trying to balance and keep momentum. It was quite a challenge. Every morning we had to do this—even in winter with snow on the ground. There were many times we fell over together, tumbling off the bike, laughing hysterically, sometimes in slippery rain or snow that would wet all three of us. Years later, my brother joked that it would have been good practice for the Olympics if Mom ever had an interest.

At the end of school, my brother and I had to walk alone back home because Mom had to work late. I recall many of those winter days, to combat the frigid temperatures, I dressed up like a cotton ball with many layers of clothes for the trip home from school. Each time, I would take a deep breath, start walking in the knee-high snow, and count the times I fell. One day, I ran in the door with excitement.

"Mom, I fell 108 times on the way home today! How amazing is that!"

(*Water Margin*, one of the most famous, earliest Chinese novels, tells the story of how a group of 108 outlaws gather at Mount Liang to rebel against the government. So, 108 resembled bravery to me somehow at that age).

Mom saw me standing there, soaking wet from the snow. As she held me with tears in her eyes, I was jumping with joy. When I noticed her tears, I tried to comfort her.

"Don't be sad, Mom. Think of it this way. After I got to 108, I controlled it well so I wouldn't fall again to mess up that number. That means I am always in control. Also, I fell not because of my uneven legs; it's the *ground* that's not even for me."

There were many other joys growing up. One of my fondest school memories is when our teacher asked each student to bring some bricks or buckets of sand to school for a particular week. Nobody knew why or what the supplies were for, but Mom was able to find some bricks for me to bring every morning to school for that week. As we saw materials in school start piling up, our curiosity built up as well. One morning, everyone was gathered at the big playground, with bricks and sand piled up in a corner.

Suddenly, the principal announced that we would build an ice rink together that day using the bricks and sand! We were so excited. Together, we made a knee-high brick circle in the middle of our playground. Teachers mixed the sand into some cement and used shovels to seal the brick walls. By the end of that day, we used hoses to fill water into the center of the brick circle we'd just made.

The next day... voila! We had an ice rink. What we didn't have were ice skates, but that didn't matter. We simply started sliding around on the ice, the whole playground full of smiles and laughter. We would play in ice and snow during break and come back to our classroom with icicles on our clothes. There was a large heating stove with a chimney in the middle of the room (which is how each room was heated back then), and we would all gather around it to heat up our clothes and frozen fingers and toes, still giggling.

I miss that simple joy during the 1980s in China. We didn't worry about rules and policies, insurance, and labor laws, etc. that we now must take into consideration. We just used what we had, worked together, and created something we wanted.

I came home and told Mom what we'd done with the bricks we brought to school. That weekend Dad was visiting from the field and told me his own story from back in 1958, when he was in middle school.

"This is how each of our generations solved our problems. We don't complain and just talk about it…we come up with a plan and execute instead," Dad said.

Like the story in ancient Chinese myth, "The Foolish Old Man Removes the Mountains," Dad once got a similar assignment: to chop off the top of a hill. On the way to his middle school, there was a hill that was about fifty meters high. Each side was too steep for young students to walk over every day. The leader of the school gathered everyone—including over a thousand teachers and students—and they devised a plan: they'd spend a whole week removing the top of the hill so that each side was sloped below ten to fifteen degrees, making it manageable for the students to cross.

Every morning that week, professional engineering teams would use explosives to blow up a portion of the hilltop. Then, it was everyone's job to use buckets to transport the gravel and stones generated from the explosion to pave the steep part of the hill. The locations that required paving were premarked by engineering teams. The whole school workforce set up a human conveyor belt, one meter apart from each other, passing buckets of gravel from the top to the lower part of the hill. It was in February and still cold, but Dad remembered seeing steam rising from everyone's heads while working tirelessly with the same common goal. At the end of that week, they completed the project together. In the end, they were able to walk to and from school without having to climb the steep hill anymore.

I was mesmerized by Dad's story and especially how it related to mine. At a young age, I learned the lesson of both self-help and the power of community. When everyone ties together as a single rope, we can pull anything away that's against us. You might wonder if these approaches to building the skating rink and making the hill easier to climb were the "correct" approaches, but the point is larger than that. I loved how during 1958 in Dad's time, and in 1985 during my time, we took a similar route: creating something from nothing, together, in pursuit of a common goal.

When you have a big community, mountains can be moved. Family is the smallest community we all have. It took many years for us to build that small community. During the coldest winter break, our family spent a lot of time inside to escape the snowy ice desert outside. Every day when we didn't have to go to work or school, we'd start a big pot of cabbage, yams, and potatoes in the morning. Then we'd sit around to talk and entertain each other until it was time to eat. That's why there are so many excellent comedians who originated from North China. You absolutely must cultivate a sense of humor if you're going to be locked into one room with your entire family for many months of long winter. So many great memories were built during the time when we were having hot pot in our little room, winter raging all the while outside our door.

While my brother had been my best friend and playmate, we drifted apart during early school years. I loved learning and was intensely ambitious. I would be at the top of my class, and there was no excuse for being second best. Dad had excelled academically, and so would I. My brother was a decent student but never received top marks. I couldn't understand why. School was my whole world, and my education was important to me. I could no longer relate to my brother who seemed much more casual in his approach to academics. Not only did I feel disconnected from him, but I also resented that he wasn't trying hard enough to be number one, like me and Dad. One time, I was berating my brother, and he burst out: "I'm just not as good as Dad and you, Sis! I'm trying my best!"

I viewed it as my personal duty to my Cao family name to be number one at everything, and I expected the same of my brother. Regardless of my frustration with him, my brother deeply cared about me and would soon teach me a lesson on what it meant to be a family. One afternoon at school, the teachers told us to pack our stuff and go home early. A winter storm with snow and flooding was expected, and school was closing early to give students time to shelter at home. My younger brother was a grade below me, and we always walked home from school separately. That day he showed up at my class door as I was walking out. Surprised, I asked him why he was waiting for me. "I don't want the flood to get you, Sis. There's going to be a big storm, and I'm picking you up so we can go home together," he said.

I realized at that moment that my brother was more than grades on tests and that I had underestimated him. He may not have been as dedicated to school as I was, but he was dedicated to me and our family. Keeping us together and safe was his top priority. He had my back, not only in words but in actions. Most of all, he has the kindest heart, to me and people around him. Since then, my brother and I have weathered many literal and metaphorical storms together, and the bond we forged that day has never been broken.

My brother and I came back to our parents and
were excited for school (1984)

2.2. BEING A ZEBRA ON A SURGICAL BED, OVER AND OVER AGAIN

I missed a lot of school because of multiple surgeries, attempting to cure my polio during my elementary years. My parents didn't know that there was no known cure for polio, and they refused to give up hope. They desperately wanted to believe the many doctors and hospitals who promised their treatments and surgeries were 99 percent effective in curing polio. They had to keep working to afford my hospital stays, treatments, and surgeries. Sometimes my teenage cousin would take care of me, but often I was alone for days and weeks at a time in the hospital.

Once during a hospital stay when I was about ten, I was prepped for surgery by getting painful injections every day. It got so bad that my entire bottom was swollen, and I would crawl under the bed every time the nurse came in to find a new place on my body to inject me. My parents had paid for the surgery, but after two months, I still had no surgery appointment scheduled. I was getting poked and prodded every day for no apparent reason. Finally, another patient's parent pulled Dad to the side and explained that they wouldn't schedule my surgery unless he gave the doctors and nurses red packets. Red packets are red envelopes with money that are traditionally given for celebrations and holidays in China. Dad was outraged: "This is insane! We're already paying for the surgery! I'm not going to bribe the doctors!" But when he saw how miserable I was, being dragged from underneath the bed day after day and held down for more injections, he started tearing up and bent his will for me.

He slipped the doctor and nurse a couple of red packets, and my surgery was scheduled the next day. That only happened once to me in 1986 in that hospital where things were not quite formalized.

The operating room and the bed I lay on were so cold that my teeth chattered. I was completely naked, not even wearing one of those flimsy paper-like hospital gowns. Next to me was a teenage boy waiting for his own surgery. There was supposed to be a curtain separating us, but nobody bothered to pull that curtain for our privacy. At ten, I was in that awkward prepubescent stage where I didn't feel like a little girl anymore. It was one of the first times I remember being ashamed that I was naked in front of an older boy. I was scared, humiliated, and alone. And so, so cold. Like a slab of meat forgotten in a walk-in freezer.

When the doctors and nurses came in, nobody explained anything to me. The nurse started painting my body with a thick brush. My ten-year-old brain thought, *They're making me into a zebra!* The icy solution brushed all over my body was to sanitize my skin in preparation for surgery, but to this day, every time I hear the word zebra, I think of that cold moment in the operating room. I felt violated and helpless, completely in the hands of these strangers who barely acknowledged me while treating my body like an inanimate object, not a person. Many years later, I read an article named "Blue Zebra," written by Haidi Zhang, who is a Chinese writer and paraplegic since early childhood. In that article, she described that when she was on a hospital bed awaiting her surgery, she felt like she turned into a Zebra. I couldn't help tearing up reading that article, knowing that there was another girl in the world who had felt exactly what I felt, and all that emotion mixed with embarrassment, shame, fear, and pain all came back to me.

I asked my parents to request only local anesthesia for this surgery. General anesthesia sometimes led to my whole body feeling numb for days afterward. Worse than that, Mom told me that full anesthesia caused me to have a slower response time for a few days after the surgery, often staring into space for long periods of time. I'd always known my brain was my most valuable asset, and I wasn't going to allow any physical repairs to jeopardize that.

During one surgery with local anesthesia on my polio leg only, I heard the doctors talking, one of them saying he would start pounding *it* in. I had no idea what *it* was. I never knew what exactly would happen during these surgeries. Doctors were like gods. We didn't ask questions. Only later did I understand that the doctor had taken a twelve-inch-long iron rod and driven it into the bottom of my foot like a giant nail. During the operation itself, I had no idea what was going on, but I felt the vibrations through my entire body from that impact. Pow, pow, pow! Over and over. Bong, bong, bong! I will never forget that sound.

For that surgery, I only had my young cousin with me because both Mom and Dad had to go back to work. The second day after the surgery, we were told to leave the hospital immediately because they needed the bed. We needed to travel by train for a few hundred miles, so Dad's friends picked me up from the hospital to carry me to the train station, where Dad was waiting. Lying on the gurney, still heavily medicated, I could only hear sounds close to my head. I heard someone say the gurney wouldn't fit through the door of the train. Dad had to stand inside the train and reach for my gurney as his friend tried to maneuver me through the window. I remember straining to see Dad's big, chubby hands—they were memorable, especially because he had a birthmark—and feeling relieved when I found him ready and waiting to catch me. I felt safe then. I knew Dad would catch me so I wouldn't fall in life.

The hospital sent me home without instructions or medication. It was common to travel to the bigger cities with better hospitals for the surgery itself and then go back home to recover and get follow-up care at local hospitals. So, there I was, held together by stitches, a metal rod in my foot, a cast immobilizing me, and the anesthesia has worn off. I was carried on my gurney to the train station to make the long trek home. Trains in China were crammed full of people, and it's hard to get in and out. Once you have a seat, you better not move. Dad had to get on a train packed with people, navigating the narrow space with his child, fresh out of surgery and on a bulky gurney. It was a real-life tragicomedy. Other than the pain after the medicine wore off, I don't remember much of the bumpy ride home. I somehow believed that medication could potentially cause damage to my brain, so I refused to take any painkillers after surgery. I could deal with pain because I knew it was just temporary. I knew my brain, however, was all I had. I wouldn't risk any damage.

Common wisdom then dictated one hundred days of recovery for any operation that touched your bones, so the cast wasn't opened until about three and a half months later. When that open-cast moment came, the doctor at the local hospital looked at the rod quizzically and pulled it out. It left a gaping hole in my foot. Nobody knew what the rod was doing in my body or what it was supposed to accomplish. I still have no idea what the point was, but I'll never forget the sound of it being hammered into my foot.

There was absolutely nothing that could stop the sickening pain. The first night after one of my major hip surgeries, Mom stayed in the hospital with me. She climbed into bed with me and held me in her arms the whole night. She begged, "My child, just cry. I know you're in pain; let it out and cry. You will feel better." But I didn't see the point.

"Crying isn't going to make the pain go away," I said. "I'd rather keep my tears for something else, Mom." Nothing would make the pain go away, and there was no good reason to make Mom feel even more horrible—watching me cry and not being able to do anything about my pain. It was a terrible situation without a solution, so I gritted my teeth and squeezed my eyes shut.

I had a few surgeries throughout my elementary school years. The frequency of the surgeries depended on how fast my parents could save up enough money. Our family was basically in a race to save money, then do a surgery to save Libo. The surgeries were usually scheduled in the fall so that my recovery in a cast would happen in colder months—where there was less risk for an infection to develop. I started dreading fall because I knew it meant another surgery—and another few long, lonely months of recovery in bed. But these lonely hours were made more bearable by Dad's library of books. No matter where we lived, how much we struggled, and how many times we moved, we always, always had Dad's books. They went everywhere with our little family and became my friends during these months of recovery.

I felt a kinship with Scarlet from *Gone with the Wind*. She might appear to be superficial or self-centered, but she is strong and will always survive and fight. In dark times, I kept telling myself what Scarlet said: "After all, tomorrow is another day!" Dad also owned many Russian and Chinese classics, especially since he spoke Russian—having learned it as a second language in college—because China and the Soviet Union were close allies at the time. One book made an especially indelible impression on me: *How the Steel Was Tempered* by Nikolai Ostrovsky. The book explained how steel is tempered, and I found this to be a fitting analogy for my own life. I grew tired of the surgeries, tired of being stuck in hospitals or alone in bed, tired of missing school, tired of my life rushing on without me. I was grateful for everything my parents had done to help me recover as much as I had, and I also knew I couldn't go on like this forever. We needed to move on with our lives, and I needed to focus on what I could do with the body and the brain I had.

I had tears in this picture, yet I was still smiling. At a young age,
I learned to smile at life, no matter what it has to offer.

2.3. DONGMEI'S DEATH (1987)

Dongmei gasped, coughed, took as deep a breath as she could, and kept talking. We stuck our heads together, giggling. The rest of our classmates were participating in PE, but Dongmei and I were excluded. We didn't think it was fair that we were not allowed in PE classes, but we also accepted the fact that life is never fair, even at our young age.

Dongmei was my best friend, and not just because she was the only other kid excluded from PE and recess. While the other kids chased each other around the schoolyard, we'd sit on the side and watch the others instead of participating. We would joke around, making bets on which kid would fall next and which kid would not pass their PE tests, just like us.

Together, we also imagined what our lives would be like without our physical limitations.

"I would be a dancer," I told Dongmei.

"I would enjoy breathing," she responded. "I haven't breathed freely for so many years that I don't remember what it's like." She gasped for another deep breath, then added, "If I can keep breathing, I can keep writing, so I would be a writer."

Dongmei and I went to the first grade through third grade together as best friends, though I was in and out of hospitals during those years and missed most of school. Dongmei had to quit school during third grade and stay home because her breathing had worsened. I didn't know if it was something else, like tuberculosis or another lung disease that Dongmei might have had. I had no way to diagnose, but I knew she couldn't hold her breath anymore. Unfortunately, her family lacked the means to provide her any medical care she may have needed to get better. After third grade, my family and I moved away. I missed Dongmei so much but couldn't stay in touch because I was traveling for surgeries, and she quit school. We didn't know each other's addresses, so we had no way to even write letters to one another. I felt powerless that I would not be able to see her again, and I kept begging my parents to find out where she was and take me there someday.

Finally, around the time I was about eleven or twelve years old, I got an opportunity to visit that town again. My parents *finally* found Dongmei's home address for me, and I was dropped off in front of her home. I was so excited to see her again, and many days before my visit, I began imagining how awesome our meetup would be. We hadn't seen each other for more than a year.

When I got there, I walked as fast as I could into their yard, calling out. "Dongmei, Dongmei, I am back to see you!"

Their yard had a water reservoir, which was about four feet high. I heard a very weak and low voice from behind it: "I am here, but don't come close." I knew that was her. How could I not get close and see her?

I didn't listen to her instructions and crept closer, finding her hiding behind the water bucket. Who I had known—my confidante, my PE companion, my very best friend—didn't seem to be who was sitting before me. Her appearance shocked me so much that I had to consciously control my facial expression. I had grown into a regular girl's build at that time, but Dongmei had shrunk to the size of a very skinny six-year-old. Her face was pale and as little as my palm. She looked almost breakable, with tiny wrists and skinny legs, unable to hold herself up or walk without grabbing on to something. She sat on a stool behind that bucket, leaning against it and just trying to catch her breath, like a small kitten near death.

My tears poured out immediately after seeing that scene.

"What happened to you?" I asked, my voice trembling.

"I just can't breathe," she said weakly, looking up at me with eyes wide. "I don't want anyone to see me like this."

"Why?"

Her answer broke my heart in two.

"I'm too ugly to be seen," she said. "I would only dirty people's vision if they had to lay eyes on me."

I sat next to her against the water bucket. I wanted to hold her hand, but I hesitated because she seemed too fragile and tiny even for that. I had no idea that not being able to breathe could affect someone in that way. I'd always thought Dongmei and I were equal in the cards we were dealt: I got leg problems, and she got lung problems. But I was the lucky one. Polio didn't kill me, but lung disease without proper treatment was killing Dongmei.

Finally, I got the courage to put my arms around her. It felt like hugging a baby bird that had fallen out of its nest. We sat there for a long time but didn't speak; I sobbed, and she gasped. During our time apart, I'd heard from someone who had visited that Dongmei's condition had gotten worse. Whenever she had visitors at her home, she would hide in the closet and not come out. I thought she was just being naughty and throwing a tantrum, and that once I saw her, I could convince her to come out and play like the old days.

I was wrong.

Life had been cruel to her. Dongmei's family was very poor and couldn't afford medicine for her illness, so she was left to languish inside the house with no hope of recovering.

After a long time, she spoke.

"If you help me get inside, I can show you my writing. I really don't want you to see me crawling back like an animal."

I held her arms as we moved inside the house, which was more like a shed with a platform to sleep on. She showed me the diary she wrote, and as I flipped through the pages, one page stuck out to me: "I can't breathe. I can't sleep. I spent the whole night trying to catch a breath." Another page: "I don't want anyone to feel sorry for me. I would be better off dead."

At the end of my visit, it started raining. She and I sat together under the roof, staring at the rain together. The scene felt familiar to me in a way, as we'd spent many hours like that growing up. Only that time, there was no laughing and giggling. There was barely even any talking.

I couldn't shake one thought: *there must be some way to save her.* She just seemed to have run out of the strength to live, like a fish out of water, constantly trying to catch a breath, exhausted. For me, I knew there were still chances to live a full life and reach my full potential; for her, there was not much runway left. We sat there listening to the rain, even though I knew she hated cold and rainy weather because it made her condition even worse. I held her against me, hoping to give her just a little bit of warmth and comfort. I knew that was all I could provide for her at that time.

I left that day wishing I was powerful enough to save my best friend and knowing that I wasn't. I begged my parents to help Dongmei. Mom and Dad said that we couldn't even afford our own medical bills, noting there were times we had to borrow money to afford my surgeries. Dongmei's chronic condition required daily medication that they couldn't afford to pay for either. Nobody we knew of could be that hero to save her.

"Maybe we will all get better over time!" I had to tell myself that, so that I could sleep at night sometimes.

About six months later, Dongmei's elder sister came to visit my parents. My parents sent me outside so I wouldn't hear the conversation, but I had a feeling it was about Dongmei. I disobeyed my parents and eavesdropped outside the door. Mom asked about Dongmei, and Dongmei's sister said she'd passed away. My tears started flowing nonstop, but I couldn't make a sound. All I could see in my head was my friend smiling on a warm day, sitting in the sunshine, free of illness and pain. Maybe she became a mermaid, breathing freely in water, swimming and exploring the wild ocean down there. Maybe she was writing in Heaven, as she had always said she wanted to grow up to be a writer.

Later that day, I told my parents I knew about it. We never spoke of her again, but I carry Dongmei with me to this day. Sometimes, when I'm all by myself, I take a deep breath for both of us, and I feel her presence with me. I keep her memory inside of me so I can live the life we both wanted and deserved. I still wish I could go back. I wish I could save her. I will forever be haunted by the image of her tiny figure hiding in her closet, until she knew it was me. She let me see her in her suffering, and I didn't look away. I couldn't save my friend, but what I can do is remember her and say her name. In 2017, I was watching the movie *Coco*, and it said the spirits of the dead only fade away when no one remembers them anymore. So as long as I live, Dongmei's spirit will never fade away, and hopefully after I disappear from this world, whoever reads this book can think of Dongmei, to keep her spirit alive. She never became what she wanted to be, but you and I will know her name, and the world will know that Dongmei existed. Her life mattered to me. Her friendship saved me in a million ways. Dongmei accepted and loved me for exactly who I was.

I wanted to reach my own full potential, and I needed to get there by building up my brain instead of my body. My parents had expended so much time and money on my medical treatment, and it was clear that I would never fully recover. I loved school and hated that the surgeries took me away from my academic pursuits for long periods of time. Around the winter of 1988, after another surgery, I told Dad that I wanted to stop the surgeries forever and focus on empowering my brain. He agreed. We both knew I needed to nurture my intense curiosity and further my academic goals. I made my decision not only based on my own disappointment with the surgeries or our family's financial situation but also due to the death of Dongmei. I needed to live with the best spirit for both of us. It wasn't worth chasing after a so-called normal body anymore.

I was ready to stop trying to fix my body and instead accept that I would have some physical limitations. I decided to *never* have another surgery again in my life to fix my polio. I accepted my body as it was from that moment.

3.

UNITED WITH FAMILY
(1989–1995)

Family is everything in my culture.
We live for one another.

There are some people in your lifetime with
whom you form impenetrable bonds, and your family
is first on that list. The values they pass down to you
and the legacy they carry and instill are both
so deep that they run in your veins.

They impact not only how you behave
but also how you approach joys and challenges
inherent to the life in front of you.

From big moments to small interactions,
we are foremost shaped by those who knew us first
and who know us best: our families.

3.1. LIFE OF FOUR

For many years and across much of North China, our family was separated. Dad was in a different field every year without his family, working his assigned survey jobs. My brother and I had to be away from both of our parents for many years, staying with relatives. After Mom reunited with me and my brother, the three of us had to move many times for her jobs, too. The four of us had never spent more than a week's time together before 1989. We'd lived in tents in forests, cabins on top of mountains, some temporary housing as base locations for survey teams, and countless places we stayed only a few months at a time.

China grew more modern over the years, and people started exploring different jobs themselves instead of taking assigned jobs. Dad kept an eye out for any opportunity that could improve our lives. He began to apply for jobs in modern cities. The goal was to move there as a family and settle down. We were all sick and tired of spending time apart: Dad was mostly in the field for nine-plus months out of the year, and Mom was taking care of two kids on her own. When Mom got pulled into field work, or her further education sometimes, my brother and I had to be sent to relatives for that period.

In 1989, Dad finally got a great job offer as the chief staff engineer in the Urban Planning Bureau in a beautiful seaside city: Dalian, in Liaoning Province. He would be leading all technical staff on survey and planning projects. Mom also got a job offer as a CPA for one of the major development zones for the city. Both of my parents had spent many years building up their own skills and credentials. They stayed vigilant for potential opportunities that would be better for our family. Their effort finally paid off, and we were able to take control of our own lives. This development meant we could stay together in a place we could call home, and the four of us could experience what having a family really felt like. The whole journey just took us thirteen years (1976–1989).

Before the move, Dad called a family meeting at our home in Qiqihar, the city we lived in at that time. He told us we needed to move to a new city called Dalian, where both my brother and I would have a much better opportunity for education. Best of all, all four of us would be able to live together, forever. (Well, to be more precise, the three of them would go first, and I'd need to stay behind for six months to wrap up the current school year before transferring to the middle school in Dalian.) Neither my brother nor I appreciated my parents' effort during that meeting, and we voiced our strong objections that we didn't want to leave our friends in Qiqihar. Of course, our parents did what most parents would do: acknowledged our concerns but disregarded our opinions. With trust, we moved forward with the plan—together. Our parents were right in the end; we had so many opportunities in Dalian, and our lives would have been totally different if we'd stayed behind. Dalian is a major international port city, the second largest city in Liaoning Province, and today it's a financial, shipping, and logistics center for East Asia. It's also one of the most beautiful cities I have ever lived in.

During the time I had to stay by myself in another cousin's care, Dad and I wrote letters to each other. I would tell Dad what was going on in school, with my grades, and things in my life. Dad would write back with encouragement, providing guidance for my schoolwork and tips in life. For that six-month period, I didn't feel left behind. Instead, for the first time in my life, I felt like I had gained a mentor through those letters.

In fall 1989, the four of us started living under the same roof. Nobody had to travel to the field anymore, and we were all able to have dinner together on weekends at the same table—my brother and I had dinner at school during weekdays. That sense of belonging made me feel safe and warm, just from simply living normal daily life, together.

Mom and Dad rented a place right next to our school while they waited for an assigned condo from Dad's work. We had two bedrooms, so my brother and I had to share a room. The last few years in Qiqihar, we'd lived in a condo that had a gas stove, a faucet, and a toilet that flushed. I was so happy to see similar things in our home in Dalian. It meant no freezing butt doing my business outside of the house and no smoke every morning trying to light the fire to cook. It still makes me smile thinking how easily someone can be satisfied with the little things people take for granted today.

Relationships are built with little moments that show love and care. I always wondered how my parents were able to build such a strong relationship for our family, and I think the reasons are in those little moments.

Dad never thought anything related to his children was little and attended closely to our needs. I recall telling Dad one morning that the pen I used for school was not smooth enough, and that night he gave me a set of new pens that were much better. One day I mentioned that I missed the persimmons we used to eat in Qiqihar. As you may have guessed, later at the dinner table, those same persimmons showed up. Mom said Dad spent the whole day searching all the stores in Dalian until he found some similar ones.

Mom showed care in similar ways. She got up every day around 5:00 a.m. and cooked a full meal for my brother and me as breakfast and also packed us yummy lunches and dinners for school. During the weekdays, we'd arrive at school between 6:30–7:00 for morning class, have lunch at our desk for an hour, attend more classes until 5:00 p.m., have our home-packed dinners together—heated by the school stove—then continue with night class until roughly 8:30 in the evening. During the weekend, we studied some more. No video games, no internet, no cell phone, no TV. By today's standard, that perhaps seems cruel, but when most people around you are living the same way, it feels normal and right.

Every Sunday morning, we could relax a bit together. Those were my fondest moments: the four of us would gather on Mom and Dad's bed, lying where warm sunlight covered us. We would just talk, sharing all the moments and the little things in our own lives. Dad would have my brother scratch his back, and we would lie in each other's arms for hours. We would talk a lot about the hard days when Dad had to travel in the field and Mom was taking care of us alone. We shared stories from our lives apart, laughing about the days when we had to poop in frozen weather outside. We truly loved that we were finally living together. Happiness was just that simple. We had no fortune at that time, but we had each other, and we had lots of love. That love was built so strong and tight that it has not faded away a bit since then.

When we had so little, happiness was so easy to get; when we had so much, later in our lives, happiness became hard to acquire. All the moments with family somehow built a reservoir of happiness while I was growing up, so whenever I needed it later in life, my memory would take me to those Sunday mornings where the four of us were together.

We all knew that we would have storms ahead of us, but we were not afraid of them. We knew that as a family that stayed together and worked hard toward the same goals, nothing could defeat us. We were all doing our share for a better life together.

We lived like that for six years throughout my middle and high school years. We ended up moving seven times in Dalian—sometimes just to get us closer to the best schools but sometimes because we couldn't afford the rent anymore—especially during the years when Dad had to start his own business. There were dark times for both me and my brother, struggling inside as teenagers. I learned later that Mom and Dad had to deal with their own challenges during that time, too, but they never let us see them. Whenever we got together for those Sunday mornings, we opened up and shared with each other. Clouds in our heads and hearts would be beamed away by the space full of light on our parents' bed. We were always there for each other and still are today.

3.2. THE JOY AND PAIN OF GROWING UP

On my first day in middle school in this big new city, I felt ready to conquer the world and show them how great I was. Right after my introduction to the class, the morning study session started, and I was defeated by the world immediately. Everyone started to recite English words, following a lead student. *WHAT IS THAT?* I couldn't believe what I'd heard. Apparently, most students in Dalian had started learning English in elementary school, so by middle school, they were already able to communicate in the language somewhat. I, however, had no education in English before that day. I was shocked, scared, and depressed immediately. For my first- to sixth-grade years—elementary school in China—even though I had missed most of school due to various surgeries, I was still able to stay at the top of the class. Mostly I was ranked number one in all my classes, and schoolwork felt relatively effortless. I thought I was just smart, but it turns out that the tables can turn simply by switching to another crowd. For the whole day, I saw other students doing things that I had no clue how to do. I hadn't even learned the alphabet at that time.

By the end of the day, I felt like a deflated balloon. When I finally got home, I burst through the door and cried out to Dad that I'd become the worst student in that whole new school. But still, I told myself that I could pick up the language quickly. For three days, I tried to memorize four English words: face, hand, eye, and nose. I just couldn't. Suddenly, it felt like nothing made any sense to me. With Chinese characters, I had somehow picked them up without a teacher. As I've mentioned, before I even began first grade, I'd already started reading Chinese classic books while lying in hospital beds. There are rules dictating how Chinese characters are put together, and I could memorize them easily and even guess the meaning of a word by examining how it was structured. For example, the character 木 means "wood." It looks like a tree with roots under the ground. The character 人 means "human," and it looks like a person walking. The two characters combined mean "resting," and they look like a person sitting next to a tree: 休.

It makes sense, right? But English, why? Why do the letters F-A-C-E put together mean something? Why not A-F-E-C or F-E-C-A? Those twenty-six characters would generate an infinite number of combinations with various lengths. There were simply no rules that I could understand, and I had to force myself to just memorize without understanding. I pulled my hair out trying, but after a whole week, I still couldn't spell those four words with confidence. It was the first time I felt desperate academically. I went to school every day that first week frustrated and in fear of failure. Nothing about this mysterious language made sense. *I must master this along with other subjects*, I told myself. *There is no way out.*

After the first week, I knew my method wasn't working. I told my English teacher that I needed some guidance. At the same time, I told Dad that I needed help. My teacher was wonderful and told me that I just need to be exposed to the language long enough to see that there *were* rules, and he recommended that I go to a place called English Corner in Dalian. It sounded fancy, but it was just an open area in the middle of a square park that people would go every Sunday to speak English to each other. There was nothing else there besides people talking. But I was in! The first Sunday, I took the bus there and listened for *four* hours as students and expats easily conversed with each other. I didn't understand a single word. Not even one! I was hoping to catch one of the four words I'd tried so hard to learn, but nobody mentioned their faces, hands, eyes, and noses. When someone attempted to communicate with me in English, I just proudly told them the four words I knew. Somehow, I was fascinated by the scene and felt excited that I could eventually learn English by going there every Sunday.

I came home glowing and hopeful, telling Dad I'd found the right kind of people to help me become a proficient English speaker. The next Sunday, I brought an English dictionary with me and started asking people to show me the words they were using to communicate. I started speaking in English by grabbing random strangers at English Corner, one after another, hour after hour. Sometimes the whole day would go by, and the last batch of people I kept there talking would beg me to let them go home. When I had nobody else to talk to, I read English words from my dictionary aloud as much as possible.

Dad had studied Russian in his school as a second language, so he couldn't help me personally. After he realized I was struggling with English, he immediately went to a tutor's market—a place where lots of students and teachers hold up signs on the subjects in which they are offering to tutor. After interviewing several people, Dad found an awesome senior college student majoring in English to tutor me. Working with my tutor, learning from people at the English Corner, and studying myself non-stop for the entire semester, I expanded my vocabulary and communication skills in this language with lightning speed. My tutor only stayed with me for that one semester, but I ended up going to English Corner every Sunday for many years until college. Around 1992, I got a Walkman to listen to cassettes recorded by native English speakers. I remember the most popular set was *Family Album, U.S.A.* My only complaint was that those materials didn't teach slang—I had to learn the good stuff from *Friends* episodes in college after 1995.

After the first semester in the new school, I became invincible in English and started ranking top in the class. The unspoken rules in English didn't need to be taught anymore, because the language had started to make sense to me. Ever since then, English has been the most effortless subject for me in school.

Mom and Dad joked with me that the reason I could succeed in studying English so quickly was because I "had no shame in me" during this learning process. They admired my courage of going to English Corner with only four words learned at that point. The fact that I would open my mouth speaking just those four words in front of those experts surprised them. Many people would feel shame around knowing nothing about a subject and might try to hide that fact from others, but I had no shame in exposing my ignorance to learn better.

I think they were right. I had always pursued learning—especially regarding what I had *yet* to learn—with no shame, and that trait carried me far.

I also started making lots of friends at school. I've always had my best girlfriends who I spent time with, but I also made secret friends with the "bad boys." One scene in middle school went like this:

"I nodded at the boy ever so slightly. He casually looked over his shoulder and then slid his knife in my desk. A few minutes later, the scene repeated with another boy. And another. By the start of class, I would have an entire desk full of knives and other weapons."

I couldn't be the strongest, so I had to be the smartest, not just academically. As the top student in every class, I used my reputation as a good girl to survive my teen years and keep myself safe at school. The teachers all liked me because of my academic efforts, so I used their perception of me to build a network of allies. I knew I was vulnerable, and I needed to secure the protection of kids stronger than me to avoid getting bullied. Some of the boys in my class, the strongest and biggest who didn't pay much attention in school, often got into fights. Naturally, they brought little weapons to school, mostly big wooden sticks, axes, and tiny knives used for fruit cutting. Of course, weapons were not allowed, and the teachers frequently searched those boys' pockets and desks to confiscate any knives they brought to school.

I struck a deal with these boys to slip me their weapons at the beginning of the day so I could keep them in my desk. I did this very discreetly with each of them, so they weren't aware of who else I was helping. No teacher ever thought to search my desk, and my secret weapons stash was never found. In turn, I now had the most feared boys in every class on my side.

Nobody dared to touch me or mess with me. My personal bodyguards took it too far on occasion. One day another student walked behind me, mimicking my limp. I didn't notice the ridicule, but one of my best girlfriends saw it and told the boys in our class. They gathered after school, found that kid, and beat him up. Turns out he wasn't imitating my limp. He had a broken leg that day. So, the kid who was wronged gathered his brothers and friends and started another fight the next day. Of course, they all got caught. The next morning, I noticed many of our boys were lined up outside of classrooms with bruises and bleeding noses, and I wondered what trouble they had gotten into this time. I didn't find out until later that day that it had been me and my limp that caused the big "oops" event. Though violence is never the solution, the fact that my friends were always looking after me warms my heart to this day.

Even though my academic success and social survival skills made me popular with teachers and students, I still felt alone and like I didn't belong. It was almost like people didn't see my leg as part of me. They liked and respected me but showed palpable discomfort with my leg. Nobody understood that rejecting a part of me was rejecting all of me. Their attempts at trying to ignore or gloss over my disability made me feel like I should do the same.

At school every morning, we had a flag ceremony, where the top student had the honor of raising our country's flag in front of everyone else. Even though I was almost always at the top of my class, I never once was given this honor. When I received academic awards at school, my teachers picked other students to walk across the stage and accept the award on my behalf, to avoid the embarrassment of me walking with a limp in front of people.

My teachers truly believed they were extending kindness to me by not asking me to stand or walk in front of an audience. They tried to keep me from being humiliated about my leg, but at the same time, they instilled in me a belief that it was something to be embarrassed about in the first place. Nobody ever asked me about my preference and how I'd like to handle these situations. Seeing my limp would be offensive to the audience. My teachers meant well and felt protective of me, but their actions unintentionally added to my shame and feelings of inadequacy. Those were not healthy thoughts.

I befriended the only other girl my age who also had polio in that school. Talking to her and sharing our experiences made me feel less alone. But one day she just disappeared from school. I couldn't find her and heard she had dropped out of school due to "psychological issues." People told me that she'd been having trouble dealing with her disability and had started thinking everyone who was speaking quietly was doing so to gossip about her polio leg. She got extremely uncomfortable with people's eyes until she couldn't take it anymore. Being obsessed with her polio and not being able to focus on anything else prevented her from staying in school. Her family took her out and moved away, to hide her from any school. I couldn't find her to ask what had happened, but I could understand how she felt. It was the same feeling Dongmei had felt before her death: being afraid that living in public with her appearance would "dirty people's eyes."

Our environment treated us carefully, but it caused a set of extreme sensitivities, making us feel that we were inferior or less capable than others. Hiding ourselves away was an easy way out—or sometimes the only thing we knew. Growing up in that environment, I also falsely believed that having a disability was my biggest weakness and that I needed to hide that fact from people as much as possible. I, along with everyone around me, also believed that my achievement academically was a natural *compensation* for my disability instead of a merit of its own. It wasn't until much later in life that I became comfortable with myself and believed my disability was just one of the attributes that made me unique. It's unfortunate that it took me so many years to come to that realization.

I never got to the point where I wanted to leave school, but I understood my friend's perspective. There are too many indignities and insults to count, and they made no sense to me. One still sticks out in my mind and has left the deepest scars. Once, when I was walking down the hallway opening a letter from a friend, a boy I didn't know was heading toward me. "I can't believe a cripple like you is worth writing a letter to," he smirked. I was left speechless, watching him round the corner. I've replayed this situation a million times in my head, racking my brain for a cutting and witty comeback. Decades later, I still haven't come up with one.

His insult didn't even make logical sense. What did my limp have to do with receiving letters? But it didn't matter; the exchange was forever burned into my mind and commemorated in my diary. I spent what felt like the whole night crying about the throwaway comment of another student I didn't even know. He's probably never thought of the incident again in his life. It was most hurtful that he had said "a cripple like you," as if I was my limp, not that I had a limp. My disability became me, my whole identity. It's as if he'd pointed at my leg and said: this is all you are.

Little things like that bothered me a lot growing up. The difference between then and now is that I've learned to fully accept myself, so nothing can hurt me now.

3.3. DAD'S BIG ADVENTURE

"There is no way we can afford to send both of you to college."

Dad looked at me and my brother seriously, then added "unless we give up everything we have right now and take a huge risk together in the next few years."

In 1992, Dad called a family meeting and said the above to us. I was about to start high school, so three years later I'd be eligible to go to college. My brother would need to do the same merely a year later. Though my parents had both worked hard for many years, they'd spent so much on my surgeries when I was younger and wouldn't have enough money for our college education.

There was a big change coming to China: before 1994, all the college education in China was paid by the country. However, starting that year, the top forty universities in China began charging college tuition and fees. By 1996, all universities would charge tuition and fees. Many families didn't see that coming and weren't prepared financially, but Dad saw what was next. He knew we must do something different soon, to afford two college tuitions for my brother and me three and four years later.

He evaluated all possible options besides starting his own business to earn more money, and they were all unacceptable to him. He knew my brother and I wouldn't qualify for financial aid because of our middle-class status. He also knew we wouldn't be able to borrow money because our family was the most well-off among people we knew. In addition, borrowing money from anyone was a scary thought, especially due to our deeply held belief that you always live within your means. At that time, we believed borrowing money should only happen under extreme conditions like urgent medical payments but not to pay for something like going to college. For many of us who grew up in that environment, if your family couldn't pay, you didn't go. Dad had crunched the numbers over and over and estimated how much he'd be able to save over the next three years before college. It wasn't going to be enough. Paying both of our tuition would require 20,000 yuan a year, and that's twice the combined income Mom and Dad made a year at that time, which is around 1,000 yuan ($142) per month.

As I saw my dreams of a college education slipping away, Dad shared a bold idea that would change everything.

Dad said he and Mom had agreed for him to quit his current job and start his own business: a geo-survey company working on surveying jobs for buildings in Dalian, so we could still be together. That meant several things. First, he would need to take on a pile of debt to buy professional equipment to get his business started. Though Dad didn't like incurring debt, loans for business purposes were considered "good debt" because they (hopefully) could be paid off quickly and would serve as springboards for additional income. Second, we would lose the apartment in Dalian where we'd finally settled because it was government sponsored, meaning it was a perk of the job Dad held. If he quit this job, we'd be homeless. Lastly, there'd be no more extra money for anything until we paid off our debt.

That sounded scary and crazy to me and my brother, but we could see the bigger picture: if this worked out in the end, we could be sent to college with paid tuition. Mom said that we wouldn't starve because she would keep her job just in case Dad failed. She fully supported Dad, and we all saw the ambition and excitement in his eyes. Besides, we had all lived in very harsh environments before without much money, so there was no fear of going back to that life together. The decision was made that night.

While China was still a Communist country, the 1992 reform and open-door policy finally encouraged more people to work for themselves and their families rather than the party and the government. Dad was a pioneer in that sense; when he started his business, he was among the first entrepreneurs in our circles. The backlash was swift. While he remained popular with many of his friends and acquaintances, this was not true of everyone. Some of his used-to-be friends and colleagues called him a traitor to the party because, in their view, starting your own business meant that you were no longer serving the party and were rather putting your own interests first. We gave back the apartment given to us by the bureau, and my parents rented a tiny room for all of us to live in together. That meant we were back to setting up a fire stove in the morning and using the outside public bathroom stalls (without toilets). Luckily, Mom's income helped keep us afloat while Dad launched himself into his new business venture, working feverishly to turn a profit and start paying back the mountain of debt he'd accrued.

To be able to purchase the equipment for his company, he needed to borrow over 200,000 yuan (about $30,000), which was an insane amount of money at that time and about twenty times their combined annual income in 1992. It helped immensely that Dad had strong credibility among all his friends. Because of that, he was able to borrow a little—a few hundred to a thousand—from each to arrive at the total amount needed. With his calculation, if the projects went well, he would be able to pay off all those debts within two years. His assumption was that he could bid on projects (like making a survey map) that only took a few days or weeks to complete, but the payment was in the tens of thousands of yuan. The skills that Dad had acquired were rare in China at that time, and his only competitor was his previous government department.

We made a plan as a family, and everyone was assigned a mission: Dad focused 100 percent on his company projects to pay off debt; Mom kept a full-time job, ran the budget of the household, took care of us, and acted as the part-time CPA for Dad's company; my brother needed to be admitted to the best public high school by 1993 since we had no money to pay for any private high school; I'd already gotten into the best public high school and just needed to stay at number one in my class and the top ten in that school so that I could guarantee getting into one of the best universities in China a few years later.

We all took our assignments, gritted our teeth, and executed them. My brother and I lost our weekly allowances, wore old clothes, and ate less-expensive food. Mom would get up every morning to set the fire in the stove to heat up the little room we all lived in, cooking all the food for that day for us to take to school; Dad worked hard in his business.

We all faced many challenges to complete our mission, but we trusted each other and provided the support needed as a tight family. My assignment was to be the best tutor for my brother so that he could get into the best public school the year after. Unlike me, my brother was popular and charming growing up, and often he would receive love letters and gifts from girls at school. Instead of sharing my concerns with him directly, I wrote him long letters to encourage him to take on his family duty to focus on his studies instead. In later years, it was interesting for me to read those letters where I shared feelings with others—I chose writing instead of conversations. We never said "I love you" directly, but we used action to show our deep feelings for each other.

Mom carried on so many tasks and never complained. We were poor, but she made sure our clothes were always clean, our food was always carefully put together and tasted good, and our spirits were always positive. Though we didn't have money and a comfortable lifestyle, we had our smiles and grace.

Dad's challenge was the biggest, but he didn't talk much about it at the time. Many years later, he mentioned that he faced lots of political battles to be able to bid on and win projects publicly. He had to use his wisdom and skills to fight with many people for things to move forward an inch at a time. I asked him if he was scared at times, and he said no, because his whole family was behind him, and he was not scared of anything. He knew we were all tough enough to live through that period.

I didn't realize until much later how much my parents quietly sacrificed during those early years of Dad's business. Or sometimes, not so quietly. I remember we had a small wooden coffee table with a giant dent right in the middle of it. As a kid, I never questioned where the dent came from. Dad only told me ten years later that one night, he was sitting at the table in the dark. He was alone and frustrated because the bidding process didn't feel fair. He suspected that there were under-the-table deals made because even when his quotes were more competitive, he'd still lose. The business wasn't going well, and he was desperate. He took a hammer and slammed it down on the coffee table in frustration, leaving the dent. It remained there as a silent symbol of how scary the situation was for my parents, even though they put up a front of calmness for my brother and me during those years.

Kids often understand more than we think, yet they can also be oblivious in some ways—at least, that was the case for my brother and me. I remember that our parents were barely home during those startup years, but I didn't know why until recently. Because our place was tiny (it was like the flat we had in the old days in Longjiang—a kitchen that was just an indoor stove with a chimney on it), our parents went for long walks at night to ensure that my brother and I had enough space and quietness to spread out and concentrate on our homework. Even in the freezing winter months, they would leave for hours, walking in the darkness, holding hands and braving the cold, to make sure we had uninterrupted study time. It feels like every time I talk to my parents, I find out about another hidden kindness they extended to us kids so we could focus on our education and have every opportunity to succeed.

I believe that in tough times, character is molded and relationships are tightened. The years 1992 to 1995 were our toughest time together as a family. During those years, we ended up moving seven times around Dalian until we got a home of our own. Each time when we needed to move, Mom would pack up everything like a pro before the move. By the time my brother and I got back to the new rental location at the end of the day, she had already finished unpacking so we could get on with our studies immediately. When things were not going well, all the turmoil was hidden from me and my brother so we could focus on what was important: our education. I have often wondered if, as a parent myself, I could ever be as good as my own.

I don't know the answer to that, but I do know that when a family stays close and has a shared goal, they can dissolve any obstacles along the way.

3.4. OUR FAMILY'S BIG WINS

The risk we took together as a family paid off in just a couple of years, and everyone accomplished their mission.

Mom did all her jobs flawlessly, supporting everyone in the family and ensuring we were all well fed to tackle our tasks. My brother was able to get into the best public high school in our district in 1993, which was a big relief for the family that year. I maintained top scores in my high school, won many academic awards, and was ready to be admitted to the best universities in 1995.

Dad won all the battles he needed to fight, too. By late 1994, he'd not only paid off all the debts, but he had also built a successful business with a team of his own. He bought an office condo to run his business and a three-bedroom apartment for our family to move into. He even bought a van for his business to do field trips more efficiently. Back then, we were the only family we knew who owned a personal vehicle in Dalian, unlike nowadays, where almost everyone owns a car.

Suddenly, we could afford things we never had before! However, Mom and Dad kept things reasonable for us: our allowances were back, but no luxury items were allowed. We knew what was important in our lives, and it was never fancy or superficial things. It was always the people that we cared about, including those in our extended family, whom Dad also wanted to help.

Our extended family is big: one of Dad's brothers has five kids, the other has four, and Mom's elder sister has four kids as well. Dad wanted all of them to achieve their life goals. Because it's hard to help everyone at the same time, Dad came up with a strategy: train some of them to be more skillful so they could, in turn, do the same for others. I recall for many years, he sent one of my cousins to school to become a tailor and another to learn geological survey with him as a field worker and driver. The premise was that once one of the kids in the family became stronger, they could start helping the others to get better over time. Dad always says, "It's better to teach someone to fish than give him a fish." Once his nieces and nephews were taken care of, his company's success allowed him to do even more in an even bigger way.

He helped Mom's elder sister with their first condo purchase and bought his two brothers their own houses, thanking them for putting him through college while raising their own big families. Everything was fully paid without any mortgage. He even bought a home for me before I went to college. It was a beautiful condo close to the sea. I tried to tell him, "Dad, I don't need it. I'm going to college." He was adamant that I would have a place to live that was my own. In case I ever got caught up with a guy who mistreated me, Dad wanted me to be able to tell him to get the hell out of my own place! "That's how I can protect you, Libo," he said. "I'll make sure you'll always have a place to call your own."

Dad was also ready to buy my little brother a home, but my brother said he was ready to deal with this world himself and managed to buy his first home only a few years after college, fully paid as well, with his own hard-earned money. Though Dad tried his best to be the safety net for us, he also taught us to stand on our own.

In 1994, by local standards, we were wealthy, paying cash for a lot of real estate and a car, and saving up for all the upcoming college fees for my brother and me. It was a completely different lifestyle after being poor for so many years. Aside from the material conveniences, I was of course most excited that I didn't have to give up my dream of going to college. Thanks to my parents' dedication and effort, my number one goal in life moved within reach.

As a teenager at that time, I didn't know that much about Dad's journey of taking our family to higher financial ground. I only knew that we were poor growing up due to my surgeries, that we were middle class once we stopped the surgeries, and that we were very poor again due to Dad quitting his job and going into big debt for his business. In the end, we became rich right before I went to college.

Many years after Dad's retirement, he started to write about his life, sending me his manuscript as he worked on it. Then, I was able to fully understand what had happened during his business journey as his stories were revealed in front of my eyes.

From 1965 to 1988, Dad had been working for the government in the field, surveying and mapping. Though working in an organization for the country, he had always been an entrepreneur at heart. Everywhere he went, he always found a way for his team to not only fulfill the country's needs but also make extra profit from the real market. This was true even though that profit was spread evenly with everyone else in the same system. He was able to use the extra profit for their team to purchase the latest equipment and increase productivity.

In 1988, right after I told Dad that I wouldn't do any more leg surgeries for the rest of my life, Dad realized he didn't need to take on any additional field work to save for surgeries. Instead, our family's priority needed to switch; it was more important to be together, to be in a place where my brother and I had access to better education and a place Dad and Mom could develop further. After lots of research and effort, he and Mom both landed their jobs in Dalian starting in 1988. After he began working in his new organization, Dad accomplished a few things in his professional life that truly reflected the Cao values.

First, after he got his new job in Dalian, he used the first two years (1988–1990) to clean up a lot of mistakes that were made by the leadership before him. For example, he identified a major mistake that was made during the Cultural Revolution (1966–1976). It was in a survey that fundamentally defined the level of accuracy of all their work before 1988, but nobody tried to understand the root cause—let alone fix it. That resulted in huge errors that failed the qualification of work from the city of Dalian for more than ten years. He was furious about such low-level mistakes having been carried on for such a long period of time. He wrote, "Someone should be sent to prison for allowing such mistakes to be in a city's fundamental infrastructure." He then relentlessly led his team in correcting all those years of mistakes, all within two years after he took over.

As a second step, after the errors had been corrected, he decided to train his team to become the most advanced survey team in China. Using the money he had earned with his previous team by taking on extra projects, he bought a computer and brought it with him to his new team in Dalian. In the process of correcting previous years of errors in survey maps, he realized that nobody in his new organization knew how to use a computer. He asked why, in such a modern city, people didn't even use the technology he'd been using for years. The answer was that they did purchase several computers, but they were left in storage for years because nobody knew how to use them. Dad set up a training program and had all his teams trained to be able to do their jobs completely using computers —no more manual work. In China in 1989, this was a significant and advanced approach.

Third, with a new team equipped with modern technology and higher productivity, Dad was able to take his team to the market and earn profit outside of the work that was assigned by the government. Dad always had a sharp eye for identifying market needs. In late 1990, during the early years when our family all settled in Dalian, he took us to travel. However, he found out that the guide map to the city of Dalian was made by another city's surveying and mapping office. He felt immediately that this was a huge, missed opportunity. Right away, he set up a technical team to make a new guide map design, with the more accurate and recent maps he led his team to make. He also set up a marketing team to get sponsorship for companies and sites that wanted to be highlighted on the map. After all the effort, it was a huge success. Those who had sponsored the guide map were very happy that it was beautifully done and distributed everywhere in Dalian, and those who hadn't sponsored it regretted their short-sighted decision. For that project alone, he was able to generate over 120,000 yuan in profit for the urban planning bureau he was working for. Dad wrote in his manuscript: "It's the leader's job to have a vision far enough and lead everyone else to a better future together."

By 1992 though, even with all those major achievements at his organization, Dad wasn't happy. All the projects were done mostly by a small team he led with a handful of people, but the profit had to be spread evenly to everyone in the bureau. He proposed another model that would include profit sharing; in other words, extra effort gets extra money. In his proposal, he wrote:

We must encourage those who are willing to put in extra effort to be rewarded more. For a small team with a handful of people that brought in over 400k yuan profit for this month, we can't just reward them with 200 yuan as their bonus, which is exactly the same as the other two thousand people in the organization. The leaders in our country have already encouraged us to move from "planned economy" to "market economy." We must adapt and leap forward as well. I recommend a contract-based reward system that would allow a fairer profit-sharing model, based on percentages for each team's contribution to the projects.

His proposal was denied. Regardless, they promised him that if he stayed, he could be the head of that bureau in the next election due to the popularity he had gained by bringing extra profit to everyone. Dad decided to resign. He'd calculated that even with that role, he and Mom still wouldn't be able to afford the upcoming college fees for me and my brother. He needed the next three years to make a significant amount of income. To do that, he knew he had to find a way to make his own rules with the skills he'd learned.

China's culture and economic climate were also at a precipice of change during that time. While my parents were working and we were going to school, Dad was always on the lookout to better our family's situation. Then came our leader Deng Xiaoping's series of speeches during his Southern Tour in 1992, which is widely regarded as a critical point in the modern history of China. Deng's speeches made notable remarks on the focus of economic development. He commented on various forms of getting people rich ("I don't care if the cat is black or white, so long as it catches mice"), and said it's OK to get rich ("To get rich is glorious"). He mentioned that "development is of overriding importance" and said that "[we] should be bolder in carrying out the Reforms and Opening-Up, dare to make experiments and should not act as women with bound feet."

Having lived through that time, I can't stress enough the importance of those Southern Tour Speeches. Until that time, ever since the People's

Republic of China was founded in 1949, a common belief had been that we should spread wealth evenly. People were afraid to own their own businesses because they were not sure if they would lose their wealth after getting rich. Many political events that happened during the Cultural Revolution scared people for life. But Deng's speeches in 1992 had a new set of political theories and policies: "The theoretical system of socialism with Chinese characteristics." This approach encouraged people to be bold, to explore the market, to own private businesses, and to build wealth. Of course, before 1992, there were people who'd already begun owning their own businesses, but those speeches reassured the larger public that it was not only *OK* but *encouraged* to do so. This was a pivotal moment in the social and economic history of China.

Many years later, American billionaire Charlie Munger—Warren Buffet's closest business partner—said in one of the Berkshire Hathaway meetings, "Former Chinese paramount leader Deng Xiaoping was one of the world's greatest leaders due to economic changes made during his tenure that opened up the nation to the West, modernized China and helped reduce poverty." I am glad someone like Charlie understands the significance of Deng's economic policies that enabled China to start decades of fast development.

Deng's speeches greatly encouraged Dad, who believed in all the same philosophies. He saw that China was opening economically and noted an opportunity in the emerging free market. He had been frustrated with the system as it was before, where he couldn't work harder for greater reward. With an evenly distributed profit-sharing model, he couldn't do more to provide for his family, because of the system. I shared a glimpse of the story from 1992 that triggered our family meeting where Dad announced he was taking the risk. Our family's win during those years also reflected wins for the country, for many other families in China also got richer starting in those years. China has grown to become an economical giant during the last thirty years, which was attributed to the open-mindedness of the leaders who embraced the market economy.

Dad was able to look ahead, prepare early by taking risks, and make sure our family could avoid any turbulence ahead of us. That was a life lesson for me: look ahead while still pedaling hard for the present. Twenty to thirty years later, his own daughter did very similar things on the other side of the globe in Silicon Valley.

Dad's big win in his adventure laid the financial foundation for the whole family to start chasing our dreams through higher education. There are, of course, things money can't buy—like people's opinions and systems we had to fight against. When those opinions are biased and systems are not flexible, they become big mountains that spread out before us. In my case, it would take me ten years of effort to climb those mountains and see the other side.

4.

"IT'S ALL FOR YOUR OWN GOOD" (1995–1999)

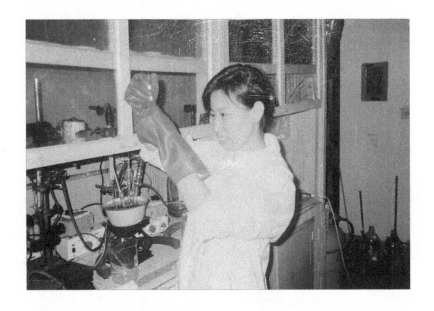

"He who controls others may be powerful, but
he who conquers himself is mightier still."

(胜人者有力 自胜者强)

—Tao Te Ching, Chapter 33

Throughout our lives, some people try to
make decisions for others "for their own good."
This sometimes comes from people or systems with power,
and sometimes from those who care for and love us.

But are they for our own good, really?
What happens when inside, we want something else
for ourselves, despite the good intentions?

The answer to this question depends on the circumstances.
Sometimes, we can go our own way, but other times,
we must take those decisions and try to move forward.
Either way, it's important never to forget what we truly want,
and never stop inching toward our goals,
step by step and little by little.

4.1. DARKNESS FALLS

"No university will admit you, because of your disability, Libo. You'd better get prepared for that!"

I had top scores and was aiming for college entrance exams with confidence. And then, the dean at my high school spoke those words.

It was just a few months away from the date I'd been preparing for, having given up holidays, summers, breaks, nights, and weekends. I thought if I worked hard enough and could become the best, I would get into the best universities in China and my life would take off from there. I couldn't believe what I was hearing, so I questioned her further.

"But I am one of the only two students who got all straight As in the nine standard tests last month, out of thousands of students around here!" I shouted.

"Yes. AND you are the only one who is aiming for the top-ranked universities, AND you failed the PE test in running. That alone can get you rejected." She calmly pointed out my obvious failure.

"But PE test scores were not counted and submitted!" I argued.

"That score was not, but your personal archives recorded the disability and will be looked at," she countered. I couldn't hide it.

"How do you know? Where are the rules written? I'd like to read them!" I still didn't believe her.

"Well, trust me, I have been in the education business my entire life," she said. "I don't want you to be disappointed later with rejections, so it's better to be prepared and seek a prearrangement with some local universities in Dalian, instead of blindly applying and getting rejections."

After all the back-and-forth arguments, I still couldn't believe what I'd heard. How did my polio have anything to do with my brain and my right to receive the best education? I insisted on looking up any written rules, but she insisted there were none written. She advised this would happen: after I applied to universities, the admission officers would see my disability record. Regardless of my top scores in academic subjects, for that reason only, I would be rejected. The recommended approach for me, then, was to have Dad contact local universities, set up appointments with their admission offices, and see if they could spare me a slot somewhere.

I didn't understand why this could happen, but I understood the risk if we didn't listen to her. If we didn't take the right approach, I could be silently rejected by the universities that I applied to, regardless of my scores. No admission office would owe me any explanation.

"It's all for your own good, Libo," she concluded.

She'd already discussed this with Dad before I'd entered the room. He'd teared up at the cruel news, but when hearing it a second time with me by his side, he sat there emotionless.

"Don't break your dad's heart," she continued. "Do the right thing and pick the safe route. I am only telling you this because I care for you!" She looked into my eyes, speaking calmly. I knew then that I must trust her; she must have been burned seeing other kids with disabilities being rejected by universities before, and she wanted to warn me with what could be ahead. In my physical exam archives, it was written that I am disabled with polio, one of my legs is shorter than the other, and I have no strength using that polio leg. That alone is a red mark big enough to wipe out all my academic achievements.

That night after I went home, Dad and I sat together for a long time quietly. I finally said to him:

"Then I won't go to college if I can't pick the best ones I chose!"

"No, you must receive a college degree!" Dad replied.

"But I can educate myself," I said. "I can learn computer science and be a coder. I can be a writer. I can be a teacher. There are infinite things I could learn and do to support myself," I insisted.

"Do you know how *cruel* this world could be to someone with a disability, without a college degree?" Dad replied, with sadness. "You won't even get a job. How would you support yourself in the future? All those things you just mentioned can come *after* you get your degree."

Looking back, Dad was wrong. Many years later, since the internet became a commodity, there are popular careers (YouTuber, Instagrammer, self-media) that don't require a college degree. Many other successful careers only require skills instead of a piece of paper from college.

But no doubt, my life in 1995 would have been easier if I did manage to get into a college and follow the route everyone else was following.

"Do it for your mom and me then," Dad said. "Stay close to us so we can look after you! That's the best for all of us," Dad finally said. I gritted my teeth and nodded, tears filling my eyes. The last six years of my life flashed before my eyes at that moment. *To be able to stay at the top in school, I've given up everything to study*, I thought. *I've never watched TV or a single movie throughout those years.* Even though Dad asked me many times to just go out and have some fun as a teenager, I always told him that I could only afford to relax after I got into my dream college. If you've ever worked extremely hard for a long period to prepare for a big win but were told at the last minute that you were not even good enough to get in the game—you would understand that feeling.

Dad finally got me an appointment with the best university in Dalian for a preadmission interview. We went into the office, and one middle-aged man was there to conduct the interview with me. Apparently, he wasn't surprised by this type of appointment, so there must have been some truth to my dean's words. He saw my top scores for all the tests in the past and knew that I was qualified for any major in their university. But he didn't ask me what I wanted at all. Instead, he first asked me to take a walk in front of him. I felt anger toward him and shame with myself at that moment: walking in front of a stranger with my polio leg so that, based on the severity of my limping, he could judge whether I was to be considered for admission. He was satisfied to see that although I was able to walk with a limp, I was fully capable of moving around without any help from others. That was the longest walk I have ever taken in my life. As I was walking across that room, my brain flashed back to that Zebra moment on the surgical bed; I was being treated as a piece of meat instead of as a human being who had her own soul.

Finally, he said, "How about you go to the chemistry department? We need lots of students there and never have enough people to apply for it, so you can have that one."

I almost shouted at him immediately: "But I want to study computer science instead. I don't want to study chemistry!"

"Oh NO, you can't have computer science; that's for *complete* talent," he said. "People we admit into that major must be perfect. It's really the hottest major nowadays!" he responded.

The meeting was over to him after that. He communicated that this was a "take it or leave it" opportunity and sent us out of his office. In his eyes, my physical limitations rendered me inadequate. I was incomplete, unworthy of the popular major at the time.

I can't remember how Dad and I got home that day, but I will never forget that admission officer's remarks about me not being "complete." I might not be the best, but I am as "complete" as anyone else I know. Quiet as I was on the outside, I was screaming loud on the inside: "I am

COMPLETE! I am CAPABLE! I am WORTHY, for my soul is as EQUAL as any other human being!" At that moment, I also wished I could yell at the admission man, just like how Jane Eyre expressed to Mr. Rochester—but in my words and condition: "Do you think I am an automation? A machine without feelings? And can bear to have my morsel of bread snatched from my lips, and my drop of living water dashed from my cup? Do you think, because I am disabled, powerless, obscure, plain, and little, I am soulless and heartless? You think wrong!"

I tried to fight back after that appointment, attempting to change my own fate. Note that the internet wasn't popular in 1995 China, so rarely did people have any means to leverage the internet for their voices to be heard. All you could find were a few websites, *if* you were lucky to have dial-up internet at home. But secretly, I wrote letters to the chairman of China Disabled Persons' Federation, without knowing their detailed address, only the city and organization name; I called hotlines on any radio station that I could look up, telling them what had happened to me and asking for their help; I wrote to a few writers I found in the newspaper, asking them to protest for me. One replied to me over the phone and said that while she was sorry to hear about my plight, there was "no reason" for her to even write about it because an article about one disabled kid who couldn't get into the college she wanted was just "strange." I also went to libraries to research anything I could learn about rules on college admission or further information about this "system" that people were talking about. In the end I couldn't find any, and the "system" seemed to be what everyone thought or believed. It was an invisible system in everyone's mind for how disabled people should live their lives. It was people's default perception of disabilities that had killed my dream.

But *what* was "it" exactly? If I couldn't identify the enemy, how could I defeat it? I felt powerless.

I then tried to hide myself for life so that I didn't have to interact with people. I felt that people were horrible, and the world was unfair. When everyone else was preparing for their final college entrance exam, my world went dark and collapsed. I didn't even want to finish high school anymore. I had always been ranked academically first in my class in high school, and I took pride in that. I didn't want to go back and see those who ranked behind me getting into top universities, studying the major they wanted, while my destination had been chosen for me already. I told Dad that people were bad, this world is full of crap, and I don't want to have anything to do with it. Dad didn't argue with my assessment, but he did tell me he wouldn't allow me to hide my entire life. I would have to get out there no matter what and deal with it.

So, I went back to school like nothing had happened. I lived like a zombie for the last few months and accepted my fate: to go to that local university, get a degree in chemistry, and be grateful for the opportunity. On the day I had to fill out my application form for college, I wrote down only the prearranged university called Dalian University of Technology (DUT), with chemistry selected as my major.[3] Then, I checked "Subject to any assignment," which meant the university had the right to assign

---

[3] The college application process in China at that time was different than it is in the United States. Schools are grouped into tiers. Those in the top tier are called "985 universities," followed by a tier called "211 universities," and then the remaining universities. There are, of course, hierarchies among the tiers as well; for example, the top five universities in 985 are the best in the country. When you fill out your application, you select from a list of schools that are organized by tier. You can only choose one from each tier—meaning if you choose a university from the 985 tier and don't get in, you automatically move to your 211-tier choice. There are no second options or second chances.

me any major they saw fit, regardless of my scores. Back in 1995, students filled in their college application way ahead of the big exam days, unlike the current system that's more scientific and people only fill in universities *after* they take the exams and already know their scores.

Knowing that my fate was predetermined and all my efforts in school didn't matter, I couldn't sleep for many nights before the entrance-exam day. During the multiday exams, I spent one entire night staring at the ceiling of my room, feeling as though my life was already ruined. There was no surprise in the end; after the exams were completed, my scores went way above the acceptance score for the computer science major at DUT. Though not my top choice, DUT was still a top-tier university in China *and* it was in my home city. I appreciated that a door had been opened for me but couldn't help feeling resentful because it wasn't fair.

After all college application forms were submitted, news started spreading about who was going to what school. One day, I was in the bathroom and overheard a conversation:

"Did you hear that Libo applied to DUT?" one girl said.

"WHAT? With her score, she could have applied to much better universities. What a shame. I wonder why."

"Well, maybe she just wants to stay where her parents are...you know, with her condition."

They didn't know that I could hear their whole conversation, sitting behind the locked stall door silently, with tears running down my cheeks.

All those scenes and feelings are still so real, strong, and vivid that it feels like they happened yesterday. But looking back now, I can't help but think how silly I was. I thought my life was over because I believed getting into the best university was the finish line, but that wasn't even a starting line in the measurement of a long life. At that age, what I didn't know is that life is a marathon, not a sprint. Every step counts, and the key is to never stop moving forward.

4.2. LOST IN UNIVERSITY (1995)

In the fall of 1995, Dad convinced me that studying chemistry at DUT was the right decision under the circumstances. But at that time, I didn't have the life wisdom I have now. Instead of taking advantage of my opportunities in that situation, I was just upset, aimless, and determined that my only goal was to get out of there as soon as possible with a college degree.

DUT's chemical engineering program is ranked highly among China's top-tier universities, and it's something they're famous for. The first day during class introduction, I was told that my entrance exam score was the highest for that major that year. I should have been pleased with that news, but all I wanted to do was to avoid studying or presenting the best of myself in that domain.

Though I appreciated the university being the one that accepted me as a student with a disability, I was extremely resentful because I wasn't accepted into the computer science major I had chosen and deserved. I tried to convince myself to be grateful, but I just couldn't. (Don't get me wrong; I love science and even competed in and won events for chemistry in high school. But once the subject was shoved down my throat, I started hating it for a simple reason: it wasn't *my* first choice.)

There were high expectations of me as the student who got in with the highest score, but I became mediocre that first year. I'd always been a straight-A student before college, but I started to get Bs and Cs and even failed one subject that I had to retake an exam to pass. Of course, I felt shame in doing that, but it was a form of self-sabotage in its own way. I felt resentful and angry, and I tried to set a distance between myself and things that were not my own choice.

Another reason my grades suffered is a simple one: I missed most of my classes. Well, to be honest, in some of those classes, I only attended when there was an exam that got counted in the final scores. I would escape to the library, flipping through books I enjoyed reading. Only right before the final exams, I would spend a couple of days reading the books and pass the subject with a mediocre score. People can't succeed when there is no motivation to succeed. I was lost, without any direction, just cruising and hoping someday I would find a way out.

I wasn't lazy though. Instead, I was extremely busy and just focused on learning random things or subjects I liked. I read computer science books in the library, participated in debate clubs, studied Japanese and German languages, and tried to learn programming on my own. Although I had no clue what I wanted to achieve, I knew I couldn't just stop learning. Every day I got up before everyone else and started to work on things that interested me.

Regardless of what happened during my mediocre and aimless academic life for the first year in college, university life itself presented lots of opportunities for fun and connection.

I made friends in college immediately. On the first day when I got to the dorm, a girl hopped down from the top bunk bed and gave me the warmest greeting with the most beautiful smile on her face. I knew then that we would be best friends forever. This new best friend also had the same character in her name as that of my best friend from childhood: Mei. The Chinese character 梅 represents plum flowers. It may sound odd translating into English, but in ancient poems in China, plum trees represent endurance and grit because they're one of the rare trees that blossom first in freezing cold winter. My childhood best friend was called Dongmei (winter plum blossom), and this new college best friend was Hongmei (red plum blossom). Hongmei and I became best friends immediately.

We had eight girls living in the same dorm room. That may sound surprising by today's standard, but it worked well for China in 1995. Imagine you have eight girls living together in the same room for all of college years. What type of friendship would that develop? There was no drama, just sister-like friendship and love. Unlike there can often be in the Western world, there was no jealousy or arguing among us roommates. Though we obviously had our differences, we all came from similar backgrounds and had so much in common. Back then, in the '90s, there was no social media to complicate relationships, and life was simpler. It truly felt like living with seven sisters my age in harmony. We embraced each other and provided care and love for each other. Without that warmth from the other seven girls, I wouldn't have survived the first year in college.

We had so many great times together in that dorm room. We'd lie in our beds each night talking and laughing, gossiping about boys. The girls' and boys' dorms were separate, of course, and we were forbidden to enter each other's rooms without getting a pass from the guard. It was always a huge scandal if a girl and a boy met at one of the dorms and spent the night together. We giggled like little schoolgirls. Never mind we were full-grown adults! In China and in most of our families, dating was still frowned upon, and sex before marriage was taboo. I'm 100 percent sure everyone in my dorm was a virgin. There was no sex ed in schools, even in college. It was the parents' job to talk to their kids about sex. But they didn't. Never. Nada. Not one word. It wasn't like we could walk into the library and borrow a book either. There weren't many books about sex, and even if you found one, you couldn't read it where anyone would see you. The information we got from each other was sparse and often incorrect. What we learned came from Western movies.

In the early '90s, video rooms started popping up in college towns. Not like a real movie theater or anything, but we didn't care. We snuck off campus for marathon movie nights at these places, a gaggle of young women, blushing and snickering the entire way there. We'd watch a whole night of Kevin Costner movies, like *Dances with Wolves*. And even though we were young women, it still made us feel like naughty little girls afraid our parents would find out. Most of the movies we watched at those overnight movie theaters were Hollywood movies released before 1995: *Legends of the Fall* and *Se7en* made us all fall in love with Brad Pitt; *Ghost* and *Pretty Woman* made us all fancy our own love in the future; and we watched *Forrest Gump* so many times and never tired of it. My personal favorite was *The Shawshank Redemption*, which made me ache and cry. I felt like Andy in the movie, locked in a cell for life, but silently digging little by little to get out. But one night, we saw something crazy: *Basic Instinct* with Sharon Stone. We weren't sure if that movie was illegal, and we didn't ask. It was so provocative that several of us sat there with our eyes half covered, totally shocked at what we saw and quietly wondering if we'd just seen porn for the first time.

Remember, the early '90s in China was a time of great change. The country had started opening to the rest of the world. Not many people had personal computers or internet access, and Western movies and music were only starting to flood in. Any sexual content was usually pirated, copied, and passed around in secret. If you got your hands on a disc with explicit content, you hid it like a secret stash so nobody would find out.

Maybe the folks at English Corner would know what real Western porn was like, I thought. After all, that's the only place where I met some real adults, and they had no connection to my family or school. So, if I were to get some materials from them, nobody in my current circle would find out the naughty things I did. I made a connection and pinged someone I knew from the old days, asking if he knew how to get ahold of real porn. We were both very embarrassed by the subject, but he agreed to help me. Weeks later, we met secretly at a bus stop, and he handed me a pirated disc with a yellow sticker on it (an indicator that the disc contained "colorful content.") That transaction was so embarrassing to us that we never spoke again after that deal.

I didn't have the courage to watch it by myself, so I found one of the senior girls who had a computer in her dorm to watch it with me. Equally curious about the subject, she said yes. We found a quiet time when everyone else was at their classes. We locked the door, shut the curtain, and popped the disc into the computer. We nervously hit the play button, expecting romance with plots just like what we saw in *Basic Instinct*. Instead, it felt like a horror movie. The noises alone made me feel like my soul had been sucked out of my body. We were disgusted first, then disillusioned. *This was what sex would be like?* I never wanted to watch that again, and I *certainly* never wanted to do it. That was the start and the end of my sex education.

I hid all the things I did in college from my parents. That first year in college was my rebellious year; the good and sweet girl who got straight As was gone. I had guilt because my parents had worked so hard to send me to college, but I had no idea what to achieve other than the degree I didn't want. I kept telling myself that I would eventually figure it out.

In the end, staying in Dalian for college turned out to be great for me. Since I couldn't find my own identity yet, I still needed my parents' moral support to keep me going. Though I lived in the dorm room during the week, I went to visit my parents almost every weekend. Sometimes, when I got busier with my exams and finals, my parents would come to me instead.

They would randomly show up right before dinner and ask me what I was in the mood for. After taking me to a great restaurant, they'd send me back to my dorm with enough delicious leftovers to last my roommates and me for days. These frequent visits seemed small at the time, but looking back, I see how much they nourished my body and heart.

It was their love that made me feel the need to achieve the goals I had in life. Toward the end of the first year in college, I decided to find a way to study computer science while continuing with a chemistry major. I came up with a plan that contained three missions:

1. Get my degree in chemistry as fast as possible so I'd have a college diploma.
2. Gain skills in computer science and be prepared for opportunities.
3. Earn my right to study computer science at a graduate school, no matter what it took.

I knew I didn't have control over everything, but I also knew I should focus on what I *could* control. My missions were set, and now I just needed to get on with them.

4.3. MISSION 1: FINISH FOUR-YEAR COLLEGE IN THREE YEARS (1996)

To complete Mission 1, I needed to figure out how to complete my chemistry degree as soon as possible.

In 1996, the university introduced a credit-based system. That was good news for me because it meant that you didn't have to take an entire four years to earn a degree. If you accumulated enough credits, you could graduate on your own time.

When I saw that news posted on the school bulletin board, I immediately made a plan: to complete my four-year college in three years. That way, I reasoned, I would have time to study computer science before getting a job like everyone else. I knew it would be impossible to pack the last year of college into half because the final courses for that major were full of field practices and lab work. That left one option: to pack the next two years into one to accomplish the goal.

I started executing my mission by mapping out all the courses I needed to take for the next two years so I could determine how to do them in one. There was only one problem: the second-year and third-year chemistry courses were on completely different campuses, so I'd need to take a bus between them during the day to not miss critical tests/labs. Cell phones were very rare in 1996, but pagers (or beepers, which receive one-way messages wirelessly) were gaining popularity. I told Dad I would need a pager so that I could receive messages from my friends who were on the other campus, just in case there was something important I needed to do for school. Dad immediately bought me a beeper for 5,000 yuan. (Note that back in 1996, the average household income per year was below 5,000 yuan. The amount of trust he had in me was incredible.)

Packing two years of college work into one year wasn't easy, especially toggling between campuses. I would often miss classes, and my friends would page me in emergency situations when there was something due that wasn't on the syllabus. When that happened, I'd rush to a phone and find out if there was a class, test, or presentation I absolutely had to attend if I didn't want to fail. One day, during lunch at a dining hall, I lost my pager and dissolved into tears. It was worth such a fortune, and I was terrified to tell Dad that I had been careless and lost something so precious. But when I finally mustered the courage to tell him, he wasn't angry. He knew that I already felt terrible, so he consoled me instead and asked if I needed a new one to continue my studies. In that moment I realized that coming from poverty, my parents certainly appreciated material things but always knew they were never as important as people. My parents retained the same values they'd always had, focusing on our family relationships and all of us supporting each other with kindness and patience.

Not many people around me knew what I was doing most of the time, including my own family. Though I did tell Dad I was going to cram two years into one, I didn't share the details of how hard that was in practice. The only person who understood me was my best friend, Hongmei; after 1997, we couldn't spend much time together because our schedules became totally different. She understood what was bottled up inside me and was always the person who cheered me up when I needed it. Sometimes when I got really exhausted at the end of the night, I would go to her campus and just stay with her for a little while. Then, I would be healed by the next day and charge back to my mission again.

Those were long days; I would say hello to the world at dawn (at 5:00 a.m.) and goodnight to the stars in the sky at midnight. Once, I was so exhausted after a set of big tests and work that I crashed in the bed of our dorm room and told Hongmei that I couldn't walk (or even hop) around anymore. My polio leg had stopped working due to constant exhaustion and sharp pain, and my whole body stopped providing strength. Hongmei would take care of me for a couple of days afterward, bringing food from the dining hall every day, until I was able to walk again.

By the end of 1997, I was able to complete two years of credited classes within a year. In 1998, I earned my bachelor's degree in chemical engineering and graduated as the first student in the history of DUT to complete all the required courses in three years instead of four.

Mission 1 accomplished.

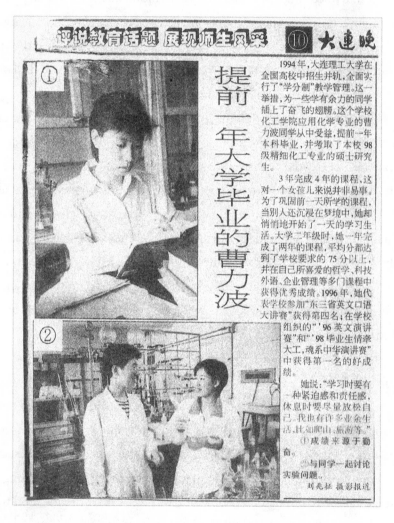

Local newspaper reporting Libo as the first student who completed a four-year college in three years at Dalian University of Technology and awards during the college period (1998).

4.4. MISSION 2: LEARN COMPUTER SCIENCE SECRETLY

The first time I ever touched a computer was around 1989, in middle school in Dalian. I remember it clearly: we were all lined up outside a lab and had been given shoe covers and hairnets to wear before stepping inside. It was a big ritual, almost holy, to get ready to enter that room. When we got in, there were computers with keyboards for us to use. After you started the computer, the fan started working hard, and white characters started rolling on a black screen followed by a blinking cursor. The teacher told us to type "dir" as a command. When we did, almost like magic, the screen responded with a bunch of things in that directory.[4] Then we'd use the command `cd` followed by a directory name to hop in there. Those were all MS-DOS commands, and it was all incredible technology to me. It was as if you were talking to a machine and it understood you, which was a powerful dynamic to experience.

A few years later, Windows 3.1x became available to us in school. That was the first time I saw a graphical user interface (GUI) on a computer. It was really mind-blowing to me, and I remember staring at those icons and admiring them for as long as my computer time permitted. There were also programs we could put on 5.25-inch floppy disks, which later evolved to 3.5-inch disks.

Until college, all the knowledge I had of computers came from just hours of precious time in middle and high school computer labs. I'd never used the internet in China before 1995. Computer classes just meant that the teacher told us to type in some commands, we found those letters on

---

[4] This was pre-GUI, meaning there were no icons to click on like we're used to today. If you wanted a computer to do something, you had to provide a specific command for that action.

keyboards, punched them in, and watched them work. I knew I loved computers and wanted to learn more about them, but I wasn't sure what was next. Starting in 1994, suddenly, computer science started gaining lots of attraction. This is likely because, starting that year, China became connected to the internet.[5] However, I had no way to connect to this thing called the "internet." At that time, computers were only in schools and universities—they were not personal commodities.

In August of 1995, Windows 95 was released, but it wasn't until late 1996 that I was able to use a computer that was bundled with Internet Explorer. The internet back then was very different than the one we know today. Google was launched in 1998, but nobody heard about it in China until many years later, and YouTube has only existed since 2005. There was Yahoo, but I couldn't find many websites that were in Chinese. To explore the internet, I would find a book that listed hundreds of URLs, including many one-pager websites that were just introductions of people or items in Chinese. Even those were very rare to find. Each time I stumbled upon one, I became excited for days. It felt like I became a superwoman who was able to communicate with someone telepathically: we weren't meeting in person, but I was getting their thoughts. The only problem was that other than reading about people or things on the internet, I didn't know what else I could use it for.

At the end of 1996, I started sneaking into computer science lectures, hoping I could blend into the sea of faces in the large auditoriums. I borrowed stacks of computer science textbooks from the library, then went to the computer lab and tried to punch in lines of code to test things out.

---

[5] "Chronicle of Internet Events from 1994 to 1996," Cyberspace Administration of China, April 11, 2009, http://www.cac.gov.cn/2009-04/11/c_126500497.htm.

Back in those days, there was only one centralized computer lab in the university. To go to the lab, you first needed to buy a punch card, each of which would have ten or twenty hours of computer time. Interestingly, to get into the college computer lab, only shoe covers were required (no hairnet like in middle school). I couldn't understand the science behind that, but I never questioned why we had to wear shoe covers to use a computer. Computers were such rare commodities back then, and maybe we had to treat them with respect.

My first programming language was Fortran, which is a language not many modern programmers are familiar with. Fortran II is what BASIC is based upon and was very popular in the mid-1990s for college students pursuing scientific programming. It's not as easy to write or maintain as more modern languages like Python, Java, C, or C++, but I still had a lot of fun. I loved feeding the computer a command and watching the program execute.

Around 1997, I finally asked Dad to buy me a personal computer so that I could continue to learn. Simply visiting the computer lab under time constraints wasn't enough any longer. Of course, it was extremely expensive and very rare for a household to own a computer at that time in Dalian...but Dad, like always, supported me without any doubt.

Having a computer at home was exciting because I was no longer dependent on the computer lab. In the beginning, I was just practicing things I learned from books by punching lines of code to run, but later on, I needed to test out if my skills were any good. Since I wasn't a computer science major and not qualified to take their exams, I decided to go after subject certificates on the market.

I studied every single holiday and vacation and began to earn publicly available certificates for computer science. For example, I earned C/C++

and Oracle certificates. I also passed the very popular certificate at that time: MCSE (Microsoft Certified System Engineer). Not only did I have to read six thick technical books all in English, but I also had to take six tests in English. Each of the tests was hours long. It took me less than a month to pass them all, and I scored so well that the head of the training facility offered me a job teaching there. That was the first time I saw that my skills could turn into money. The offer was 100,000 yuan per year—an insane amount of money in China in the late '90s. I didn't take the role, but that offer felt like a successful proof of concept for me; what I was doing was working, and there was a future in it. I knew if I wanted to come back to the teaching job, I could, but I didn't let the money distract me from my mission. I became a certificate hoarder, even getting one certificate that claimed it would allow me to do import/export business with computers in Great Britain! Dad supported me financially for all the fees and associated costs to earn those certificates, without any questions or doubt. I would come to Dad every few months and tell him I needed some money to get another certificate, he would give me the money, and I would pass each test with flying colors.

At one point, I had many friends in college. But during my certificate-hoarding time, I became a lone wolf due to my own crazy and special schedules. I would run between campuses for college classes during the day, visit labs in training facilities at night for computer science training, visit labs during the weekends to catch up on some missed homework at school, and spend many nights at home with my computer practices and experiments.

I didn't know if and when I would ever get to formally study computer science, so I took every class and course that came with a piece of paper showing my proficiency. Looking back, I know I accumulated all those certificates to prove that I could do it, that I should have been accepted into the major, and that everyone was wrong about me. This, unfortunately, led to me wasting a bunch of time on certificates.[6]

At this juncture, I also wanted to understand how the server and client communicate between networks. The only server networks I knew were training facility computers, and the only outside network computer I had was the one at home. So, I would spend the weekend at a training facility lab, trying to set up a live IP address with a port that could be connected from outside of that network. I would then rush out of the lab, take the bus to my home, and try to ping and connect to that IP/port I had set up at the lab, just to see if I could connect. How the internet worked was (and is) fascinating to me. Retrospectively, this feels almost like a comedy. If only I'd known there were things called laptops, I could have saved those bus trips to get to my desktop at home. Regardless of my ignorance then, I was able to do programming on my own through various certificate training and understand most of the computer science basics. Although that knowledge and those skills felt very surface-level, looking back now, I gave all I had to gain them, without any mentorship or guidance in that domain.

I didn't know when to call this mission complete, so I just continued it. I had no idea if my approach would work someday, but I knew I had to keep trying to get prepared in case any opportunity were ever to arrive.

What I *didn't* know back then was that, many years later, those certificates got me a chance to be admitted to a computer science major in another country.

Steve Jobs once said, "You can't connect the dots looking forward. You can only connect them looking backward. So you have to trust the dots will

---

[6] Some programming humor for my fellow computer aficionados: if there is ever a crisis in setting up a company's network infrastructure with Windows NT servers, my MCSE certificate proves that I am qualified to do that, at least in the late '90s.

somehow connect in your future. You have to trust in something—your gut, destiny, life, karma, whatever."

When I read that many years later, all my dots immediately connected backward.

4.5. MISSION 3: EARN MY RIGHT BACK TO STUDY CS

I needed to figure out how to be accepted as a computer science student—if not in college, then in graduate school.

Switching majors in the same college was unheard of, as was transferring. There was an invisible system that disallowed those changes. To apply for graduate school to study computer science in China, I had to first get a degree in that major. I couldn't do that, so it was a dead end.

Or so I thought.

I didn't know how to untie the knotted situation in front of me, and graduation was coming up. Out of panic, I applied and was accepted into graduate school at the same university, still as a chemistry major. I had no idea what to do with my life and how to get it on the right track, so I figured I might as well just continue with the path that I was "allowed" to be on.

However, one night during summer break in 1998, I found myself browsing randomly in the library and stumbled upon some news that would change everything: there was a book on applying for graduate education abroad. It listed all the scholarships in graduate school from universities abroad. And switching majors or schools seemed so simple! The book said you just transferred credits over to the new one! All it took to apply was a bachelor's degree, a Test of English as a Foreign Language (TOEFL), and a Graduate Record Examination (GRE). Then, you could be admitted to a university abroad.

The more I read, the more my body started to shake with excitement. This book didn't specifically say anything about people with disabilities or exclusions; instead, it just included all the requirements. *And I could meet all of them!* They didn't mention PE scores! They wouldn't even know I had a disability! As I flipped through the book, I thought, *If they don't ask about disability, I don't have to tell. Then, it's not considered lying, right?*

I'd heard of a few people going abroad to pursue graduate school, but I'd never imagined that I could be one of them. I'd always been told to stay put because of my disability, but this book listed everything outside of "staying put."

I wasn't sure if what I read was accurate, so I went online immediately and visited a few university websites to verify their application process. It was *true*! None of them mentioned anything about a PE score, and bachelor's degrees didn't require a PE score either. I knew I could do this. At that moment, I believed that somewhere in this world, I wouldn't be at the mercy of strangers who refused to see past my limp. They would see my strength. I needed to get there.

I searched more about how to take the requisite tests and found a training company in Beijing called New Oriental School that specializes in training for TOEFL and GRE tests. I took a bus home and told Dad I needed to go to Beijing to attend training school and would need 3,000 yuan for my summer there. Dad gave me the money, and I dashed out to the train station. That same night, I was on the train to Beijing for my training. I was in such a hurry that I couldn't even tell Dad about the details while at home. From the train station, I called home and told Mom and Dad that I needed to go abroad for graduate school, and to start that process, I needed to be trained to pass all the graduate entrance exams. Dad said I sounded like I knew exactly what I was doing, and I must do it immediately, so he didn't doubt me. I wasn't that vulnerable high school girl anymore. I was twenty-two and ready to make my own decisions in life.

I arrived at the training campus of the Beijing New Oriental School, which was located on top of a mountain and functioned as a closed system—designed for students to stay there without interacting with the outside world for several months. The isolation was a form of immersion; we just studied together to prepare for the exams, day and night—and it worked.

By early 1999, I'd completed the TOEFL and GRE tests and had started applying for universities abroad, especially interested in graduate programs that might come with a tuition waiver and full scholarship program. Of course, I was only qualified for a chemistry major, so I picked analytical chemistry (DNA sequencing, for example) as a research field, knowing that I would use computers quite often for that type of research. I had to apply to many universities abroad to increase my chances of acceptance.

Doing all those things myself wasn't easy, especially because the only guidance I could find was from a bulletin board system called "MIT BBS" —a forum where university students in China could ask questions. I couldn't even make a phone call to the United States if I'd wanted to. How would I look up the phone numbers? Instead, I had to try to figure out all the steps to apply on my own.

There were many universities in the United States to choose from, so I made a list of those that didn't charge application fees nor require extra GRE major tests (that also cost a lot more). I'd asked Dad to pay for all my certificates and tests already, so I felt guilty at the thought of asking for more money to support expensive application fees. I remember looking at Stanford University with its hefty application fee of $75 and crossing it off the list immediately. Ohio University caught my eye because their chemistry department decided to waive the $30 fee for applicants, so I immediately loved that university. How considerate of them! It's funny how such little things can influence our decisions.

As long as they didn't charge an application fee (or had a very low fee), I would apply to them. I also applied to universities in any countries that had graduate programs listed, such as those in Hong Kong, Singapore, UK, New Zealand, and so on. I had no problem footing the bill for the postage.

Getting all the application information from each university's website was challenging in many ways. First, I thought I ought to find a site that listed all the universities and URLs for their application pages. Unfortunately, I couldn't find such a site, so I started guessing. *The White House is a powerful organization*, I thought. So, I typed in "whitehouse." Unfortunately, I didn't know the extension should be ".gov" and instead I used ".com." That was the day I stumbled upon my first ever internet porn, which is not a comforting thing to do by accident.

Another challenge was internet speed with a dial-up modem. If you don't know what it is, it's basically a modem you get that can tap into your home telephone line. In this system, when you are using the internet, your home phone won't work, so you need to be prepared before you log on. I would write down all the URLs I planned to visit, open that number of Internet Explorer windows and pretype the URLs offline, then click on that dial-up modem icon on my computer. The dial connection would start with about twenty to thirty seconds of sound (Du... number dial sound, static... beep-boo... beep... static... if you know, you know). Once the quiet started, you knew you were in this wonderland of the internet. I would then go to each window to refresh that URL, navigate to the application page, find the file, start downloading to the local disk, then move on to the next pretyped URL until I'd downloaded all the packages. Then, I'd disconnect the modem as quickly as possible because it was a pay-by-the-minute setup. (So, instead of calling it "surfing the internet," I'd say that was a quick dip in the internet sea.)

After I sent out all my application packages in late 1999, all I needed to do was wait. A few months later, offer letters started arriving. I received some full scholarships from UK universities and US universities. Ohio University offered me a full tuition waiver and a full PhD scholarship with $23,000 a year to cover my living expenses. What's more interesting is that they had a DNA sequencing field as well as an "intelligent instrument" field in the chemistry department, meaning I would be able to develop in both computer science and chemistry in those combined fields. I made my decision to accept that offer. Within the week, I apologized to my advisor in graduate school at DUT and quit the program. Without any passion, I couldn't succeed. I would just be wasting their time as well as mine.

Dad supported my decision. When I'd first applied to DUT, he was convinced there was no other way forward for me based on what we'd been told. This time, there was not only potential for me to succeed but a high probability.

The night before I flew to the United States for my graduate studies, Dad packed a family photo for me to always carry wherever I went. On the back of that picture, he wrote:

No matter where you go, what you do, do not ever forget you came from China, and never bring shame to your mother country. Stand tall and strong! Remember who you are and where you came from, always!

My parents helped me pack all the allowed suitcases for an international flight, which included two giant ones and two carry-ons that, combined, outweighed me (I was eighty-eight pounds then). My parents were very concerned about me dragging that luggage—at almost three times my weight—to the other side of the globe.

On the day of my departure, my entire family saw me off at the airport in Dalian, China. I was brimming with excitement and ready to go. I was pushing a clunky baggage cart piled high above my head that held everything to get me started with a new life on my own. However, from the back, I must have looked quite forlorn. Mom wept, and even my brother welled up with tears at the sight.

"Sis, you look so tiny, but here you are, marching forward into your new life!"

"Don't worry. This is what I wanted," I said to him. "I got this, and nothing can stop me!"

I squared my shoulders, used all my strength to push the cart, and limped forward without fear.

5.

DUAL GRADUATE DEGREES AND A JOB (2000–2004)

Many great writers, philosophers, and artists
throughout history have used the phrase "move mountains"
to note some degree of impossibility.

And yet, we try.

Confucius said, "The man who moves a mountain
begins by carrying away small stones." This is similar to the story,
"The Foolish Old Man Removes the Mountains."
But what makes a person choose to pick up small stone after
small stone? What was going through the foolish old man's head
in that story? What makes us think we can accomplish
seemingly impossible goals, and why do we try even
when we know we might not succeed?

I only began to understand the foolish old man when
I started to carry away small stones of my own and discovered that
anything is possible with perseverance and great determination.
Regardless of the outcome, deep in my soul,
I owed it to myself to try.

I knew that I would have to earn it every step of the way.
But I also knew I was worth it.

5.1. WHEN IN ROME (SEPTEMBER 2000)

That trip from Dalian to Athens, Ohio, took me more than forty-eight hours. The flight needed to stop at Beijing, then another major transport in the US before reaching Columbus, Ohio, followed by a two-hour drive to Athens. Flying from Dalian to Beijing for the first time, I chose to stay overnight in Beijing to avoid missing the connecting flight to the US because I was concerned the layover time was too short. That trip was the first time as an adult that I realized how lack of accessibility in a country's infrastructure could so deeply constrain someone with a disability.

First, I needed to take all my luggage to the overnight accommodations in Beijing instead of leaving it at the airport for my next day's flight. Unfortunately, I realized that there were many places I needed to climb stairs (there were some elevators, but the ones that did exist were often out of service). So, I would leave my cart at the bottom of the stairs and carry one piece of luggage at a time, one stair at a time, with the strength of one leg. Each staircase took me ten to fifteen minutes to climb with all four pieces of luggage, using all my strength. Just when I thought I was done, there was another one ahead of me. One time I was so excited to see there was an elevator after a landing, but I was soon disappointed to learn it was taped off for maintenance. When I was with packs of people, often someone would offer help, but I usually declined that help. Somehow at that age, I was so proud and stubborn. I believed that I must do things on my own if I had even a slim chance of succeeding. What I didn't know at the time, though, is that not everything is worth proving. Knowing when and how to accept help graciously was a capability I had yet to learn.

Finally, I made it to Columbus, Ohio. I was weary and sweaty. At the same time, I felt ready to learn, adapt, and find my own feet in this new land.

Many universities have a Chinese Student Union for new international students. We can contact them ahead of time so that pick-ups can be scheduled. On that same flight, there were a couple of new graduate students heading to the same new destination. Courtesy of one of those scheduled pick-ups, we met with a warm senior graduate student to continue our trip...which meant another two hours driving to Ohio University.

My idea of America was based on movies and TV shows: the glitzy skyscrapers of New York City, beautiful suburbs with manicured lawns, and thriving neighborhoods with lively storefronts. By then, other than English study materials, I'd only watched the series *Friends* and dozens of Western movies. What I saw flying by outside as I pressed my forehead against the cold glass was none of that. Outside, there was nothing but farmland with the occasional dilapidated shed, rural towns with bleached-out neon signs atop vacant businesses, and peeling paint on small family homes. It was nothing like the large, modern city of Dalian that I had just come from with buildings that would have towered over everything I saw. I felt a little disillusioned with my first look at this country, so completely different from the vision in my head.

To complete this "fresh off the airplane" experience as a new Chinese graduate student, I summarized it into a multiple-step process.

Step 1: Get to Your New Apartment, and Don't Ask Too Many "Newbie" Questions

The apartment I'd arranged before landing was called Athens Garden— a large, affordable housing complex that historically rented to low-income families and graduate students. Walking by some apartments, I smelled something sweet in the air. "If you wonder what that is, it's the smell of weed," said the senior graduate student.

"What's weed?"

"Don't worry. Plenty for you to learn."

I stopped asking.

Step 2: Get a Phone Card to Call Home, and Tell Them Only the Good Things

Since overseas telephone calls at that time were paid by the minute, I talked as fast as I could for that first call to Mom and Dad. I told them that I'd made it to my new home, and everything was great. Then, I hung up.

Step 3: Pay Up–Get a Financial Reality Check

Back in 2000, the banks in China allowed each person to exchange a maximum of $2,000 to take abroad. Dad wanted to equip me with a lot more to start with, so he utilized a side channel to exchange another $10,000 for me. Unfortunately, after he gave out the Chinese Yuan, we were told that our money was stolen, and we would receive no dollars. Long story short, $2,000 was all I got, but I told Dad that it would be plenty with my scholarship and hoped he didn't feel too bad about the loss. What I didn't know was that there are things called rent deposits and up-front fees from the university. I also learned that my scholarship was only paid monthly— and only beginning *after* one month, not up front. Before I realized what had happened, only $300 was left in my pocket. I knew I'd need to survive with that amount until my first scholarship paycheck arrived. The problem was, I had no idea how much even food would cost for a month, or if there were any unknown bills around the corner soon.

I've heard a saying before: "People don't grow up gradually; they grow up instantly at a certain moment." I finally understood what it meant. I grew up at that moment, holding that last $300 in my pocket and knowing it was all I had to survive in a new country for at least a month. Before that moment, I was so ignorant. I thought that I could conquer this new world with my skills, wisdom, and willpower. But on merely day one, I got a big slap from this new world, informing me that I knew nothing about it and I had nobody to fall back on. I realized that for all my years living in China, Mom and Dad had sheltered me from every storm. Though we'd been both rich and poor together, my thoughts had never needed to be on money. It was always their job to make money, calculate money, and provide for me and my brother.

I also realized that there was a type of emotion that I had never dealt with before until that moment: fear. I was really scared that I would run out of money soon and was too proud to borrow from anyone; I feared not knowing how much bread and milk would cost; I feared getting sick and not being able to afford to go to the hospital. A million potential situations started to cause a storm in my head, and worst of all, I had nobody to share that fear with. I was merely being dragged around by others, paying for one thing after another.

Step 4: Get a Mattress to Sleep on for the Night

My next step was to go mattress hunting—on the street. (That is not a typo.) Why look on the street and not in a store? Well, to start, I was low on funds. Secondly, those experienced seniors who voluntarily took care of the newbies knew that nobody by that time would be in the mood to pay for a mattress. I was told that simply hunting around the neighborhood close by on move-out days could yield one. So, another new grad and I started hunting for mattresses on the street. That's something that I had never done before.

Very quickly, we saw some mattresses lying around the neighborhood. *But how do we get them back without a car?* we wondered. I walked back for help and was surprised to find out one of my roommates had already kindly put a mattress in my room. Many years later after I graduated, I gave everything in my apartment to the incoming graduate students for free to get them started easier. My possessions weren't worth much, but I knew they could be worth a lot to those who had nothing. I always remind myself to pay it forward with random kindness to those in need, for I received so much from others.

Step 5: Cry Yourself to Sleep for the Night

Though this step is not explicitly communicated, it was one we all worked through privately.

The first night was tough. Due to jetlag and the excitement, I couldn't sleep... and not because of the lumpy mattress, which I reminded myself to be grateful for, but because of the insane quiet outside. I'd never experienced that before. Growing up in villages, I'd heard crickets chirping, dogs barking, and frogs croaking at night. After moving to the city of Dalian, life carried on at night as if it were daytime. Nights were full of people dancing in the town squares all the way to midnight, full of teenagers yelling, kids laughing, and buses honking. The smells of barbecue wafted through the air, and vendors sold handmade goods at every corner. China's nights don't sleep and are not lonely. But there in my Athens Garden apartment, after darkness arrived, it was as if the quiet took over. No animal nor human sound. I'd never known what true loneliness meant until that night, which was totally different from the loneliness I felt because of my polio. I was away from all my friends and family and everything I was familiar with. In this new country, I knew nobody, and nobody knew me. The people on the other side of the wall were only neighbors or roommates. Nobody had any responsibility nor was obligated to help me with anything. The empty contents of my new home in Ohio matched my aching insides. I had been considered incomplete because of my physical limitations, and now I felt incomplete without my family by my side. Truly alone for the first time in my life, I did cry myself to sleep that night... but I'm not the type to "let it all out." Instead, I cried quietly so that my roommates wouldn't hear. The physical pain from surgeries didn't make me cry, but somehow being alone at night in a different country broke me down.

Since it was an unspoken step, nobody told me how long it would last. It took me several months of nights like that before the loneliness faded— which only happened because other challenges began to hit, and there was no time to cry anymore.

Step 6: Look for Acceptance and Be Able to Laugh at Yourself

Surviving the first week wasn't any easier, though looking back, there were quite a few moments that were comedy material. That's why Step 6 is a natural progression.

To get my first paycheck from my scholarship, I needed to work as a teaching assistant while completing my PhD program. *How am I capable of teaching others when I barely know how to live in this country?* I wondered, the thought swirling through my head.

Before I arrived in the States, I thought my English was great and there were no language barriers for me. That feeling lasted until I started living here.

When someone greeted me "What's up?" I would lift my head, look up carefully, and say "Nothing really!" People would laugh, but I didn't get the joke until someone later explained to me that it was merely a hello.

When someone greeted me with "How is it going?" I started answering the question, only noticing that the person who asked the question had already passed me and kept walking. *Why would someone ask me a question and just walk away?* That question was in my head for many days until someone explained to me that not all questions are meant to be answered. It was just another hello disguised as a question.

I ended up in many embarrassing situations, especially as a teaching assistant. One of the professors I worked with had a heavy Australian accent. In my very first week, he asked me to do something and handed me a stack of papers. I looked at him, nodding, saying "yes, yes, OK," and turned to leave. He called me back and repeated himself. I had no clue what he was saying, but instead of asking for clarification, I just said again, "OK, I'm going to leave now." I was so ashamed that I couldn't understand him that all I wanted to do was get out of that situation. Was I supposed to grade these papers for him? I would have to find another Chinese grad student and ask about it.

The professor may have seen this behavior before and kindly asked me, in a very slow and clear way, "Libo, do you understand what I'm saying?"

I looked down at the floor, "No, I don't." I felt like a fraud. What was I even doing in this country being a teaching assistant when I couldn't understand the simplest instructions? The professor had a great idea, though, and wrote down what he wanted me to do on a slip of paper. Seeing the words without hearing his accent, I understood he wanted me to stay at this desk and do the work right there. As the weeks went on, I got used to his accent and was able to understand him better. That same professor also taught me how to guide other college students to hold test tubes correctly, and he realized that I didn't know what each of my fingers was called. So, I would hold one finger at a time and repeat to him, "This is my thumb, this is my index finger, and this is..."

"No, no, no, Libo!" he said, bursting out laughing. "You don't do that in this country. Holding up your middle finger by itself is not acceptable."

Still seeing me confused, he continued.

"That means "the f-word" in this country."

(Apparently, I didn't watch enough American movies to learn that part of the culture.)

My instinct in those early situations was to run away and avoid any confrontation that might make people think I wasn't smart enough or didn't deserve to be there. I felt lucky to have made it to graduate school with a full scholarship but was terrified that the opportunity would somehow all be taken away from me once they found out I wasn't that smart. Those feelings are called imposter syndrome; I was constantly worried people would find out I didn't belong. But at the time, all I knew was that I had to survive one way or another, and faking it seemed like the best way.

Many moments were quite embarrassing. Those were not at all what I'd imagined before coming to America, but now I know it is natural when you are in a new place. I found that people largely understood where my confusion came from, or at least they *tried* to understand. Many even went so far as to help, making me feel welcome.

In one of my classes, I had a professor from India. No matter how long I sat there trying to adjust my ears for different tones, I couldn't figure it out:

was he speaking English? Because of all the exams I'd taken before coming to the states, I'd gotten used to the American accent (and even the British accent). And though this professor *sounded* like he was speaking English, I couldn't understand a single word.

Of course, I had an accent myself, but I could not—for the life of me—understand my professor's heavy Indian accent. I kept wondering why I could communicate easily with one Indian graduate student, but I couldn't recognize *this* professor's accent. Later, I was told by my Indian friends that based on which part of India people come from, their accents can sound quite different to foreign ears.

Luckily, that class was based on the study of algorithms, and numbers have no accents. I got an A in the end, but my biggest accomplishment was (slowly) learning to understand different accents in the country I was now calling home.

Step 7: Deal with Stomach Homesickness

Athens is a beautiful university town with a population of less than 25,000 …and more than 20,000 are students at Ohio University. As you might imagine, that means there were not many choices for international food. There was one Chinese buffet on the main street, but when I tried to enter, the smell of fryer grease hit me as soon as I opened the door. I was immediately sick to my stomach; that was (and is) *not* Chinese food but rather an American creation.

I was homesick, but most of all, my stomach was really homesick. There were many international students and quite a few Chinese graduate students I befriended who had similar feelings. One day, while reminiscing about home-cooked Chinese food, one of the other students said there was a place in Columbus that served authentic Chinese noodles. The five of us decided to give in to our cravings and packed into a car to make the four-hour round trip to Columbus for those famous noodles. We arrived at the restaurant with visions of tasty lo mein made from scratch.

What we got instead were six-dollar bowls of noodles that the staff took out of a bag and boiled in a big pot! It was tragic for all of us homesick Chinese students hoping for a taste of home. For weeks after, we laughed about spending hours crammed in a car for the worst noodles we'd ever had.

I started preparing myself some simple meals that were affordable, efficient, and comfortable for my stomach. To save time, I would cook large batches of porridge with chopped vegetables and eggs, freezing them in blocks for quick meals.[7] This meant I was able to spend just fifteen to twenty minutes preparing myself a whole week's worth of food that was nutritious, low in calories, and a comfort to my stomach. Of course, the porridge blocks didn't compare with fancy or home-cooked meals, but my stomach homesickness problem felt temporarily solved. At one point, I became fed up with the situation and cooked myself a full table of authentic Chinese food. I invited my friends over, and we ate it all. I wasn't a great cook, but after watching Mom cook at home so many times, I was able to mimic her way of cooking. It turned out to be the best meal I'd had since I'd landed in the States.

Step 8: Accept and Embrace Cultural Differences

The first holiday I spent in the United States was Halloween. I was in the lab, working late (as usual). Some of my graduate friends found me there

---

[7] Porridge is a starchy base, like oatmeal without any sugar, to which meat and vegetables can be added.

and refused to leave until I agreed to come celebrate with them. I had no costume, so they put a wig on my head and stickers on my face and called it good. I figured I'd give it an hour and then make my way back to the lab to finish my work. Little did I know what I was about to experience.

As we walked down Main Street in front of campus, more and more people kept spilling out of buildings and alleys, crowding into bars, and clogging up intersections. It was a giant, outdoor Halloween party, and the booze was flowing. On Halloween, people can drink outside on the sidewalk, but not on the street itself. The longer the party wore on, the more students found it hilarious to hold their drinks while dangling their feet over the curb. The cops on duty would move toward them, only to have the pranksters pull their feet back. The especially brazen ones would jump into the street and goad a cop to chase them back onto the sidewalk. It was a game of whack-a-mole that cops couldn't win. As a perpetual rule follower, merely *watching* students defy authority like that was exhilarating.

But that was not the most shocking thing.

After that, we made our way to a multilevel building that housed several dormitories. A throng of people was already crowding around, chanting something I couldn't quite understand.

"Show your tits! Show your tits!"

As if this alone wasn't scandalous enough, the next moment I caught a glimpse of a girl pulling up her shirt, flashing the crowd to a roar of cheers. I have never again seen that many boobs in one night. Boobs of every color, shape, and size. I could not believe my eyes. To say this was a culture shock would be putting it mildly.

My mind flashed back to the night before my flight to the States. Mom pulled me aside and asked me seriously:

"Do you know what is most important to a woman before marriage?"

"Independence?" I guessed, confused.

"No. Virginity!" Mom said firmly, with a straight face.

"Oh Mom, please don't talk about that!" I cried out, running away from her as fast as I could.

These are examples of what I call cultural differences. When they'd hit me in the face in times like this, I felt as if I had landed on an alien planet. At that time, I believed what my parents and culture had taught me was the correct way, but I took in these new experiences mostly with curiosity and amusement rather than judgment. Looking back now, I know there is no right or wrong. However, there is definitely a huge difference between how people think and behave based on where they come from.

Thanksgiving was a much calmer affair but no less strange to me. I spent it with a few Chinese graduate students and some other friends from my department. It was an early version of Friendsgiving; we each brought a Chinese dish and then gathered to eat and talk about home. I was very confused about being invited to a feast and having to bring some of the food myself. Potlucks are not a thing in North China. If you are invited to a feast, the person or family hosting usually does all the cooking. It was interesting to see that the Chinese students, after living in this new country, had very quickly started to adopt a culture that was not our own.

Sometimes the culture shock was mutual. Once, there was one American grandma who saw me eating a bowl of fast noodles (known as ramen) in the cafeteria, and she started a friendly conversation.

"Do you have fast noodles in China?" I was shocked that she asked that question.

"Not only does China have fast noodles...China has everything you have ever seen—and many things you've never seen before as well!" I answered.

At the end of the day, it takes time to get to know someone and their culture. As long as you are willing to learn, cultural differences don't have to become barriers between people. We are just different... and that's what makes this world so beautiful.

Step 9: Changing the Opinions We Thought Were True

No matter where we grow up, we all form a set of opinions that we think are true—without realizing those opinions could be flawed.

For example, in 2000, one opinion I had about myself is that I looked ugly... and not only because of my polio leg. I also thought my face was ugly, my whole body included. In Chinese culture, being humble is a top virtue. Growing up, when I looked in the mirror and told Mom that I thought I looked pretty, she would smile and call me "shameless." My parents, who love me so much and have always been willing to sacrifice anything for me, have not been able to tell me even once that I looked good. Instead, Mom and Dad told me not to pay any attention to how I looked.

"Libo, you have polio and look ugly, so your only way to get ahead is to work hard and equip yourself with skills!"

What my beloved parents told me, others in China verified. I even asked my graduate school boyfriend in China if he thought I was pretty. His answer?

"Well, with short hair, you *could* look cute."

One day a few months after arriving at Ohio University, an American boy smiled at me.

"You look really beautiful in that dress!" he said.

I was shocked. It was the first time in my life anyone had ever said such a thing to me.

He must be lying, I thought. *What does he want from me?*

"Oh no, I am not. Stop saying that!"

He smiled again, affirmed what he'd said the first time, and then walked away.

That was odd, I thought. But similar things happened a few more times, and I decided to consult my friend Lazlo about what was going on.

"Of course you are beautiful," he told me. "And you should learn to take a compliment like that by simply saying 'thank you.'"

I told my parents the news: that I'd learned I was beautiful. They said they were happy that I was confident enough to think that, but that they'd always loved me no matter what. In time, I realized that people are more inclined to give compliments to others in Western countries and, more importantly, that beauty exists in everyone.

This step took me many years to complete, with many people's help. But at least I learned initially to nod, smile back, and say "Thank you" to compliments without feeling uncomfortable.

Step 10: Becoming Independent with a Car

I was able to survive the first month on $300 until the first paycheck arrived. With my scholarship of around $23,000 a year, I was expecting to receive about $1,900 a month. I recall looking at my first paycheck and scratching my head hard: Taxes? Social security? Insurance deductions? I had no idea what those things meant.

After the deductions, I received less than $1,200.

My goal was to save enough for a car before winter came because to me, having a car meant having independence. I figured I'd get one first, then learn to drive it. For instance, I couldn't do my own grocery shopping without a car, so I had to eat the cheapest food close to campus: hamburgers and fries. After eating that type of food for a while, I gained ten pounds within the first couple of months. Not that I cared about how I looked, but extra weight combined with polio made walking that much more difficult, and I could feel my energy dropping. I needed to get healthier food by grocery shopping for myself.

Lazlo, one of my roommates, was a sweet Romanian man who had an old clunker he had bought for $500. Lazlo was generous and helped me out a lot, always asking if I wanted to tag along when he went to the grocery store, so I didn't have to drag my bags through the snow. We'd get into his car, and often it wouldn't start right away. He'd say, "Just a sec," he'd get out of the car, and—while smiling sweetly at me through the windshield—he would proceed to kick the car violently a few times until it started. Then, he'd get back in the driver's seat, he'd turn up the music, and we'd be on our way. I simply thought that's how old cars were fixed. It was only later, when I tried to use that approach to fix my own car, that I realized not everything could be fixed by kicking the hood.

For many weeks, either Lazlo would drive me for grocery shopping, or I would tag along with other Chinese graduate students. But I needed the freedom a car could provide, especially as the weather began to chill and snow was in my future. I knew that walking in snow meant that I would fall often. That wouldn't be a problem normally, but in this new country, I couldn't afford to get sick from a bad fall.

Snow did come, and I did get sick...with a fever instead of a fall. One day I had to leave campus early around 1:00 a.m. because I was running a fever and couldn't pull my usual all-nighter on campus studying. I didn't have a car and couldn't trudge through the snow all the way home to my apartment with a throbbing head and burning cheeks. My only option was to call the university's shuttle to get home. Waiting outside of my lab for the shuttle to arrive, I sat there in the freezing cold with my fever raging and my thoughts spinning. *I'm never going to make it,* I thought. *I'll fail all my classes because I'm sick and I can't study and there's too much to do and I'm so tired, and my to-do list is never-ending. I'm going to lose my scholarship and get kicked out of the university and will have to go back home to China with nothing.* I felt desperate and hopeless, sitting there with my boiling insides in the freezing cold of the gray Ohio winter, wondering what I was going to do.

And what I did was wait for the shuttle, go home, sleep it off, and wake up the next morning feeling like I wanted to conquer this new world and make it mine again. There would be many more low points, but I was learning already that they would only be temporary. I sometimes lost my footing or experienced a setback, but I had a goal and a plan, and I would never give up. Accepting that my life would be a roller coaster with extreme ups and downs was something I had to remind myself of constantly.

I knew I had to get a car to avoid that situation again. I started to calculate the numbers. I rented the cheapest apartment I could find for $170 a month, all utilities paid! I didn't spend much on food, either. After the first few months, I'd saved over $2,000 already and knew it should be enough to buy a second-hand car. However, I wasn't sure who could help me. Lazlo had already helped me so much, and everyone else I knew was super busy as well, so I didn't want to bother others with my problems.

One weekend, a tall American guy wearing a suit knocked on my door. With a kind smile, he asked if he could help me with anything. I'd heard that he was a Jehovah's Witness and that he tried to convince new graduate students to join their religion during weekends. So, I told him that I did need help, but I wouldn't believe in God even if he helped me. He laughed and said he would love to help me without anything in return. His name was Jim, and to me back then, he was a true angel sent by God.

I told Jim that I needed to buy a car but only had $2,000 for it. Jim said he knew just the right place for me. I hopped in his car and left a message for my roommate to call the police if I was not back later that night. I was desperate, and Jim's angel-like smile made me trust him enough to hop in his car after meeting him for just a few minutes. He took me to a junkyard, and a guy sold me a car right there. It was a beautiful white Mazda and only cost me $2,000, the exact amount I told them I had with me. They said it was a "salvage car," meaning the insurance company had deemed it damaged beyond repair. But the guy said he'd fixed it up, and it looked great to me.

After getting my car, I asked other graduate students to teach me how to drive within a weekend. I also went to a car shop prior and asked if they could modify my vehicle to help me drive with my polio leg. They installed a stick-like contraption that would allow me to use both pedals, but it cost a whopping $600.[8]

I practiced for about four hours and passed the driver's license test later, all within a week. I was extremely proud of my proficiency, though now I'm aware of how dangerous things could have been for me and others on the road. Once, when turning left at an intersection, I stopped as the light turned red—even though I was in the middle of the turn. "What are you doing?" my friend cried out next to me. "Red light means stop...right?" I responded.

---

[8] Later, when I arrived in California, I learned that my desire to drive "normally" by using both feet was misplaced. People typically use the same foot to drive, not both.

Luckily, Athens, Ohio, is full of local roads. It wasn't until many years later when I started driving in LA (and being yelled at while driving in LA) that I realized more training might have helped. I also knew nothing about cars or how to take care of them. Many years later, I learned that a car needs things like "oil changes," which I did not do during the three and a half years I owned that Mazda.

About six months later, my car started to make all kinds of noises, especially when the weather was cold. During the winter mornings, I would get up early, dig my car out from the heavy snow, turn it on, then hear loud squeaking noises. It was so loud that I would wake up many people living in that same apartment complex. I would either sit in the car, ducking my head to avoid being seen, or run back to my apartment until that noise stopped. I was afraid people would see that it was me who woke them up with that annoying sound. The large squeaking noise would go away after a few minutes of warming up and would run fine on the way to school… until next time when I had to start the car in frozen weather again. You may wonder why I didn't have it fixed. Well, not only was I very cheap, but I was also extremely busy with my schoolwork and barely had time to sleep. Oftentimes I would get up at 6:30 a.m. to start the day and work until 2:00 a.m., wondering if I deserved to get a few hours of sleep. I was happy that I could avoid walking in deep snow in Ohio with that Mazda, which I called my "white horse."

First self-cooked feast in the United States (2000).

5.2. SURVIVING THE FIRST YEAR (2001)

My story of surviving the first year in a new place is, like it is for many, full of wins, losses, and a lot of learning. To accomplish my mission in this manner, I had to work through another set of steps:

Step 1: Don't Get Kicked Out of the Program

During orientation for new graduate students, I realized that what I'd gotten was just an entrance ticket to the program. It turns out that all the PhD candidates were required to pass a "qualifying examination" before we were formally accepted into the program. The exam is intentionally broad and designed to assess our proficiency in fundamental areas relevant to chemical engineering. I was shocked to hear about that. *I was already qualified, and I need to be qualified again?* But that was just the first step.

After the qualifying exam, I needed to pass a set of "comprehensive exams" to "demonstrate my ability to formulate, refine, and present a proposal for original research." Each exam included a three-hour written test. I learned that not only must I pass those exams, but I must receive at least an A- average to continue receiving any scholarship from the university.

I'd never failed academically in my life until I got my first midterm grade back in one of the graduate courses: 67 out of 100.

While this may seem acceptable to some new graduate students, this grade spelled catastrophe for me. It meant game over. Unless I could achieve almost perfect scores for the rest of midterms and finals, it would be hard to get an A- at the end with that first midterm score. I wanted to hide my face and run to my room to pack up my belongings and go back home to China. Instead, I went to see my professor, Dr. Dewald. I didn't understand why I'd received such a low score when I was sure I had answered the questions correctly. The professor told me that my answers were all factually correct but that those were not the answers to his questions. It turned out that I hadn't understood what he was asking on the test and only provided the facts I'd learned from the book. I asked him how I could ensure that I'd always provide the right answers to his questions. He gave me a tip: if it's not in the notes he wrote during class, it's not the right answer.

During every class, he would scribble in his tiny handwriting until he'd filled the four big boards multiple times. I needed to ace this class despite the massive amount of information I had to retain somehow. In my desperation, I decided to memorize everything. I recorded his entire lectures and every letter he wrote on those boards. Each night, I'd pack my sleeping bag and head up to the library upstairs in the chemistry department. I would sit there memorizing every word, telling myself that I just needed to get through this and survive. Many mornings I got woken up by the sound of janitors vacuuming the library floor around 5:00 a.m.

I got a 98 and 99 on all the following exams, which I needed to balance out my score. I ended up with an A- for that course. I went back to my professor to ask him about the few points I missed.

"You missed a period."

I knew he was messing with me by saying that, but in another way, I realized he wanted to make sure that I knew there was room to improve. You might say the professor was a stickler, but he taught me a valuable lesson early on: details matter. Dr. Dewald took his work seriously and showed respect to his students by paying attention to every little detail. I appreciated him for instilling in me the importance of accuracy and conscientiousness. He was tough but fair, and—as I would learn soon enough—never minced words about the reality of my situation.

Somehow, I was able to score well in the rest of my courses, pass the qualification exam for the PhD program, and gain a little bit of confidence back.

Step 2: Set Solid Feet on the Road I Am On

When it came time to select a direction for my PhD program after the first semester, I wondered how to best accomplish my desire for completing a graduate-level computer science degree.

One day, another Chinese senior graduate student, Chen, approached me with a question: his PhD advisor, Professor Harrington, had given him a mission to recruit the best new graduates to his lab. Chen said he thought I was the best in that crowd and had come to convince me to pick Dr. Harrington. Their area of expertise was chemometrics, a scientific area to extract information from chemical systems by applying data-analytic disciplines such as statistics, applied math, and computer science. (Basically, I only needed to analyze data with math and computer science skills.) That was a field that I'd never known existed before, and it felt like a perfect match for me. I accepted the invitation. What I didn't know then was that Chen would become a lifelong friend of mine and would help me in so many ways, academically and later in life.

Dr. Harrington's group had several research focus areas, one of which was to develop algorithms that performed real-time signal processing, modeling, and interpretation. I immediately fell in love with their lab during my first visit. At least six Sun workstations were sitting on center desks, which—at that time, in my eyes—were the holy grail of computers. These super-computers could run multiple complex models at once, allowing you to do so much more than what was possible with a singular unit. In China, those types of computers were only provided for one of the Olympic math model competitions I was involved with—and there they were, in front of me.

WOW, I thought. *What a luxury that they can have computer clusters in a private lab, on their own, and no usage time limits!*

I spent so much time on those computers in later years and had the greatest fun with them, building models, running simulations, and some-times just letting them run algorithms during the weekends, just because I could!

Dr. Harrington was also quite a character. He was usually in his office, programming with both of his feet up on his table, keyboard on his lap, and typing like crazy. During our first lunch together, he finished his meal, then looked at my half-eaten burger and fries, and asked, "Are you going to finish that?" Once I said no, he grabbed my plate and finished for me, leaving me there dropping my jaw. (That is a good old pre-COVID-era story, of course.) He was extremely casual, straightforward, open-minded, smart, and fun to be with. I owe my deep gratitude to him for any of my success under his supervision.

Step 3: Getting Admitted to the Road I Desire to Be On

I loved chemometrics as my PhD program, but it just wasn't enough computer science for me. So, I looked for another graduate program to take at the same time.

After some research, I found out there was a master's program at Ohio University that focused on computer science combined with advanced mathematical algorithms. Graduate students needed to take a total of fourteen related graduate courses to complete a master's degree. Due to the tight relationship between the two fields, I would be mostly coding with algorithms in that program. *This is the perfect computer science program for me*, I thought. However, to be qualified for admission, I had to have either a math or CS undergraduate degree, and I had neither. My undergraduate degree was in chemical engineering, but I'd taught myself a lot and had taken as many classes and courses in computer science as possible.

Finally, I thought, *all the certificates and credentials I'd hoarded won't go to waste.*

I decided to apply for the program despite not meeting the specific criteria. I wrote up a personal statement that told my story, explaining all the work I had done on my own. I needed to capture not only the official credentials I had amassed but also everything I'd taught myself. Explaining my determination in achieving academic and career goals regardless of challenges is a key part of my story. I also explained that I was currently a PhD candidate in chemometrics and planned to pursue this master's degree in tandem with that line of study. When that was done, I sent my package with the stack of certificates I'd obtained over the years.

Then I crossed my fingers and waited.

The admissions officer was intrigued by my story and invited me for an interview. He first asked me if my story was true, that I couldn't study computers as a major due to my disability. I told him yes, and—though I wanted the opportunity badly—I couldn't afford to spend another four years getting a BS degree in CS first. He listened attentively and was impressed by all the certificates I was able to acquire because normally people would do that only after they graduate with a bachelor's and are training for a job.

Still concerned, he questioned me further.[9]

"You will be taking graduate-level computer science courses that require two or even three prerequisite undergraduate classes. Can you really keep up?"

"I've looked at all the courses, and I know that I already have the fundamental knowledge and skills from my college years in China. For example, this certificate is comparable to those two prerequisite classes."

"Do you plan to quit your current PhD program and focus only on this program instead?"

"No. As long as my department allows it, I want to pursue both at the same time. I've made my commitment to my advisor already."

"That's an insane amount of work. How would you manage that?"

"I've packed two years of work in one before, during my college years. I am great at time management. This is a much harder one, but I've planned out the schedule already. In theory, it should work."

"Do you know that you must maintain an A- average for all graduate courses to keep your scholarship?"

---

[9] These are not direct quotes but rather how the conversation went to the best of my memory.

"Yes, I am fully aware that once I drop below A-, I will lose my scholarship."

"To be fair, you also need to do a teaching assistant job so we can waive your tuition here. With your PhD program, you could be doing two jobs at the same time but only getting paid by one."

"Deal!"

He chuckled and looked deep into my eyes, trying to decide if he should give me that opportunity.

I don't know if it was my insistence and determination that convinced him, but he decided to admit me to the program, waived the tuition, and provided a TA job for me in their department.

Walking out of his office, I burst into tears.

For the first time since the day I was rejected back in 1995, I'd finally gotten an admission ticket to a door I'd always wanted to enter—one that I'd felt was closed forever. There I was, six years later, limping through that door with my head held high.

To many people, opportunities like this one are so easy to get and are often taken for granted. To others like me, we have to walk an extremely long way to get there.

I didn't ask his name, but whoever he is, wherever he is, I owe him a great debt of gratitude for giving that young Chinese girl with a polio leg the opportunity she deserved.

Step 4: Get Permission for Dual Graduate Degrees

Instead of only pursuing this new master's degree, I'd already made up my mind to do both at the same time. I loved chemometrics as an interdisciplinary field that solved real-world problems by applying algorithmic skills. But it would be a tough conversation for me to convince the chemistry department to allow me to do both programs at the same time. I'd heard that some other students had attempted that before but had all been rejected. There was a firm belief that to achieve a single PhD program, you must concentrate with all the energy you already have.

I told Dr. Harrington about my decision, and he called a meeting with me and Dr. Dewald, the department's dean, in his office.

(Yes, it was *that* Dr. Dewald, who had taken off a mark because I had missed a period.)

"Libo, this has never been done before in the two-hundred-year history of Ohio University. Do you understand that you're setting yourself up for failure? You'd be at a big risk of losing your scholarship and going back to where you were...with neither degree."

It sounded harsh, but Dr. Dewald didn't mean it as an insult. He truly cared about his students and our success. He had a job, and that was to prevent me from blindly walking off a cliff.

"You will be doing double the work while keeping all your grades up. And the second year, we have comprehensive tests, all of which a lot of graduate students couldn't pass and had to drop out. Are you ready for all that?" he asked, eagle-eyed and serious.

Neither Dr. Dewald nor Dr. Harrington knew my story and where I came from. They didn't know I only had one option in my mind: full force ahead. I looked at him and said, "Maybe nobody's ever done it before, but I could be the first one!"

I knew what was at stake. I knew my failure, if it happened, would be devastating. I knew that I was risking everything. But I had not walked this far to give up just because nobody else had done it. I had seen many people in the Cao family who had become the first ones to do courageous acts. I had never been the Cao who stops at a road just because nobody has ever walked on it before.

I knew I could lose, but I couldn't yield. It was a battle I must fight.

Dr. Harrington and Dr. Dewald hesitantly agreed to let me do it. They could not argue with my determination, but I don't think they truly believed I would be able to pull it off. I don't blame them; I didn't believe it myself at that point. I just knew it was a fight I had picked with my fate and that I couldn't back down.

We were all very clear that I would be held to the same standards as everyone else and that if I failed, I was out of the program. As I walked out of the meeting, I felt Dr. Dewald's eyes like laser beams boring into my back. I shook a little, knowing the risk was extremely high—but I also knew that if I didn't take that opportunity, I would regret it for the rest of my life.

I also made up my mind that I would finish both degrees within the next three years. I imagined one day in the future, walking back into that office triumphantly, putting both of my diplomas on the desk, declaring, "I won!" It may sound silly, and I never followed through on this little fantasy, but my imagination allowed me to visualize myself as a success regardless of other people's opinions.

Libo in front of her white horse in Athens, Ohio. This old Mazda salvage car made so much squeaking noise during cold winter mornings (2001).

5.3. I CAN LOSE, BUT I CAN'T YIELD (2002–2003)

In Chinese, we have a saying: 无知者无畏. This is directly translated to "The ignorant are fearless." You can also call it "the fool's courage."

That basically described what happened to me. Everyone who warned me about the challenges of the dual degree route was right.

In the chemistry department, starting the second year of the PhD program, are a set of comprehensive exams. Each month, a subject was sent out for students to study on their own. We would need to find out everything about that subject, which could be one area that's emerging from a recent scientific study, a complicated scientific approach/equipment, or anything in between. At the end of that month, we would be quizzed by a three-hour written exam. This required a method of studying that I had never done before. In the past, I'd learned how to read a textbook and take an exam based on content from that textbook. But to be simply given a scientific subject without any study material? That changed the whole game. Not only did we need to learn all the factual aspects of that subject, but we also needed to research current trends and recent studies, discover who published what paper on that subject that shared that new opinion, and determine how we thought about it. The whole process lasted ten months with ten subjects. Each graduate student needed to pass at least four out of ten. If it sounds like passing four out of ten is easy, it's not, when you consider that those tests were added on top of our regular graduate courses. Plus, we also still needed to maintain an A- average. They were very time-consuming as well because we needed to find our own study materials and conduct our own learning. It was an energy-draining process, and many PhD students dropped out during that period. On top of that, I still had to conduct research work in Dr. Harrington's lab so that I could start publishing papers, which was a requirement for PhD candidates.

Additionally, I was working. In the computer science program, though the name was teaching assistant (TA), the job was doing the whole thing instead of just "assisting." It included preparing for the class, giving lectures, making assignments, and grading assignments. Basically, the assistant *is* the teacher. I also had to sign up for three to four graduate-level classes each semester to be qualified as a full-time graduate student in that department.

To sum it up, I needed to take a total of six to eight graduate-level classes per semester with grades no lower than A-, do a TA job for my computer science master program, do an RA job for the chemistry PhD program, and pass monthly comprehensive exams for the PhD program.

I came up with a plan of attack to manage it all.

I signed up to teach the earliest classes available, at 8:00 a.m. By 9:00 a.m., I could then take my own regular graduate classes in different buildings. After 6:00 p.m., I would get back to my chemistry lab and work from there for the whole night to get homework and lab work done.

With that plan in place, I believed I should be able to keep up with all the work daily. There was only one problem: no time for sleeping. I started to research if people really needed to sleep to live and found a thing called the "power nap." Problem solved: if I was able to take small power naps during the day, then I would have the whole night working. In theory, I thought it would work. It had to! I needed ten to twelve uninterrupted hours to code effectively every day, which I only had when the world around me was in bed.

So, that's exactly what I did. I approached the problem systematically, giving up sleeping at night and using fragmented time during the day between classes to take power naps. While sleep deprivation is a form of torture, it was the only way I could squeeze enough hours out of the day to complete all my work. I averaged about four hours of sleep a day but would allow myself five or six hours sometimes, if I started feeling too light-headed. Sleep deprivation affected my body in strange ways. It felt like walking on clouds, like my entire body was lighter than it should be, almost untethered to the earth.

I'm glad I was young, in my mid=twenties, because I can't imagine myself surviving that type of insane schedule today.

I would wake up early in the morning and go teach my classes at 8:00 a.m. Then, I'd curl up in a corner somewhere for a quick power nap before my own classes started. Sometimes I did that in the library, sometimes in my car in the parking lot, and sometimes I could go back to my apartment for a nap. I managed my time down to the minute because I couldn't afford messing up my schedule for even one day. If I fell behind, the consequences could be devastating. Throughout the day, I attended my chemistry and computer science classes while trying to finish all my classwork and home-work. I was also grading papers and exams. If I had breaks between classes, I'd get some sleep wherever I was. At night, I'd buy four hamburgers and stack them up on my desk in the lab to eat while I programmed through-out the night. Years later, I discovered the science behind what I did. Our bodies *can* function with short periods of deep sleep.[10]

And while it was exhausting, it was also glorious. My lab with computers was paradise to me. Remember back in China when I had to take the bus back and forth between the two computers I was using in the lab and at my parents' home? Now I had all these computers to myself late at night. I was ecstatic! There was only one time I recall when I hit a wall and had to skip all my classes that day. I went home, slept an entire day, and started over the next morning as if nothing had happened. It felt like I could drain all the energy out of my body and then reset with one good night's sleep.

Now that I'm in my forties, I'm in awe of what my body accomplished then, and very aware those times are over. If I must pull an all-nighter with my team now, I know I'm not myself once 3:00 a.m. rolls around. I must take a rest to ensure that exhaustion doesn't lead me to make errors and create more problems for myself and my team. I always push up against my limits, and I know myself well enough to be smart about it.

My greasy diet of Wendy's hamburgers and lack of sleep caught up with me over the semester, leading to an extra twenty pounds—on my small frame. This quickly became a problem... again, not because I was bothered

---

[10] Jamie Ducharme, "People Are Sleeping in 20-Minute Bursts to Boost Productivity. But Is It Safe?" *Time*, January 30, 2018, https://time.com/5063665/what-is-polyphasic-sleep/.

by my appearance but because the extra weight put additional strain on my polio leg. It became even more exhausting and difficult to walk for long periods. I couldn't do much about my lack of sleep, as there were simply not enough hours in the day for all my work. However, I could make changes to my horrible diet. By then, my porridge preparation skill had reached its master stage. I would be able to spend no more than three minutes dumping oatmeal, rice, frozen veggie and meat bits, and spices into a slow cooker in the morning and setting the timer for it to cool down later. When I dropped by home, the porridge had solidified for me to cut into squares and take to labs as a meal. It was almost like making my healthier and cheaper granola bar, and it was sugar-free and soothing to my Chinese stomach.

My brain was constantly buzzing with the computer science problems I was trying to solve, and more than once, my obsession with the subject led to awkward interactions. One day, another Chinese graduate student startled me out of a midday power nap with a phone call, asking to borrow my umbrella because it was raining. I'd been immersed in a tree data structure for my class, and in my sleep-deprived state, I told the other student that I couldn't loan him my umbrella.

"I just built this tree data structure, and this umbrella points to the root node of the tree. Before I can loan you my umbrella," I told him, "I need to create another pointer for the root node, or else I will lose the whole tree structure, and the program will crash."

After a moment of confused silence, the voice on the other side said, "Uh, never mind, Libo," before hanging up. I was so consumed with solving this problem that it didn't occur to me until a day later what had happened. I called the graduate student up to apologize for not letting him borrow my umbrella. He laughed and said he understood that I was in the "flow," and that happens to people who get crazy with their classes sometimes.

While I had taught myself computer science theory from books and memorized entire algorithms, I'd never had regular access to a computer to practice coding until I was assigned homework in my degree program. I was studying alongside many young graduate students. After completing my very first computer science homework assignment, I asked one of them how long it took him to finish. He said ten hours.

It had taken me one hundred hours to finish that same assignment! Ten times longer than everyone else!

For that first assignment, I first tried to code it up on Linux, which is the operating system everyone was using to submit their final work. However, I had forgotten that most of the graduate students in CS had already been trained with the debuggers on Linux, and they were all very good at using command-line–based tools. I had only coded before with debuggers on Windows. I couldn't make progress after the first ten hours, so I requested help from Chen, my senior friend in the same PhD program under Dr. Harrington. Chen spent that whole night in the lab with me, showing me how to set up the environment I was familiar with—Visual Studio—debugged my program there, built up a first library, then cross-compiled it to run on Linux. There were differences here and there, and I had to adjust for both platforms to work, but that process worked for me under extreme time pressure. That was such a long night of learning for me.

After that first hand-holding, I told Chen I got it, and I used the same approach to code up all my homework that semester. During the summer break, I had to catch up with command-line tooling on Linux so that I could be much faster and better the following semester.

I owe my eternal debt to Chen (and many other friends like him) who gave me much-needed help in life during those years. Many of them were great cooks as well, and whenever I got to a point that my stomach couldn't handle porridge anymore, somehow, I would get an invitation from one of them telling me that they'd cooked too much and needed my help finishing it. It was those friends from China who looked out for me and were invested in my success as well. They spent their time and energy being there for me when I needed them, and I will always be grateful for their support.

I had a big computer science assignment like that every two weeks, and thanks to my support system and my own determination, I learned quickly and became faster. Ultimately, I matched my fellow student's speed in completing my assignments.

Of course, I had my meltdown moments as well. One night, around 2:00 a.m., I went home early (yes, you read that right) from the computer lab because I was so exhausted. It was the Mid-Autumn Festival—a Chinese holiday during which all family members get together to celebrate—and I was missing my family badly. I was tired from months of endless work on little sleep and little food, and I was ready to give up. I wanted to go home. Because I was barely awake, I ran a stop sign on my way home. A police officer pulled me over, and when he knocked on my window, I burst into tears. It was the last straw. I started apologizing over and over, rambling to the officer, "I haven't slept for months, and my head isn't working. My family is celebrating together today without me, and I miss them. I'm so tired. I can't do it anymore."

The officer looked at me calmly. "It's not safe for you to drive like this. I'm going to get back in my car and you'll follow me. I'll guide you home and make sure you'll get there safely." It was such a relief to experience this small act of kindness from a perfect stranger, at a moment when I felt lost and alone and ready to give up. When we got to my apartment, the officer told me to take care and didn't issue me a ticket. It was a small gesture that meant the world. Still, for a long time, I wondered why a cop was waiting at a stop sign around 2:00 a.m. (Later, during my party days in Silicon Valley, I understood that's when the bars close.)

Things started turning around after that second year in Ohio, and I began to hit my stride. I did all my jobs right, kept all my grades above A-, passed all my comprehensive exams, and not only Dr. Harrington was happy with me, but professors from the other program were happy as well. I pulled off the hardest year and no longer felt like I was precariously close to losing everything daily. I started to feel more confident about my academic career. The only downside was that twenty extra pounds that I couldn't get off. When I came to the US, I weighed eighty-eight pounds. The first year, I added ten pounds, and the second year twenty pounds. I blamed those burgers and decided to never eat a burger again, especially from Wendy's. (I consumed four per night while coding, and I knew it wasn't Wendy's fault.)

I was out of the woods for the most part and allowed myself to consider a trip home to China for the end of summer break in 2002.

My family back in China at that time didn't know what I had signed up for. Every week, I would give them a quick call and tell them that everything was fine and perfect; I was just busy. Before each call, I would take a deep breath, swallow the tears, and only tell my parents the good things. It wasn't until decades later that I had a conversation with my brother where he confronted me about those phone calls home in the early years of graduate school. By that time, my family had heard bits and pieces of the challenges and hardships I'd gone through. Small and big tragedies that seemed funny now that time had passed but that were terrifying to me while I was going through them. My brother was upset that I hadn't been honest about my struggles, but I only wanted to protect my family from worrying about me. What could they have done from thousands of miles away? I didn't want to cause them pain.

Because I had been singularly focused on academics, I spent barely any money, except for what I needed for my rent, food, and car. Four hamburgers a day are not that expensive, and neither is porridge. Though I was doing both RA and TA as my jobs for the second year, I was only able to get one payment instead of double. Still, I was able to save up $8,000 in two years from my scholarship alone, which was a lot of money for any twenty-six-year-old graduate student in 2002. I decided to take $5,000 back to China as a gift to my parents and save $3,000 as an emergency fund for the following year. I didn't want to risk losing that money while transporting it back to my family in China, so I came up with an unconventional (and highly uncomfortable) idea. I bought a giant pair of granny panties and sewed multiple pockets onto the panties, two in the front and three in the back. I stuffed those pockets with the bills. While the TSA didn't question my secret stash, I spent a painfully long flight with wadded-up money in my underwear.[11]

When I finally made it home, I pulled Mom aside, who could not stop laughing when I emptied the money pockets in front of her. Bringing money back to my family was my way of showing that I was doing well enough by myself that I could afford to help support them if needed. I wanted to give them a small token of appreciation for always taking care of me. Dad retired from his company in 2000, the year I moved to the US. His mission had been to make enough money to send my brother and me to college. Together my parents had achieved much more than that initial goal. They were set up financially and no longer had to work. They owned a big

---

[11]   It was legally allowed to transport cash that's below the amount of $10,000.

enough portfolio of real estate. Both their children were going to college and building lives of their own. They didn't accept my $5,000, but I refused to take it back. It's still sitting in a savings account somewhere, untouched. It is a privilege to know that our entire family is financially taken care of, and we no longer have to worry about what to do with this $5,000.

It was wonderful to spend time with my family, and the visit filled me up emotionally. The love and pride I felt from my parents and extended family kept me going once I was back in Ohio. Nothing could stop me from completing what I had started.

Many of the projects and assignments I completed helped me see my majors—chemistry, math, and computer science—in a different light. They turned from interesting but abstract concepts to real-life applications. Throughout my academic career, I created math models and algorithms to streamline the elevator system in a big hotel complex, to determine the relationship between any two given people in a complex genealogy software program, and to estimate how long it would take for a hazardous chemical to pollute a system of waterways. You wouldn't think an elevator system should be that difficult to design. The problem comes in when you introduce randomness into a model. Different hotel guests on different floors at different times using multiple elevators to go up or down is about as random as you can get. That project gave me nightmares for months. Even nowadays, I ask interview questions for young graduates to see if they know how to debug multithreading programs efficiently.

But the beautiful thing was that I realized computers with algorithms could solve real-world problems—some small, some large, but all impacting the lives of real people. One especially memorable project was Dr. Harrington's lab collaborating with the government for antiterrorist initiatives.

One day, Dr. Harrington walked into the lab and said to me, "You are Chinese; you must be good at math. Do you know how to do Laplace transform?"

(Dr. Harrington didn't always care about being politically correct in his communication.)

"Yes, Sir, I can do any transform you need," I replied confidently. "Laplace, Fourier, Wavelet...you name it; I can transform it!"

Dr. Harrington laughed, handed me a stack of material, and said, "The project is yours. How much do you want for your next year's scholarship?"

I was shocked. I didn't know such a great opportunity would be provided to me. At the time, I was paid $23,000 per year as a research assistant while pursuing my PhD. So, I went brave and asked for $26,000 per year, then waited for a response. Dr. Harrington said, "You got it!" then left me with my mouth open.

I later learned that the project came with a $100,000 research fund, and I could have asked for a lot more. Lesson learned: never name your own price. Ask the others to name it first because you might be surprised. That project was to develop real-time signal processing algorithms to be able to detect potential chemical weapon residues in the air efficiently. This was after the 9/11 attacks, and the government had heightened concerns over mitigating potential terrorist attacks. I helped build models for devices that could collect chemical simulant data to identify potentially toxic airborne materials, the rate at which they spread through the atmosphere, and which other chemicals to deploy to mitigate the risk.

It turned out that my combined skillset in applied math, computer science, and analytical chemistry made me the most productive researcher. I was able to take on many projects that others couldn't and publish papers at a much higher speed than others. I was also able to apply many machine-learning algorithms to solve problems in the chemistry domain. For example, I could train a model that predicts the type of explosive chemical "sniffed" by ion mobility spectroscopy (a type of electronic nose), like a highly trained explosive-detection dog. Many years later, I got a call from someone either from the government or FBI, questioning me about getting paid for such graduate work. I thought it was a spam call. Turns out the government, over a decade later, was tracing payments for antiterrorism work to anyone who wasn't a US citizen. I had to tell them that their process was flawed. There wasn't any requirement for people conducting the study to be US citizens, and all research work and results were published in papers afterward.

Time flies when you're busy learning. I completed all my other master's program requirements by summer 2003 and started focusing solely on PhD research after that. In late 2003, Dr. Harrington surprised me:

"Libo, you're ready to graduate!"

I was confused. It had only been three years since I'd come to the US in 2000. One PhD program usually takes at least five to six years to complete, and I was pursuing a dual degree. He explained to me that since I had already published several required papers and accumulated enough credits, I only had to write the final dissertation and complete the final PhD defense.

He recommended I focus on finding a job for a seamless transition out of academia and into the next chapter of my life.

Before I knew it, I had already completed all the programs I'd set out to complete. I'd won the battle!

But who would hire me? I really didn't know where to start.

5.4. THE JOB THAT FOUND ME (APRIL 2004)

In late March 2004, I presented a paper at an industry conference in Pittsburgh, Pennsylvania, on data compression and classification algorithms. One hiring manager from a Silicon Valley startup in the semiconductor business came to find me after my presentation. One of his employees happened to be my grad student friend, Chen, who had worked there for a while but quit the job for another opportunity. Highly recommended by Chen, they asked if I was interested in his position... mostly because they were happy with Chen, and I had the same background as him.

The hiring manager interviewed me with many technical questions. He was well prepared with data sheets and issues they had encountered in day-to-day work. After a long interview, he was pleased with my answers and problem-solving skills. He extended an invitation for a formal interview in Silicon Valley, California. I was thrilled by the success of the first interview and flew there soon after that.

That visit began with a full day of technical interviews plus a PowerPoint presentation I had to give to the hiring committee. I excelled and advanced to the last interview with the CEO. At that point, there were no technical questions left to be asked. Nothing else left for me to prove my proficiency. He asked me only one question:

"If the world was perfect, what would you do differently?"

I paused. *Was that a trick question? Was he trying to trap me?* In the end I answered plainly and honestly.

"There is nothing I would do differently. I have had the life I wanted, and it went the way I wanted it to be. I have no regret in any of my decisions in the past, and I wouldn't change a single person in my life that meant so much to me. I would change nothing!"

Looking back on my answer now, I wouldn't change it. I don't wish for pain or suffering, but at the same time, I know I gained self-knowledge in those moments. In a perfect world without pain, how would I recognize ease and relief, happiness, and contentment? How could I know what true peace and harmony feels like if I'd never been through struggle and chaos?

On the plane ride back from California to Ohio, I received my first job offer from the company. They wanted me to start working immediately for them, without getting my final degree. Once I finished writing my dissertation in six months, using my spare time, they would pay for my expense and time going back to Ohio for my final PhD defense. They even asked me how much base pay it would take for me to accept their offer.

That was the first time I'd ever done a job interview and the first offer I'd ever received in this new country. I had no idea how to deal with it, so I turned to Dr. Harrington and asked him how much I should ask for. I was thinking about doubling my scholarship. Dr. Harrington instead said, "You're a PhD! It's a big deal! Ask for no less than $90,000 a year!"

I told the hiring manager that my advisor thought I was worth more than $90,000 for my first job. I was terrified, expecting them to tell me that I wasn't worth that much. In fact, I was willing to drop down to $50,000 if they'd asked me to.

The company representative paused for a moment and said calmly, "We will make it $95,000 a year plus stock options, but you need to accept our offer immediately."

"I accept!" I said, trying to keep my voice calm. I believed I'd shamelessly taken advantage of their company and worried that they would regret their offer later. Maybe at that moment, the feelings were mutual . . . maybe they also thought that I was a steal for them and worried that I would regret it on the other side of the line.

Regardless of what I had achieved by that time in my life, I didn't have confidence.

I know what you're thinking: *If you didn't have confidence, how did you come all the way to another country and attempt to tackle the impossible?* The answer is that my courage was not coming from my confidence but rather from my willingness to fight for my right to live equally to others. My goal was simple, to get what I deserve, to overcome whatever was in my way so that I could *survive* on my own in this world. My parents taught me how to work hard, stay focused on goals, grit my teeth, swallow my tears along the way, and keep moving…but they never taught me to be confident. Staying humble is certainly a virtue that Asian culture taught me, which is valuable. However, as a side effect, I forgot how confidence is equally important to someone's life.

Looking back, I could have asked for a lot more, and they would have paid a lot more to get me signed. I also wasn't aware that I could negotiate and ask for things like "sign-on bonuses" and "relocation fees," etc. Those are the costs I paid for my lack of confidence or knowledge at that age and state in life. However, I have no regrets about that decision at all. I am extremely grateful for my first company, which gave me the initial offer I needed before I even graduated. I didn't have much confidence in myself before, but that offer provided me with the first bit of confidence I very much needed. We can always accumulate more wealth later in life, but gaining the confidence to believe that I was worth something to someone was a lot more valuable to me at that time.

Now, as the head of an organization at my current company, I pay close attention to salary equality. I work with my staff and HR partners to eliminate any gender pay gap or inequalities for people at the same job with similar performance. I would encourage other leaders to also extend this fairness to their teams.

5.5. MISSION COMPLETE, GO GET A LIFE
(OCTOBER 2004)

In April 2004, less than a month from the time I presented at the Pittsburgh Conference, I started my new job in Silicon Valley.[12] It all happened so fast that it felt like a dream to me.

My starter job title was "Software Scientist," which was a unique title in Silicon Valley. Why? Because the job required research work that a scientist would do: forming a hypothesis for a problem, experimenting, collecting data, providing a solution to the issue, and verifying with a conclusion. Since most of the work required coding as a software engineer, *software* is also in the title.

For the first six months, I worked for at least twelve hours a day, thinking that I must earn my high salary by working as many hours as possible and being as productive as possible. During late nights and weekends, I would work on my dissertation. I didn't think I deserve to have a life yet.

My dissertation went well with the first draft but was quickly returned for polishing. After seven major revisions of going back and forth with my advisor and the dean, I lost faith in doing it right. At that time, my dissertation was about two hundred pages. One of those revisions was returned with the feedback that I needed to do a "self-review." The reason? Dr. Dewald

---

12   The full name of the conference is Pittsburgh Conference on Analytical Chemistry and Applied Spectroscopy.

found a missing period on my reference page, again! He said something I will never forget: "If I can't trust you getting your periods right, how can I trust you getting your data right and any other facts right?"

To complete a qualified PhD dissertation, not only do the contents of the paper need to have merit, but all the references must also comply with the American Chemical Society (ACS) style guide. The ACS style guide itself is a full book, listing how to refer to any sources quoted depending on the source type. For example, if you want to refer to one of the papers I published, you must do it exactly in the format below to meet ACS style requirements:

Cao, L.; Harrington, P. D.; Harden, C. S.; McHugh, V. M.; Thomas, M. A. Nonlinear wavelet compression of ion mobility spectra for ion mobility spectrometers mounted in an unmanned aerial vehicle. *Anal. Chem.* **2004**, *76*, 1069–1077.

You can't miss any period; you can't miss any space; you must bold what needs to be bolded and italicize what needs to be italicized. There is no room for inaccuracy in science.

I felt ashamed that I couldn't make my dissertation perfect, but it taught me that it's not acceptable when something is *almost* right. Instead, things are great when *everything* is right. Paying attention to all the details is a basic requirement in my PhD training, and I've benefited from that training throughout my whole career. I do have this fear that when this book is published, Dr. Dewald will buy one and tell me that I missed a period somewhere in this book, again!

I redid my dissertation many times. Finally, around the tenth revision, it was accepted. In October 2004, exactly six months after I started working, I flew back to Athens, Ohio, and completed my PhD defense. Dr. Harrington congratulated me and told me that I should proudly call myself Dr. Libo Cao from then on.

Starting from September 2000, when I first arrived in this new country, to October 2004, when I completed both of my graduate degrees, it took me three and a half years in school and half a year at my first job. I fulfilled everything that I had set out to do and was very satisfied with the results. I thought of that moment of success a million times when I was struggling. But now that it was over, I really didn't know how to have a life. I'd never spent any time outside of studying and working.

Am I successful now? If so, how come I didn't feel it? If not, what next?

Suddenly, I realized that I had free time and had no idea what to do with that time. I searched "What do people do for fun," and the first thing on people's list was outdoor activities.

Ah, sports! Those things I was told to avoid doing during all my PE classes.

"I am a grown-up now, and I can do whatever I want," I said loudly to my polio leg, the words bouncing off the walls in the otherwise empty room.

After working for half a year, Libo flew back to Athens for her PhD defense (October 2004).

6.

PERSEVERANCE, PRIDE, AND A CENTURY RIDE (2005)

"Battle not with monsters, lest ye become a monster, and
if you gaze into the abyss, the abyss gazes also into you,"
said Nietzsche.

I viewed polio as my abyss. My weakness.
What pulled me into dark places.

But Nietzsche also famously said,
"That which does not kill us makes us stronger."

Polio didn't kill me. But before I could see it as my strength,
I knew I had to come to terms with it.

The journey to acceptance may have been
a hundred miles long, but it is the most worthwhile trek
I've ever taken. And the destination?
Pride in who I am—all of me.

6.1. CAN I RIDE A BIKE?

I was eight years old and watching people from our window, feeling the sun hit my shoulders. It was a rare day during this time in my life because I was not on crutches, nor was I wrapped up like a mummy recovering from another surgery. I loved watching people passing by on the street, and I often wondered what their life stories were.

It was rare for me to feel that happy and free during that time in my life. I hated my polio leg, so much so that I often told my parents that I just wanted to cut it off. It was weak, shorter, skinnier, and I had to have surgery after surgery to try to fix it. These surgeries meant I had to miss school to recover, and the last thing I wanted to do was miss school. Everything I didn't like at the time felt like it had at least something to do with the polio leg. It was ugly and stopped me from doing the things I wanted to do.

When I brought this up, Mom always told me that though my polio leg looked different and wasn't as useful as my healthy leg, it was still valuable.

"Your leg is *real*. It is a part of you that is connected by blood," she reminded me. Later, as an adult, I would internalize this message, even going so far as to talk to my leg to come to peace with it. I thank my leg for staying alive with me and keeping me moving forward.

But at that time, I was eight years old, and I did not yet have that maturity of thought. I *hoped* that Mom was right about me one day loving my leg because it is a part of me, but I did not know how to make that happen. And for once, I was thinking about other things, like the warmth of the sun on my skin and how nice it felt to be walking down the street on my own.

Then, it happened. A chance encounter that would plant a seed—one that would not fully bloom until twenty years later.

I heard him before I saw him, the clinking of the chain and whooshing of air: it was a boy, and he was riding a bike. Everything about the scene felt glorious to me.

"Freedom!" I yelled as a feeling of awe welled up in my throat like a lump, watching him from the window. That night, I told my parents my plan: I was going to learn to ride a bike. That way, not only would I get to fly through the wind like the boy I saw, but it would also stop people from seeing my limp. The only problem was that to learn to ride a bike, I needed a bike to practice with.

"That's my girl," Dad laughed as I explained my goal. "You got it. But make sure you don't fall too much." Two days later, I had a bike.

Two days after that—and after countless crashes, bruises, and scars—I did not have a bike any longer. My parents worried I would break my already not-so-useful leg, or worse. Though I didn't want to stop pursuing my dream, I understood their fear... especially after crashing into the neighbor's storage building.

Not even a day after I was forbidden from riding my (now damaged) bike, my brother saw that it was still rideable and hopped on. Within just a few minutes, he was riding that bike like he had known how to ride his entire life. He had healthy legs and was able to learn the skill so quickly. Before I knew it, he had claimed my bike as his own. The sense of freedom I was drawn to after seeing the neighbor boy whoosh past on his bike mere days before felt far less tangible then. *How can a person with polio learn to ride a regular bike?* I wondered. *Is it even possible?*

It would be years later before I'd try again.

I was all alone in a new country—the United States—for graduate school. Too proud to ask for rides from friends and without the funds to buy a car myself, I had to find a solution to my transportation problem. This is when the idea of biking, again, entered my life.

One of my friends was brave enough to lend me his bike so I could try to learn. Unfortunately, his generous act did not end well for me. After a series of significant falls, I came to the same conclusion my parents had come to all those years ago: a polio leg and a bike might mix someday, but it was not worth the risk.

It specifically was not worth the risk for me then because, at the time, I was preparing for my PhD qualification exams, trying to apply for a second degree in computer science simultaneously, and studying at least fifteen hours a day. Not only did I not have enough time to be down from a potential injury, but I also thought about my family back home. They had always been there to catch me when I fell. But this time, they were thousands of miles away.

The dream of riding a bike—once again—gave way to practicality. I weighed the risks, and what I could gain simply wasn't worth what I could lose. A few months later, I got my first car with my scholarship money, leaving my transportation troubles in the dust.

The dream of riding quieted again, but—much like it did when I was eight years old—it never left completely.

6.2. THE CHALLENGE OF A LIFETIME

"Libo, we know you can achieve anything intellectually, but you might never be an athlete," my friend Bill said. He was trying his best to be pragmatic and kind while delivering what he knew was likely an unwelcome observation. "There are just limitations."

During the early Silicon Valley days, I socialized to make some friends in this new home. Many of them were enthusiastic cyclists who often completed long rides together during their weekends, and Bill was one of them. Some of the rides were one hundred miles long: they called these rides "century rides."

"There are lots of ways to be an athlete," I said to Bill, the wheels of motivation already turning in my mind. "I may not be fast, but I know I have endurance. If I can do one of those century rides you guys did before, I would be an athlete then, right?" After the confirmation from Bill that riding a bike for one-hundred-plus miles would qualify me as an "athlete," I said "Deal!"

My mind was made up. And I not only had the desire; this time, I also knew I could afford the risk. I was done with school, had a job with excellent health coverage, and had enough savings that I could afford to be out of work for a period, if necessary, due to injury. For the first time in my life, the timing, risk assessment, and desire around learning to bike all came together.

The only problem? Before I could ride one hundred miles, I had to learn to ride one hundred feet. I had to learn to stay on the bike without it toppling over. I had to learn how to pedal with only one good leg. In short, I had a lot to learn.

I knew step one was to find a bike, so I purchased one from an ad on Craigslist. Later I would discover that all bikes are not created equal: I'd gotten a heavy twenty-four-gear mountain bike, and what I needed was a light road bike. But at the time, I had a bike, and I had determination. After wrestling the heavy contraption into my car and then into my apartment, I set a plan: the next day, Saturday, I was going to learn to ride. Nothing was going to stop me this time!

For the first few hours of that Saturday, people in my apartment complex saw a twenty-eight-year-old woman struggling to ride a bike around the parking lot. I even saw a dad teaching his young son at the same time—and the child was doing far better than me, at least at first. After a couple of hours, I'd learned to make adjustments and was able to stay on the bike for a short period.

Many people aren't familiar with how polio can affect the body. I cannot speak for all people with this disease, obviously, but I can share what the process looks like for me.

Being far skinnier and shorter than my left leg, my right leg is mostly decorative. I use it much like a stick upon which to briefly support my body weight as I walk. If my right leg is to bend for any reason while it is holding my body weight, the chances of me falling are 100 percent.

In learning to bike, I made a few adjustments. To get the bike started, I learned the left pedal must be in the right position to give the bike enough momentum once I hopped on from the left side. Once things got going, I learned to always assess any upcoming climbs. If it was a short and relatively flat hill, the trick was to speed up as much as possible ahead of time so by the time I hit the little hill, I could cruise through with as much leftover momentum as possible. If it was a steeper or longer climb coming up and speed alone wouldn't do the trick, I learned to slow down, lean to the left to get off, and walk the bike over the hill. I also learned the best way to restart if my balance was off: when my right foot fell off the pedal and I was unable to get it back in place, I had to promptly move all my body weight to the left side, get off, and restart.

I practiced and practiced riding around the parking lot of my apartment complex until eventually, using the adjustments learned over time, I had fewer crashes and was able to get on the bike in fewer than three attempts. Success! I felt I was ready to leave the parking lot and ride on the road. Once I was on the road, each time I saw a car (even one far away), I got nervous and fell off the bike.

Not too long after that, I traveled to Solvang, a beautiful Danish town in Southern California, to see for myself what a century ride might be like. As Bill started his ride, I called another friend who had come with us and let him know that I was going to try a test ride myself on the road and would call him in about an hour. Instead, I called him back in about five minutes.

"I crashed; there was a stick on the road, and I'm bleeding now," I told him. "So much for my first century."

After that, though I was a little disappointed, I felt more excitement than anything. I found a grassy area that had more forgiving places to land, and the more I practiced, the more my fall-free rides progressed... as did my passion for the sport. After that, I finished a twenty-five-mile family ride and made it through the first twenty miles before crashing severely due to a stick in the road. (Later, I'd learn how to avoid obstacles in my path without catastrophe, but these were still the early days of my biking journey.) Regardless of the accidents, I knew I was growing. And, for the first time in my life, I knew I'd found a sport that I enjoyed! It was an amazing feeling. It's worth mentioning that I completed that twenty-five-mile family ride by following a mother and her six-year-old daughter the entire trip, because that's how fast I could keep up. I recall that at the beginning of the trip, the little girl was puzzled as to why an adult stranger would be following them. She kept looking back, but once she and her mother saw how fast I could go with an obviously broken leg, they got used to it. Any time when they were pedaling hard uphill, they would look back at me, and the girl would yell, "Come on, let's go, keep it up!"

That was a fun ride! While I was still learning, that ride helped me gain confidence that I could be as good as a six-year-old girl, at least.

6.3. TEAM IN TRAINING

After my crash happened at Solvang due to a little stick on the road, my desire to complete a century ride didn't change, but my approach did. I decided I needed professional help, and my friend Fey pointed me in the direction of Team In Training (TNT)—a nonprofit that assists those who want to take on endurance challenges while raising money for the Leukemia & Lymphoma Society. They became a wonderful resource for me, and I loved the good cause of the organization. While training with them provided guidance and support, it also provided me with another challenge: riding in a group.

When I saw a single-profile style riding group, my first thought was, *How many people am I going to crash into today?*

The first day with the team was calibration day. We had coaches looking at everyone's bike, making sure each was toned and calibrated correctly—I'd never known that was a thing. After Coach did the initial calibration of the bike, pumped my tires to the right pressure, and adjusted the seat to be appropriate for my height so that I could ride longer and more comfortably, we all needed to do a "warm-up" thirty-two-mile ride to decide which riding group we should belong to. This was so we could ride in smaller groups throughout our training. I was terrified, but Coach Don looked at me and said, "Don't worry. It's more like twenty-five miles!"

I survived the initial calibration ride with the company of Coach Don for the entire trip. I was assigned to team "Apple," which meant the slowest team category. But that didn't matter to me. We were all just happy that we had completed the first ride successfully. That "warm-up" ride for initial calibration was my longest ride at that time.

On early training rides, though the team was encouraging, I made sure to always ride in the back. That way, if I crashed or had to push my bike up a hill due to the slope, nobody behind would have to wait on me. I remember that for the first ride, I was slow, but more importantly, I felt safe being with a team of people who took care of each other. I realized that maybe my big crash before hadn't been about a lack of skill but rather the result of a subconscious belief that I couldn't control my bike as well as others could. TNT taught me that while my riding strategy might need a bit of adjustment compared to those of others, my capability was never in question.

Later, I learned how to ride with a team to rotate positions within the group mode. When you're doing anything in a team, especially riding as a unit, communication is critical. For example, if one rider sees something on or near the road ahead, they'll relay that to the rider behind them, so they know to avoid it safely. Once, the rider in front of me said, "Man and a dog!" What I heard, though, was what I repeated for Fey behind me: "Man on a dog!" I'm thankful she wasn't taking a drink from her water bottle at that exact moment, or I'm pretty sure I would've had water sprayed all over my back.

I met many good friends during my time with TNT, including George and his wife, Charlotte, who were both in their mid-fifties. Charlotte had similar post-polio problems, and we bonded over both our shared struggle and the tips we'd learned about working around our challenges. For example, I could not use clipless pedals like other bikers because my right foot isn't straight, and the leg didn't have the strength to adjust its angle. Even when the foot was correctly put in initially, I couldn't clip in and out of the right pedal later. Eventually, George helped me install a clipless pedal holder on top of the pedal, which mostly kept my right foot in place during the ride.

Some differences are difficult to work around, though. Each time we approached a stop sign as a group, I knew it would take me quite a bit of effort to get back on my bike and put my right foot into the pedal holder again. To avoid that, I would try to ride slowly and zigzag to avoid dismounting—which sometimes worked and sometimes didn't. A few times, I scared my teammates with this zigzag trick, and other times I'd miss a traffic light and have to stand there, embarrassed, as the whole team waited for me on the other side of the road. There were certainly moments when I thought my team would be better off, both faster and safer, without me. Coach Don was especially kind to me in these moments. He told me that during one of his charity rides, his bad knees caused him to slow down his whole team, and he'd felt horrible—but he'd have felt more horrible if he'd given up. In these moments and others, he and the rest of my TNT friends helped me keep my chin up, made me feel like I wasn't alone, and reminded me of how far I'd come.

To get ready for our century ride, we needed to train continuously. Every week, we needed to finish several hours of leg-muscle training ourselves at home, and every Tuesday we met as a team to do "hill repeats." That's a fancy way of saying we had to climb a local hill up and down seven times. Every weekend, we needed to complete many hours of outdoor rides. We climbed almost all the mountains around the Bay Area. We rode in all kinds of weather. We ate carbs afterward together without any diet control. We laughed. We started developing inside jokes and greeting each other with phrases like "How is your butt doing today?"

We were doing a big, important thing together as a team, and we had a lot of fun working toward it together.

The more we trained, the longer our rides became. Once, while approaching the sixty-mile mark on an especially hot day, I felt a sharp pain in my polio leg and heard a clicking sound.

What are you complaining about? I thought. *I'm not even using you.*

I hoped the discomfort would ease, but a few minutes later, I decided to take a break and check. The moment I got off my bike, I knew something was wrong: my polio leg wouldn't bend at all. The whole team had to wait for me, and (again) I felt horrible for holding them back. I gave up that ride, and Charlotte, our support captain, took me back in her car.

Once home, I researched what the strange clicking noise and pain might mean. I discovered that polio is not a stable disease. New muscle weakness can occur as well as general fatigue and exhaustion with minimal activity, muscle and joint pain, breathing and swallowing problems, sleep-related issues, and more. On one online forum, I even found that in cases of exercising, someone's "good" limb could lose strength because of overcompensating. It's called post-polio syndrome (PPS), which is a disorder of the nerves and muscles that affects many people after many years of having polio.

While what I did find was discouraging, what I didn't find felt like a glimmer of hope: despite the stories of and data on endurance exercising post-polio, there wasn't concrete, scientific data that told me overexercise would definitively cause permanent and irreversible damage to my body. I held a few graduate degrees myself that focused on data analysis, and if people did not do their experiments and draw a scientific result based on a statistically evaluated figure, I did not see any reason for me to trust their conclusion.

As I saw it, I had two choices:

1. I could minimize my physical activity and live carefully for the rest of my life, or
2. I could do what I love and try my best while I can, knowing that I might end up in a wheelchair later in life.

My answer? Option two, without a doubt. Deep down, polio or not, I am still just that little girl who wants to live her life fully and reach her full potential in life. Don't get me wrong; I bit my tongue and gritted my teeth when it hurt, and I used medicine to reduce the swelling from the exercise.

But I kept going, even though it wasn't always pretty. Specifically, on my twenty-ninth birthday, I took a pretty bad spill going downhill after a sharp climb. The speed of going downhill always felt dangerous for me. In this case, I'd made a sharp left and, before even realizing it, landed on my face really hard at a speed of twenty-five to thirty miles per hour. After the initial impact, I rolled over several times on the concrete road, and my bike was thrown out far away into the ditch. For a long moment, my brain just went blank. I couldn't recall what I was doing, and I just lay there. Luckily there weren't any cars going by, and one skilled rider came after me and pulled me to the side of the road to wait for help. I lost two front teeth, got blood all over my face, elbow, and knee, and had many scrapes around my body. Later that day, my polio leg caught up to me: even touching the ground lightly sent a shooting pain in my joint, and I had constant, bone-deep pain in the rest of the leg.

So, I couldn't walk for a bit...but I could hop—a skill, remember, I honed during "Bunny Time" in the hospital as a child.

6.4. ONE-HUNDRED-MILE RIDE
WITH POLIO

When the century ride we'd been training for was just a few months away, Ben—the seven-year-old we were fundraising for via the Leukemia & Lymphoma Society—lost his battle with the disease.

There's no other way to put it: we were shattered. At the same time, I tried to remember that Ben's life was so beautiful because he'd touched so many people, including those he'd never met. What do our lives mean to others? What do we have to leave behind for the world to remember us by? For Ben, that answer was rooted in so much love.

When I started with TNT, my reasoning centered around the bike; I wanted to improve, and I wanted to reach a goal I'd set for myself. It was no different from any other goal I set for myself at that time, and it was the only approach I knew: set a goal, work hard for it, overcome hardships, and make it come true. It was as simple as that.

Being a century rider, though, grew to mean more than a goal to me. While it was very much about the bike and the distance, it was also about the joy and laughter I found with my TNT teammates. It was about the pain, failure, and frustration we helped each other through. It was about the support and love we felt for the group and the cause.

So, when the countdown for the ride started, emotions were high to say the least. I remember lying in bed the night before, giving a little pep talk to my polio leg.

Listen, let's make a deal, I thought. *If you behave well tomorrow, I will keep you for the rest of my life and feed you a painkiller every now and then if it hurts. But if you are not being supportive tomorrow, I'm going to chop you off this winter. Deal, naughty little leg?*

After a couple of seconds, I felt her reply with that subtle pain she sometimes gives me as a signal of communication between us.

Deal!

The ride we needed to finish was called the Mammoth Gran Fondo, at Mammoth Lakes, California—a 102-mile range at 8,074 feet elevation with 6,643 feet of climbing.[13] On the big day, we found out the weather would cause a fifty-mile-per-hour wind against us, which made just staying on our bikes challenging. Still, we rolled out steadily in the chilly morning air. I was wearing a new pair of shoes, and the shape of the shoe didn't fit properly in my bike cradle. Because I don't have control over my right foot, I couldn't just slip it back in, so I had to use my hand to keep putting it back in place. This caused me to drop out of the pace line and fall to the back because I didn't want to cause an accident for anyone behind me. I moved slowly, steadily, and silently to the first stopping point. There, Coach Don told us Deadman Summit was right ahead—a scary name for a hard hill, and one we'd have to attack with a ton of wind. Surprising even myself, before I knew it, I was at the summit without much trouble—showcasing just how good Don's training had been!

Going downhill, though, was *not* a piece of cake. The descent was long and bumpy. Imagine moving at least forty miles per hour with every crack in the road vibrating your bike, the wind whipping you around at the same time. At that moment, all I could do was grit my teeth, hold the handles tight, and focus: any mistake could throw me off the bike and result in broken body parts.

The ride was bearable before the third stop. After that, hell started: long, seemingly endless climbs in unforgiving wind—something hard with two working legs, let alone one. At times, I had to get off my bike and walk it, but I was in good company. Others on my team were doing the same thing. At the fourth stop, Fey commented that we all looked like rabbits, our eyes red from tearing in the wind.

---

13 "Gran Fondo: 102 Miles," Mammoth Gran Fondo, accessed February 14, 2023, https://mammothgranfondo.com/gran-fondo-102.

Butts and brains numb, we had a snack and climbed back on. Everyone was having a hard time, not just me, but we tried to have fun at the same time. There was music playing, and we even Hula-Hooped at some aid stations. When we reached the point where we only had ten miles to go—and were told it was mostly flat—we were ecstatic. And I was relieved that, so far, my leg had kept her promise.

But the last ten miles proved to be the worst ten miles, a sentiment echoed by even the most seasoned athletes at the race. The wind against me, I could only go about four miles per hour, each rotation of my leg sending a sharp pain all the way to the bone.

I kept asking my dedicated coach, Devan, who stayed with me the entire time, a question that I now know (as a parent) is a very annoying one, especially to have repeated: are we there yet?

I drove myself crazy thinking that we'd surely gone the ten miles yet feeling like I was barely moving, inching along the road painfully. Time stood still. For the first four sections of the race, I'd been surrounded by people. For the final section, it was only Devan. I'm grateful for that because, on one of the last descending hills, he shouted, "Slow down! Cattle guard here!"

Thank God he did that because, at the speed I was going and with my bike-controlling skills, I could have knocked myself out without that warning. After that, it was back to the grueling, slow fight against distance and the wind.

Finally, I heard Devan shout the words I'd been wanting to hear for hours: "It's the finish line! I hear the music!"

Reinvigorated, I pedaled ferociously and with every ounce of energy I had left until I finally saw my fellow TNT friends. They shouted and applauded as I rolled across the finish line. As I stepped off the bike and felt the heft of the medal proudly declaring "one hundred miles," I burst into tears. George took off my helmet, and both he and Charlotte hugged me, my tears soaking their shoulders and those of Coach Don and Fey. We all celebrated there at that finish line, and I would not trade that moment for anything. It took me eleven and a half hours to complete the ride.

That night, after a brief resting stop at the hotel, I changed into a beautiful dress and went to the dance party. Fay, Charlotte, Coach Devan, and all the rest of our girls on the team danced like there was no tomorrow.

I made peace with my polio leg after that night. I not only accepted it, but I am also very grateful that I can walk with a limp, for many others who have far greater physical limitations can't even do what I am blessed to do.

The weakness I used to see in myself turned out to be my strength.

Libo Jane Cao learned to ride a bike this February and on Sept. 10 she will cycle in a century, which will be a 100-mile trek in the High Sierra and Mono Lake area.

Her weakness fuels her strength

By ANNE WARD ERNST

Libo "Jane" Cao has no excuses, only goals. And in spite of the polio that limits the strength in her right leg, Cao is about to achieve her latest goal—to complete in a century ride.

On Sept. 10, Cao will cycle 100 miles in the High Sierra and Mono Lake area in a fundraiser for the Leukemia & Lymphoma Society's Team In Training.

"She's going to finish the century if she has to crawl across it, and I don't think she'll need to crawl," Charlotte Rogers says.

Rogers is the support and gear captain for Cao's team. Her job is to supply water, food, encouragement and an occasional push.

On a training ride on Old La Honda Road—a hilly training favorite for cyclists and known for its difficulty—Cao was having a bit of trouble getting up the hill. Rogers, who follows behind the team, says Cao stopped, turned to her and asked for a "push" to get going again.

Standing nearby and watching were three cyclists unaffiliated with Team In Training.

Rogers says the trio noticed Cao's impairment and asked if Cao was cycling with one leg, which Rogers confirmed.

"They said, 'Oh my god we will never complain about riding this hill again,' " Rogers says.

Cao's physical limitations were caused by polio. Her right leg can only carry the pedal around while her stronger left leg does the pumping. But this has not prevented her from

➤ **Strength,** *page 8*

SEPTEMBER 7

San Jose newspaper reporting Libo's Team In Training ride
(September 2005).

7.

RESET, RESET AGAIN IN THE PROCESS (2006-PRESENT)

*In the ancient poem "Bamboo and Rock" from the Qing Dynasty
in China, Zheng Banqiao (1693–1765) wrote:*

Through broken rocks, my root strikes deep,
I bite the mountain green and won't let go.
From whichever direction the wind hits,
I persevere through millions of blows.

咬定青山不放松，立根原在破岩中。

千磨万击还坚劲，任尔东西南北风。

*If your roots are strong enough, there is no fear of wind,
no matter how hard it hits you.*

*I survived windstorms with the strength of my deep roots,
after wind carried me, yet a seed to this new land.*

*In planting myself here, I sprouted new roots for myself and future
generations deep and far by passing on my stories.*

7.1. LEARNING FROM REALITY (2006)

The ambition I had wasn't born of a drive to be rich or conventionally successful. Instead, based on where I came from, my ambition was to survive, live a good "normal" life, and pursue something I could be proud of.

And my life was, at that time, feeling even better than "normal." It was great! I enjoyed my work because it was meaningful. I spent my days making scientific instruments with intelligent algorithms that enabled chip manufacturers to be much more efficient and economical. I also enjoyed the people I interacted with at work and the friends I made in social circles outside the office.

As an immigrant, I was on a working visa (H1B) that I knew would only last for a period. To truly get clearance to work for a company long term, though, I'd need to apply for a green card. So, in 2005, I started pushing for an application even though I hadn't yet been there for the year-long waiting period. Other coworkers were also in the same boat. However, Metara was a startup company and didn't have many resources to help employees with their immigration-related work. They provided an immigration lawyer for us to consult with and paid those fees, but we were on our own for the rest.

I decided it was worth it to work with the lawyer they provided and get the ball rolling. My green card journey is worth including as an example of how challenging the process can be for immigrants. In the end, you can judge for yourself if the system makes sense.

Spoiler alert: even after I got my PhD, to get my green card, the whole journey took me over six years.

Step 0: Select a Category to Apply for a Green Card

There are many employer-based categories of green card applications. For simplicity, I picked the category of second preference (EB2). The first preference (EB1) option would have required me to ask many professors to write letters of recommendation to vouch for me as an outstanding researcher. It can be a faster route, but I hated to bother anyone else with my problems. Besides, how could I ask someone to help prove that I was an "outstanding researcher?" EB2, on the other hand, only required candidates to have "advanced degrees or exceptional ability."

After I chose EB2 as my category of application, I also took the liberty of helping others choose the right categories for their respective situations.

But before I—or any of us, for that matter—could apply for a green card, the Department of Labor (DOL) required that we obtain a "labor certification" through a system called Program Electronic Review Management (PERM). One of the purposes of PERM is to allow the officials to determine if the company has made every effort to hire an American worker for the position. We could only move forward with our applications once the company proved that they couldn't possibly find an American for the job.

Step 1: PERM Listing—Post My Own Job for Americans to Apply

According to the lawyer, the first step was to create job postings for the jobs we currently held. Why? Because we had to prove that no Americans were as qualified for our roles and could perform them better than we immigrants. I asked the lawyer, "What if an American applied for the job, and it turns out they can do that job. Then what?"

"Then you as an immigrant shouldn't be hired for that job, and you are not qualified to apply for a green card!" My lawyer replied.

I couldn't challenge that whole immigration system, so I started executing the steps based on what I'd been told. And I'd been told that people look in "help wanted" ads in newspapers to find jobs.

I ran into our CFO's office and asked him, "Where do I find all the newspapers?"

"Mission City!" he replied.

"Wow, Mission City is so far away. It's OK. I will drive there this weekend and find newspapers!"

"No, not *Mission City* in the Bay Area. I mean the Mission City Cafe right around the corner. Just grab newspapers from there."

And I did. Then, I gathered the job-posting information we needed and asked the company to sponsor the listings in those newspapers and some digital spaces. There was nothing left to do but wait, hoping no American with stronger qualifications would apply for my job. Talk about awkwardness!

Step 2: PERM Proof—Collect Evidence That No Americans Can Do My Job

My green card journey was a do-it-yourself process, as the lawyer was only there to consult. That meant I needed to help receive all the resumes submitted, conduct any necessary interviews, and collect all the information required to prove that I was more qualified than the American applicants.

We had to wait for many months for this period to be called complete. Because my job at that time required a PhD in chemistry or related field *and* extensive coding experience with an advanced degree in computer science or math, I received only a few resumes. I conducted interviews, but nobody even met the basic requirements.

What a sigh of relief!

I packaged all the materials and evidence, had the company sign them, and shipped them off to our lawyer for the next steps.

Step 3: PERM Compensation Check– Prove That I Am in a Highly Compensated Position

After we had collected all the evidence to prove that our company couldn't have found any Americans to fill our respective roles, we needed to prove the job type was one worth hiring foreigners. In other words, we needed to prove that we were paid above the required minimum for that type of job. It was supposed to be an easy step.

Big surprise, it turned out that my $95,000/year as a *software scientist* didn't even meet the minimum requirement for PERM qualification. For my role in the Silicon Valley area in early 2005, I needed to be paid at least $105,000/year to be qualified for PERM. Two other Asian women who had other roles in the company also didn't meet the minimum. I gathered the other two and, together, we decided to ask for a raise. We went nervously to the CEO's office and asked for a pay increase so that we could meet the minimum pay requirement for our green cards. Our wishes were granted.

I couldn't believe that the first time I asked for a raise was for immigration reasons, and I couldn't believe our company didn't bat an eye to approve my request. I began to realize then that it would've taken the company a lot more money to replace us.

After the pay raise, I had to accumulate enough paycheck stubs (along with many other forms) to submit to the immigration office. After many months of preparing, I submitted my PERM paperwork in August 2005.

The filing date is important when it comes to PERM because when you submit determines where you fall in various queues throughout the green card process. And those queues can take years.

Step 4: I-140 and Paperwork with Huge Queues

The Department of Labor approved our PERM a few months later, in December 2005, paving the way for our employer to submit Form I-140 (Immigrant Petition for Alien Worker) with USCIS. My form was submitted in December and approved about a year and a half later. The I-140 form ties the employer and employee together such that if an employee were to switch jobs before the next step, this process would need to start all over again. I wasn't worried about that part, though, because at that time, I fully planned to stay with the company forever. Loyalty was my way of showing gratitude for the opportunity they'd extended to me.

If things went smoothly, I would go to Step 5 . . . but if life were perfect, it would be no fun.

Around fall 2006, the company had an all-hands meeting and introduced a new CEO. We were told that our company wasn't doing well, our previous CEO had stepped down, and the new leader was going to turn the company around quickly. This new CEO came from New York, and he promised us he wasn't going back until he did just that—turn the company around. He wore nice suits, he looked credible, and I trusted him.

Just a few months later, there was *another* meeting with *another* announcement. This time, the new CEO told everyone that we'd run out of money, that the company would be in shutdown mode, and that he was going back to New York to spend the Thanksgiving holiday with his family. We never saw him again.

I couldn't believe my ears. *But he'd promised!* I thought. *How could someone promise something, not fulfill it, not apologize, and just call it a day?* I realized then that I had put too much trust into the man with the big title and fancy suit. I respect everyone equally until they teach me not to through their actions. *If you're not impeccable with your words, I have no respect for you.* That is the moment I learned not to simply give my trust to people due to their titles and social statuses.

On top of losing our jobs, we were also told that while the company wanted to provide us with back pay, we might not even get that for the work we'd done now that the company had gone belly-up. It was a catastrophic situation for me, and I was on the phone with my immigration lawyer immediately. For immigrants like me, the law requires that we have consecutive paychecks. From paycheck to paycheck, you can't have more than a ten-day gap on your working visa. If you do, you become an "illegal immigrant" on paper.

In other words, I had to get another job. And I had to get one fast. My status in this country depended on it.

Finding a job back in 2006 was not as easy as it is today with connection tools. There was no LinkedIn to go search, for example. Still, I knew I had to get moving. By the time I understood what was at stake and all the red tape around it, I calculated that I only had about eight working days to get a job offer.

Game on!

I first updated my resume and uploaded it to a few websites. Since I'd gotten my first job during a conference, I searched for nationwide conferences that would be upcoming in the next two weeks. On the same night the company shut down, I registered for job fairs at several conferences, booked the flights for those conferences, and sent out emails to any recruiters I could find online for any potential interviews. Though I was hopeful, I still had to be ready for Plan B. Over Thanksgiving, I packed up my whole apartment just in case. I knew that if I didn't get an offer in time, I needed to be ready to fly back to China and find a job there.

I will be OK, either way, I told myself. *I've got the skills I need to be independent anywhere in this world. In about ten days, I'll know where fate takes me. And I'm ready for whatever that is.*

30，知识和技能的积累，使她们在职场已经具备一定的资历，但始终在挖掘最适合自己的土壤，寻求着自我突破。

我更喜欢有挑战的工作

2004 年 4 月，曹力波从俄亥俄大学化工博士毕业的前昔，她被 METARA 聘任为化学计量学软件科学家到加州硅谷工作。每天，曹力波和同事们一起开发、研制、推广应用尖端技术产品，工作都很有挑战性，也很紧张。

METARA 是一个只有 50 个左右员工的高科技产品公司，没有人知道公司的发展前景如何。"我依然深深地爱着这份工作"，"我知道很多人企求一份稳定的工作，我可以偶尔享受平静的生活，可是并不安于平静。作为一名硅谷的工程师，我更喜欢有挑战的工作，让我不知道前方的路是什么样的，并且我能够看到每天自己工作的成效。也许几年以后当一切都稳定下来，工作失去挑战性的时候，就是我该离开的时候了。"

刻苦学习，努力工作，再学习新的技能，再更努力地工作，是曹力波到硅谷大半年的生活模式。在国内的时候，曹力波用三年的时间念完化工专业本科四年的课程，申请到奖学金后，到俄亥俄大学念化学博士，第二年她申请到同时念数学/计算机硕士的机会，在美国三年半的时间里，她完成了别人平均需要 6 年半才能完成的分析化学博士和计算机硕士学位，一直是在"很艰苦地向前奔走"等等。等稍微复习，曹力波发现，事业确是人生中一个很重要的环节，但生活本身却是全部，自己的生活缺少了很多东西。

于是，曹力波决定在努力工作的同时，开始发展自己的生活了。在硅谷这个世界精英密集的地方，曹力波在半年的时间内，利用各种渠道广泛地结交了各个领域的朋友。她和 IT 工程师讨论各种 IT 技术，并建立了几个有实力和潜力的企业工程师作为未来的商业建设伙伴；向营销人员请教销售技巧；从学生朋友那里拿到日语和西班牙语的语言教材，拷贝到 iPod 里，开车的时候练习；雇佣值得信赖的金融分析师朋友来管理她的股票和证券账户、长期投资计划。

曹力波说自己"像一个饥渴而无知的孩子用全部的力气去汲取自身所没有的知识，学会在每次各种重大决策之前征求专业人士的意见。她对所有的事情都好奇，所有的事情他都愿意去尝试，希望能找到让自己真正钟爱的事情。

2005 年 6 月，曹力波代表公司申请了 METARA 自动质谱仪数据分析引擎专利。2005 年 8 月，她得到了一次非常可观的加薪作为鼓励。2005 年年底，曹力波挑战越野体能完成了一项 160 公里自行车越野赛。2006 年，她计划在硅谷买下自己喜欢的房子。

两年前，曹力波到 METARA 面试。开着车在硅谷转悠了一圈——SUN、GOOGLE、ADOBE、CISCO、INTEL……感觉世界有名的大公司都在硅谷，空气中都是一股科技的味道。METARA 的 CEO 面试曹力波的问题是：如果这个世界一切事情都是完美的，你会做什么？"如果世界是完美的，我可能还在做我正在做和我将来计划做的事情——学习、工作、恋爱、家庭……因为我在意的一向都是过程，而且一切我曾做过的事情，我都很高兴其中有苦、有甜、有艰辛、有失落，因为那才是真正的生活。换句话说，如果生活在一个完美的世界里，我并不见得会比现在过得更开心，或者说更感受到自己在活着。"曹力波笑着回答。（陈倩山 / 文）■

> 生活中有些风浪的时候，是我笑得最开心的时候。变化的生活让我感到生命的乐趣，否则如何证明自己还在积极地活着呢？
> ——曹力波

Libo on the "30 below 30" list for a technology magazine in China while still working at her first job (2006).

7.2. DASH IN A FLASH (2006–2008)

Right after Thanksgiving, a nontypical and talented recruiter named Katherine called me from Dash Navigation, a local startup. The company was developing the first internet-connected Personal Navigation Device (PND). Back then, navigation wasn't common on mobile phones yet, and there were no Google or Apple Maps. My first company had made multimillion-dollar instruments that only a handful of people in this world understood, so I welcomed the idea of moving into the consumer product space.

Katherine arranged for me to interview with one of the co-founders, Mike, the next day at 5:30 p.m. After we talked for almost an hour, Mike said I'd answered all his algorithm-related questions flawlessly. Confidence boosted, I went into a daylong onsite the next day and was presented with an offer just the day after. Without hesitation, I accepted their offer right there. I did not negotiate terms or compensation. It was just in time! My official H1B transfer started with Dash on December 7, 2006, the exact date of my deadline to avoid a paycheck gap.

After I accepted the job, another two offers came through. However, I declined them. I'd already committed to Dash and was grateful that they'd saved me from immigration complications by acting on my paperwork with lightning speed.

There was another reason I picked Dash. Not only did their offer come first, but also at that time, their technology was revolutionary. If you speak tech, they were a PND HW loaded with stripped-down Linux OS, navigation app, point-to-point connectivity between devices for live traffic info, and even with live (Yahoo) point-of-interest (POI) search capability. If you don't speak tech, you just need to know that it was the Android before the existence of Android, just not on phones! At the time, the company also had investments from the two most prestigious venture capitalists (VCs) in Silicon Valley (which rarely happens). To them, Dash had the potential to make a big splash.

I formed many friendships at Dash. There were so many kind and talented people! I especially connected with the other co-founder, Brian—a tall guy with a gigantic head that was packed with enormous amounts of knowledge. He became my mentor right away. Anything related to the Maps and Navigation domain, he knew it all. To understand some algorithms he used in the code, I would ask him a question, then he would pause for a few seconds. Just when I'd started to run out of patience, he would start talking slowly, drawing on whiteboards, explaining from the beginning, going back to fundamentals, peeling layer by layer. The next thing I knew—three hours or so later, usually—I fully understood everything about the subject. Over the course of my time there, I learned the whole life cycle of the technology: from raw Maps data from vendors to making navigation applications running on embedded devices.

As I was fascinated by the massive amount of knowledge in Brian's head, I found out that he was also the co-founder and CTO of a company called Telcontar (1996–2003), the leader in the field of Location Services from the end of the '90s to the early 2000s.[14] Telcontar provided consumer-oriented location services for Google Local, Yahoo, Rand McNally, and almost all the big-name navigation services on a private-label basis. It also provided telematic services for companies such as BMW, Ford, and Mercedes-Benz. The technology was so influential that even in

---

[14] Mark Gibbs, "Telcontar's Drill Down Server Is All about Location," Network World, November 21, 2005, https://www.networkworld.com/article/2315896/telcontar-s-drill-down-server-is-all-about-location.html.

2010, you could find its major footprints as a core dependency in many companies' backbone location services.

For the first many months, I would spend all my spare time at night studying our code base, which was mostly written by Brian. His code was very hard to understand but brilliantly done once you did. But it wasn't just *that* I wanted to understand. I wanted to understand everything about the technology, top to bottom, whether it was directly related to my role or not. And I did, using my free time to study other people's code. Every day before lunch, I would show up in people's cubicles and ask if anyone would join me for lunch so that I could pick their brains on their areas of expertise. Leveraging lunchtime was a great way for me to build relationships, learn from the best, and not feel guilty about consuming others' working time. I learned so much from our software architect, Baron, QA manager, Ean, and many others with high technical aptitude whom I still admire to this day. In Silicon Valley, you must know your stuff. With so many smart, talented people working on creative solutions, skill is the differentiating factor. It would've been a shame if someone like me, in her early career, did not leverage the talents of those surrounding her. I felt like a sponge, trying to soak in as much knowledge as possible.

Initially, my role was to fix algorithm-related bugs for navigation, but very quickly I realized those bugs came from upstream of the data pipeline. I started to learn more about data so that issues could be stopped upstream. To catch problems earlier, I built regression test systems and partnered with QA teams to ensure issues were eliminated earlier. Before I knew it, I was promoted to supervise data products and build systems. The day I was promoted, one male engineer in my group came to me and said that due to his religion, he couldn't report to a woman. I told him that while

I respected his religion, unfortunately I couldn't change my gender just for him, so he had to accept that fact or transfer to another team.

He transferred, in the end.

Dash's product was announced during the Consumer Electronics Show (CES) in 2007—one of the world's premier technology events—and CNET reported on this revolutionary connected device on January 8, 2007.[15] One day later, the iPhone was announced. But at that time, not many people realized what the iPhone really meant for the PND market in the future, because Maps and Navigation had always been running as embedded SW or on PND instead of on a cellular phone. The app-store-concept iPhone was still in its infancy at that time. Later, as we know, that whole ecosystem changed the world on how anyone could develop apps on mobile phones—and in just a few years, any PND would be obsolete due to free smartphone apps. That said, many features that Dash had created—differential Maps Data update, for instance, which can generate a tiny data patch for a complete nationwide over-the-air Maps update—were so advanced that not even current modern major players are caught up, fifteen years later in 2023. That's how good Dash's software package was.

At that CES, we made a big splash by being the first to market with navigation connected to the internet, with live traffic-sharing features and live POI searches. I was part of the crew demonstrating the device, and we were surrounded by so many bloggers and technology enthusiasts the whole day at our demo booth. One day, when everyone else went to lunch and I was alone in the booth talking to customers, two men walked in casually and asked for an intro of the device. I immediately recognized

---

[15] Kevin Massy, "Dash Express Turns to Navigation 2.0," CNET, January 8, 2007, https://www.cnet.com/culture/dash-express-turns-to-navigation-2-0/

one of them: Google's co-founder, Larry Page. I introduced our product comprehensively. Larry asked why the device was so bulky (all PNDs were bulky then), and I told him we'd enclosed a super powerful antenna for the best GPS signal and were internet connected—just with Yahoo search instead of Google search. After they left, our COO, Rob, ran into our booth to find me, with excited eyes. "Someone told me that you were talking to Larry from Google?" he said.

"Yes," I said. "Maybe they're interested in us!"

Soon after, I heard Dash's board had received an offer from Google with an amount that was ten times more than the VC investment at that point. To this day, I don't think there is any correlation between my encounter with Larry at CES and that offer, but we were all sure that Google had its eyes on us for a while. After the offer was presented, Dash's management was in favor of accepting the offer because the technology would be wrapped into Android, predicting it would become big. It wasn't only lucrative but also evolutionary, meaning it would change the whole smart device industry—offering an operating system that worked on smartphones, or any embedded device, that's affordable and accessible to people all over the world. Before the iPhone existed, Android was viewed as one of the hottest technologies in Silicon Valley. Ultimately though, the offer was turned down by the VC representatives on the board because they believed that Dash should go all the way to IPO instead.

In March 2008, we started to prepare for big-box sales, leading with our lighter and prettier model called Dash Express. We knew our product needed to be sent out for the first technical review article, and we picked the writer to be Walter Mossberg (who wrote technology columns for the *Wall Street Journal*). There was only one problem: our live traffic feature only worked when there was at least another device that hit the traffic *first* on the same route. That way, the traffic information could be shared immediately over the air. Devices that came after would benefit from that info, similar to the Waze app feature many are familiar with today, which became a billion-dollar business.[16]

We had a dilemma: before we had any sales, how would we get the data necessary to make Walter's device function as it should? We needed the seed data ahead of time, and a team of us was chosen to get the mission completed. First, we discovered Walter's daily commute route and the rough time he would hit that route. Then, we hid in our car early in the morning and started our drive just a bit earlier than Walter. Why? So that when he used our device for his commute, he would benefit from the traffic information we'd already shared from our devices. A few weeks later, we saw a great review come out from Walter titled "Dash's Car Navigator Gives Smart Directions, If Others Participate." He wrote:

> They could talk to each other via the Internet and share information on how fast traffic is moving on the roads they have just traveled. And they could also use the Internet to let you search for places of interest, get map updates, or even receive new destinations wirelessly.[17]

Things were going well—and then, in late September 2008, the stock market started dropping significantly.

All the VC-funded startups could sense the tightness from investors. On September 30, 2008, Dash announced that we needed to do a round

---

[16] Waze Mobile was acquired by Google for $1.3 billion in June 2013.

[17] Walter S. Mossberg, "Dash's Car Navigator Gives Smart Directions, If Others Participate," *Wall Street Journal*, March 27, 2008, https://www.wsj.com/articles/SB120657844534867167.

of layoffs of about 30 percent of the workforce. Many of my coworkers lost their jobs that day, but I kept working hard and kept being optimistic.

But the stock market didn't rebound. Instead, it kept crashing to a new low week after week. When that happens, VC firms are very cautious about investing more in any startup. At that time, no smartphones could run turn-by-turn navigation, and traditional in-car built-in navigation systems didn't have all the connected features Dash had to offer. It wasn't a lack of value with the design or technology, nor was it the belief that Dash couldn't win if more money were fused into it. However, facts are facts: without the next round of funding, a startup like Dash with over one hundred employees just wouldn't survive. Leaders of the company tried their best to get us the funding we needed, but 2008 was the most serious financial crisis since the Great Depression due to subprime mortgage issues that spread to all industries. Lehman Brothers filed for bankruptcy on September 15, 2008, and the avalanche of bankruptcies and company shutdowns lasted for years after that.

The bad news kept coming. Next, I heard a rumor that Dash needed to have a second round of layoffs. In late October 2008, a member of management pulled me aside, and he told me that Dash needed to lay off about 70 percent of the remaining employees the following Monday. He then indicated that I didn't need to worry because my name wasn't on that "cut" list, based on his sources. I really loved the company and people so much that I wasn't worried. I wasn't even thinking about looking for another job. My mental model was this: Dash had saved me when I needed it desperately, so I would stay with Dash as long as I was needed.

On the morning of November 3, 2008, ironically two calendar days after the date my first company shut down, Dash announced that 70 percent of the company was laid off. This included most of the leadership, my entire team that built maps and content on devices...and me. They'd decided to only keep a small handful of people just to keep our service running and support the products we'd already sold. My mentor, Brian, had to stay with the company, but the other co-founder, Mike, was on the list. That made sense because, after all, Brian was a one-man army.

It felt like déjà vu: there I was, in a different conference room. With a different company. With a different CEO telling me the same thing I'd heard only a few short years before. This time, though, it felt different. Rather than abrupt and insincere, the communication from *this* CEO was honest and genuine, and we could feel his deep sadness about the news. He was on the layoff list as well. It was done with warmth. Even though we had no money left for layoff packages, our HR team set up group com-munication emails with lists of companies that were still hiring. We knew we'd all tried our best, that we'd had something truly great, and it was just bad timing for a startup without a solid financial foundation. It wasn't anyone's fault.

I organized a farewell lunch at a local restaurant for everyone who got laid off that day. We drank, toasted each other, and said our goodbyes. We set up a Google Group to stay connected and asked everyone to help each other in their job hunting. We were all sad, but we were all smiling at the party.

I kept it together for the farewell lunch, but as soon as I got home, I dissolved into tears. This time felt personal. I'd experienced one startup shutdown, but everyone was in the same boat that time. However, this time, it was a layoff. Even though I could understand the 70 percent selection was purely due to business, I couldn't stop wondering why I wasn't picked to be in the last batch to keep things going. Was I not good enough? What could I have done differently? I thought my name wasn't supposed to be on the "cut" list. What had changed? My head was spinning as scenes from the last two years whirred through my mind.

There I was: sitting at home, alone, crying, and feeling defeated and worthless. It was my first layoff, and it felt like I wasn't needed by the company I'd loved. It took several minutes of crying before I could collect myself enough to consider the question that I could feel crystallizing in my head:

What is different about my value between yesterday and today?

My answer came quietly and clearly: *nothing.*

I realized at that moment that nothing had changed. My knowledge, experience, skills, and determination had not changed. While how this world treats me might go up and down, just like how this company treated me before and after the layoff day, depending on that day's circumstances, my inner value remains the same. How could I let other people's perception of me define my own value? How could I doubt myself when the variance of the outside world had changed, but my entity as a constant within it hadn't changed at all? How silly was it that I, as someone who studied science, was not able to see the logical flaw? Why would I cry over the *variance* instead of focusing on the *constant*?

I wiped off my tears, got up, and laughed at my own silliness. I would allow my sadness to come from the loss of a connection to a great company, but I would not allow it to come from self-pity.

After all, this time around, without anyone around me knowing it, I was fully prepared—financially and status-wise for immigration. My father had taught me that we need to see far ahead and become fully prepared for anything that could come at us in this life. Because of his guidance, I was more than ready when that second crisis hit me in a similar manner.

Fool me once, shame on you; Fool me twice, shame on me.

7.3. HOW I NEVER MAKE
THE SAME MISTAKE TWICE (2008)

Sadness aside, I wasn't panicking at all. Right after I'd joined Dash at the end of 2006, I'd looked at my life and made a few plans to ensure I could catch myself from falling when the rug was pulled out from under me. Besides working hard to gain more technical skills, I'd been building safety nets, and they were all ready by that dark, massive layoff day of 2008.

Safety Net 1: Instead of Hitting the
Immigration Wall, Pave a Path around It

I was forced to switch jobs at the end of 2006. Even though I'd gotten an offer, any new job would have reset my immigration status. Recall all those steps all the way to I-140 in previous chapters? I'd have to start from Step 1 again. Though Dash had much better immigration support and I didn't have to hunt for newspapers and post my own listing, our lawyers still had to follow all the steps. The priority date would be reset after another round of submissions. By layoff time, I'd barely gotten to the same step in that second round by 2008.

So on paper, I was in the same boat as two years prior. I did, however, have a slightly better time window to work with. The massive layoff happened on 11/3/08, but Dash committed to providing the last paycheck for everyone, to cover till 11/15/08. I didn't care about the money, but that date was critical to my immigration status. A two-week gap after my last paycheck would have been 11/30/08. That meant I had to sign an offer by that date, giving me about one month, instead of just a few days like last time.

However, I'd paved another path already in case I couldn't land another job within a short period. I'd gotten a Canadian green card, without living in Canada. I knew that a green card would allow me to apply for another type of working visa, which was much easier to obtain and not as time-sensitive. I could just take a short trip to Canada, then return to the Valley anytime, as long as I had an offer in hand.

How did that happen? Well, right after I joined Dash, I started researching all visa types that would allow me to work in the US easier. I found out that if I have a green card from Canada, I can get a TN visa to work in the US. To get a green card in Canada, instead of the mountains of paperwork, I only needed to be qualified based on their scoring system. With my degrees, skills, and field, my score ranked highly for a green card application. In late 2007, I started my application. By mid-2008, Canada had issued my green card. Their scoring system was really that simple: you show that you deserve to have the green card, then you get it. It only took one package to apply, and I was notified via email that my green card was granted.

All I needed to do was go to Canada to get it in person.

A small episode happened during that trip, which was supposed to last just a couple of days. I landed in Vancouver, got my green card, and planned to board the plane on my return trip. However, I got stopped at the immigration office. The officer pounded on his computer, and after a while, he told me that a thorough background check needed to be conducted before I was granted entry back into the US. After 9/11, immigration tightened its review process on potential threats by putting extra background checks on sensitive groups of people. The officer looked at me like I could be a threat to the national security of his country.

Am I a potential terrorist? I wondered, shocked. *Me? What is going on?*

"Could this be because of the chemical weapon detection research work I did in graduate school?" I asked him. "Does that make me a potential threat? It shouldn't. That work was *antiterrorist*."

I didn't get an answer. I also didn't get a timeline for how long the check would take. All I knew at that time was that I needed to stay in Canada until my security clearance was complete. This made me nervous because I had heard horror stories about this background check. One graduate student back at Ohio University was denied entry after his summer break, for example, because his major was related to aircraft control. After 9/11, that was an extremely sensitive subject. He stayed in China and waited. Before his departure from the US, he was single. After he came back, he was already married and had a child... that's how long a background check could take. Instead of waiting in Canada, I booked a flight back home to China and enjoyed spending time with my family. Luckily, only about one month later, I was able to fly back to the US after my background check was completed.

With a Canada green card in hand, I had options.

Safety Net 2: Become Financially Secure

I never cared about money until I became independent in 2000. Having enough money in hand provided many extra choices that I wouldn't have had otherwise. I also didn't want money to be the reason that I had to work. But when I realized money was important, I sought to understand it better. I have always believed that if you want to learn something, you might as well learn from the best person in that domain. I can't remember which year I started reading about Warren Buffet, but his investment approach was so simple: invest in value stocks and let time and the power of compound interest take its course. On top of that, his modest lifestyle allowed him to accumulate wealth at an early stage of his life. Before his biography, *The Snowball* by Alice Schroeder, was published in late 2008, I was able to read many of his shareholder letters as my early financial education. Early on, when I couldn't afford even one share of Berkshire Hathaway, I bought top stocks in their portfolios. As soon as I could afford his company stock, I bought it (and still hold it to this day). Of course, there were times I made rookie mistakes (like buying a mutual fund that had a high load), but I learned from those mistakes quickly and managed to avoid the pitfalls of the stock market after a couple years. I firmly believe in buying value stocks and holding them for the long term. Keep it simple. Warren Buffett was once asked: "You're the second richest guy in the world; your investment thesis is so simple. Why don't more people just copy you?" To which Buffett replied, "Because nobody wants to get rich slow." I, however, have believed in his simple approach from a very early stage of my life, and I have never minded getting rich slowly. Starting as early as 2002, I put almost all the money I could save up to work for me. Over the years, I've bought no- or low-load mutual funds, cash-flow-positive real estate, triple-net-lease (NNN) type commercial real estate, and many more financial products to make sure I could get rich slowly. I used the power of compound and just accumulated my wealth little by little, year over year.

To have more money to invest, I lived a modest lifestyle. During graduate school, I could save more than 50 percent of my income after tax due to low housing costs and low expenses. After I started working, I could save 70–90 percent of my after-tax income every paycheck. For several years in Silicon Valley, instead of renting a one-bedroom, I rented a small room in a house that I shared with others for only a few hundred dollars. I spent little on food and purchased necessities at second-hand prices. All my savings went into either the stock market or real estate investment.

I was never a financial guru, nor did I want to be. I just wanted to feel secure financially...and I accomplished that goal. I was grateful that by the time I got laid off at the end of 2008, I was financially secure enough that I could live for many years without working. I was very proud of myself that I was able to remove money as a key factor from decision-making at a very early stage of my life. Money became only a factor of how much a company values its employees, and to me, speaks primarily to fairness.

Safety Net 3: Build Skills That Fit in a Larger Job Market

After my second job, I started to become more aware of my own skillset, personal strengths, and weaknesses. With my education and background, historically, I had leaned toward algorithm development, which is why companies in related fields had been interested in me as a contributor. But I found out gradually that a specific domain expertise can also limit someone to fit into a very specific job market. On top of that, due to my nature, I couldn't just look at the problem domain that I was assigned to. I had to understand *it all*—how other parts of the company functioned, for example. I also began expanding my domain of expertise in many other areas. I started spending many nights and weekends building random systems in domains outside of my core competence, while doing my day job. Those skills not only broadened my view, but also helped me grow in a leadership role faster. My original intention was mostly based on curiosity, but I began to fall in love with some of the new skills. By the time the layoff happened, I was not only able to stick to my own domain of expertise, but I could also fit into many other software roles a company would need. That flexibility gave me enough confidence to tackle the job market with my safety-net skills.

When I was forced to job hunt again, I was confident that I could do it well because I had spent time and energy developing a large set of flexible skills. I was, of course, still very interested in consumer products in the exploding navigation technology that started moving onto cell phones instead of staying on PNDs. I set my target companies to be consumer-based, profitable, pre-IPO, and no more than ten miles from where I lived. The great thing about Silicon Valley is that there were tons of companies that fit that bill. I interviewed with several startups that met those criteria and, by November 21, 2008, I'd received three offers already.

I accepted an offer from Telenav. They provided white-label (meaning the company name is hidden behind that of another brand) navigation applications for almost all the major mobile companies, such as AT&T and Verizon. For example, the AT&T Navigator and Verizon Navigator were both made by Telenav and were prebundled with phones sold by carriers. By that time, Google Maps already existed, but turn-by-turn navigation providers were still dominated by carriers who used white-label SW from companies like Telenav or traditional built-in car navigation. The company was very profitable and on its way to IPO.

At least *that* company would survive with its own income during the financial crisis! I also loved the people I interviewed and the company culture I experienced.

This time around, even though I was still under pressure to sign an offer within a set amount of time, I looked out for my own best interest. I managed to negotiate a much better salary, a sign-on bonus, pre-IPO shares, and a long vacation.

I wasn't green anymore.

My bet was right. Telenav was great to work for and successfully went to IPO in May 2010.

But a new offer aside, I needed closure with Dash. Right after I got my verbal offer from Telenav, I texted Brian and Ean, who were still working as the last batch in the office. I needed to see them. I drove as fast as I could back to Dash's office and saw Brian and Ean, standing there waiting for me. I walked as fast as possible to them and threw myself into their arms. Brian patted me gently on my back for our long emotional hug, in silence. We didn't need to say anything to understand each other. People started gathering around us, and the emotion of sadness spread like a dark cloud above us. The office that used to be fully packed with people and laughter was now mostly empty and quiet. To lighten the mood, we started to recall all the good times we'd shared together—the special memories, the inside jokes. Dash was such a special company, and the stories at Dash alone could be written into an awesome Silicon Valley TV show, the real one that's full of nerdy and witty stories, fun and funny as well. I told everyone that I was all good, with an offer in hand already, but I just needed to say goodbye to those who were still left there to hold the fort down.

The company had designated our previous COO as the CEO to keep the light on. About nine months later, Dash was acquired by Research In Motion (RIM, makers of the BlackBerry) for "an undisclosed sum," which was significantly lower than the total invested value. Instead of making ten times the investment by selling to Google for hundreds of millions in early summer of 2008, the VCs sold Dash to RIM at a loss rate in May 2009.[18] The difference was only one year, and stories like this happen in Silicon

---

[18] Sharon Gill, "RIM Acquires Dash Navigation," TU-Automotive, June 8, 2009, https://www.tu-auto.com/rim-acquires-dash-navigation/.

Valley all the time. Timing can cause a technology to succeed or fail in the blink of an eye.

7.4. DESERVE TO BE HERE, AFTER TEN YEARS OF BEING HERE (2010)

The 2008 financial crisis caused a huge dip in 2009, and the housing market dropped to the bottom around 2010. Those were the hardest times for many people. However, for those who were able to prepare, it was a wonderful time to invest. I kept investing like usual—and even more aggressively during those years—because stock prices went down so significantly. I took Warren Buffet's words to heart: "Opportunities come infrequently. When it rains gold, put out the bucket, not the thimble."

Even before the IPO, Telenav began to face challenges in late 2009 when Google offered free turn-by-turn navigation on Android phones.[19] The company lost the profit from its application on Android devices quickly, but profits from the rest of the cell phone market remained strong.

After joining Telenav at the end of 2008, I had to start my green card process for the third time…but I was on a faster track. I wasn't allowed to change jobs due to my immigration status unless I was ready to start the process all over again. Luckily, I loved the unique company culture, the work, and the people I became friends with.

My immigration papers kept stacking up, step by step, year after year. After ten years of legally staying in this country, I finally received my green card by the end of 2010, which gave me the right to permanently live on this land.

---

[19] Dan Moren, "Google Unveils Free Turn-by-Turn Directions for Android Devices," Macworld, October 28, 2009, https://www.macworld.com/article/200842/android_turnbyturn.html.

I finally deserve to be here, after ten years of being here!

With this card, I could switch jobs freely without having to worry about any time gap in between. I'd envisioned the day that I would receive this piece of plastic so many times. *I will be so excited!* I thought. *I've been waiting for so long.*

Surprisingly, that day was just like any other day for me. I felt numb after so many years of filling out form after form, waiting for one step after another. By the time I received the green card, I'd reached a point in my life where I was already capable of living in any country with the lifestyle I chose to live. One thing did change with this piece of plastic, though. As I mentioned, due to this immigration status change, I was able to freely change jobs anytime I wanted to, without any immigration consequences. In the past, I'd always been forced into a situation to hunt for a job quickly or face leaving this country when the allotted time to secure employment was up. Now I had the freedom to choose when and where to work and whom to work for. Oddly, I wasn't sure what to do without life pushing me to the next step.

Somewhere along the way, I started to have more of an urge to explore wider technologies outside of the domain I'd accidentally gotten into. The technologies in maps and navigation were fascinating, and that's where I could do large data, distributed computing, cloud services, UI development, test and automation... but I didn't want all the knowledge I had accumulated to be applicable to only maps and navigation. I needed a bigger platform with a more diverse portfolio in the company—a whole ecosystem for all technologies to thrive in. I wanted to jump out of my comfort zone and start over in a completely different technical domain, to see if I could succeed. That said, Telenav treated me well, and I didn't have enough motivation to start looking for that much bigger platform.

On October 5, 2011, Steve Jobs passed away. His biography was released on October 24 of that year. I bought that book immediately and started reading it at night. One story really touched me: one Sunday morning, Vic, a Google app developer, received a call from Steve Jobs. The conversation went like this:

"So Vic, we have an urgent issue, one that I need addressed right away. I've already assigned someone from my team to help you, and I hope you can fix this tomorrow. I've been looking at the Google logo on the iPhone and I'm not happy with the icon. The second O in Google doesn't have the right yellow gradient. It's just wrong and I'm going to have Greg fix it tomorrow. Is that OK with you?"

When I was reading the story that evening in bed, I recall lifting my head, almost jumping out of bed, unable to contain my excitement. *I am going to Apple!*, I thought. *I think Steve Jobs just touched my soul.*

I was so inspired to know that the very successful CEO of Apple, who had millions of other things he could have been doing on a Sunday morning, cared enough about the second "O" in the Google logo that he called to have it fixed immediately.

This may sound like I had an overreaction to a very small story. But it represented so much more to me. I wanted to work for a company that truly cared about its products, to the extreme that the right shade of color in a tiny letter matters a lot. That level of enthusiasm and attention to detail was something I'd never thought of but could relate to strongly. People must have that type of love and dedication to make products that have the potential to put a dent in the universe. *I am not sure if I could ever put a small dent in the universe*, I thought. *But at least if I make it to Apple, I will be among people who have ambitions to do just that.*

At that moment, I made up my mind to work for Apple. I had a few friends working there at that time, and they'd tried to persuade me to join the company for quite some time. I had always said no, though, because I didn't "get" Apple at the time. I loved their products, but their secretive culture was something I didn't understand. Whereas Google talks a lot more openly about what they do and how they do it, nobody knows what is going on at Apple until it's time for a product launch or big reveal. Only after I read Steve Jobs's book did I begin to understand a bit why: when you are trying to build something so carefully with all your passion and pride, hiding it until it's ready is the best thing before it can be properly introduced to this world. That surprise and delight when people find out at the right moment meant everything.

After I closed the book, I pinged one of my friends at Apple and submitted my resume on October 26, 2011. I went through a few phone interviews just a few days later, followed by two series of onsite interviews within two weeks. I received an offer from Apple on November 18, 2011, which is less than a month after I read Steve's book. In 2021, I received the ten-year anniversary gift from Apple, the metal block that stays on my desk and will for the next decade to come. I can confidently say I wouldn't trade the experiences I've had at Apple for anything else in the world. I am deeply proud of our mission and humbled to be part of it.

When I first arrived in this country with a student visa, many potential outcomes ran through my mind—including going back to China and spending my life with my beloved family and friends there. But life kept pushing me to the next stop, and I went along with it.

At the point of this writing, I've spent about half of my life in China and half in the US. Whenever there are political conflicts between the two countries, it pains me deeply. I love the kind people I have met from both countries with my full heart. I've cried and laughed in both lands. People in any country are worth being loved and seen for all their humanity and potential.

Many immigrants choose to stay in the United States because it's one of the places where we can achieve our own potential. But wherever we stay, it won't change where we come from and the blood that runs through our veins. The heritage we all carry with us makes us unique, strong, and powerful. The diversity we all bring to the table makes this land a wonderful place.

8.

LOVE, MARRIAGE, FAMILIES, AND KIDS (2007–2014)

If I love you—

I will never be a spoony bird

Repeating a monotonous song for green shade

. . .

I must be a ceiba tree beside you

Be the image of a tree standing together with you

Our roots, entwined underground

Our leaves, touching in the clouds

With each gust of wind

We greet each other

. . .

—EXCERPT FROM "TO THE OAK TREE" BY SHU TING

This is part of my favorite poem that best describes the romantic love I wanted, and eventually found, in my life.

Seeking that love takes belief, confidence, patience, and perseverance. Before that, being fully prepared for it means loving yourself and your life without it. Only when you are truly happy with yourself can you be happy with the right person.

And my "right person" had been out there all along. I just had to go through eighty-two dates to find him.

8.1. ALL THE BRUISES AND SCARS

I've viewed romantic love the same way I've viewed having a luxury item in my life: it's expensive to acquire, it's hard to maintain, and I don't *have* to have it.

Growing up, there was a boy I liked starting from my last year of middle school until all the way to college. That silly, ambiguous, warm, butterfly feeling filled my young and fragile heart. Even still, that's about six years of having a crush on someone, but I never had the courage to tell him. Why? I didn't think I deserved that thing called love because of my polio. During high school, just passing him accidentally in the hallway would brighten my whole day. We would look into each other's eyes with a smile each time we passed by. After we both went to separate colleges, we started writing letters each week to each other, sometimes daily, just to share our lives. However, neither of us would move one step further from our deep friendship. In what would ultimately be my last letter to him, I shared that I was pursued by someone in my college. He never wrote back after that, and I never knew how he really felt about me.

To be fair, I wasn't sure if I'd known how I'd felt about him, either. Was it love? I'm not sure, but I just know he was someone I wanted to share my life moments with. I was afraid that if I moved one step further, he would reject me, and I didn't want to risk ending the friendship I valued so much.

The boy who'd pursued me in college started dating me discreetly for a few months. But when he returned from a break, out of the blue, he refused to see me. I sought him out to ask why.

"My dad found out I am dating someone with polio and said that if I were to continue, he would break my leg as well. We can't continue anymore."

And that was the end of it.

That hurt...not because I had any deep feelings for him but because I was judged by someone I hadn't met, all because of my disability. With that one prominent label on me, it seemed that nothing else mattered. Suddenly, I realized what Dad had said to me before leaving for college was true: *Do you know how cruel this world could be to people with disabilities?*

Of course, I was loved by my family and many friends, and I experienced countless acts of kindness from random strangers, growing up in China. That is one reason I was able to walk so far in life and keep limping forward. But occasionally, discrimination gave me a reality check. When I was young, I thought that if I became excellent in other dimensions, people would see me differently. I believed I could compensate for my disability by excelling academically, being successful in my career, building wealth, and so on.

I was wrong.

After I'd achieved all those things, nothing changed. I realized that people who loved me without my achievements still loved me the same, yet the people who had bias and discrimination against me didn't change their opinion either. They may have shown respect on the surface, but I could tell that in their hearts, they still felt I was not enough. Incomplete.

I did find someone during my last year in college in China who saw me as a complete and equal individual. We were just classmates at first—until one night when he told me he liked me and asked if I'd be his girlfriend.

"What will your parents think?" I'd asked. "Would they agree?"

"I make my own decisions," he'd said.

"Then yes!" I smiled and accepted his invitation.

We ended up dating for three years in China, then I waited for him to join me in the United States for two more years. In the end, he ended the relationship with one email. The email was short, unceremonious, and didn't even include an explanation.

I had an idea why he ended it, though. A long-distance relationship is hard enough, but ours had also been reduced to me crying on the phone and him listening. It was as if I had used up all my toughness throughout the day dealing with others, and the side of me he got was all vulnerability and tears. We were living completely different lives without any idea of when we'd see each other again. Though I understand why it ended, I was still very sad about the loss. He was a link back home…a link that was now broken.

I had no idea how to grieve this loss properly, so I did what I'd seen in movies. I bought a pack of cigarettes and went to a park alone at night. I sat on a bench in front of a lake, staring glumly ahead. The lake was beautiful, and ducks were swimming in front of me. My tears started running down as a lump caught in my throat. *Those ducks are in pairs*, I thought. My head started to play the love song we used to sing together: "The most romantic thing I could think of is to grow older together with you slowly." I'd never smoked before and didn't know how. But I lit one cigarette after another, awkwardly holding it up to smoke, coughing some, then wiping the tears— which could have been coming from the smoke, pairs of ducks, or the love song playing in my head. It was getting dark, and the park was closed. My self-mourning ceremony came to an end when a park cop approached me and told me to go home. I didn't know how long he'd been watching me. He probably thought I'd throw myself into the lake at any moment.

I wasn't suicidal. I just didn't know how to grieve a broken heart.

I packed up my stuff and went back to the lab. I allowed myself to be immersed in sadness for just a few hours. Then, it was time to go back to work. My mouth felt like I'd been licking ashtrays all day long. I promised myself to come up with a different mourning ritual next time, without smoking. I was glad to be so busy with school that I had little time to dwell on my failed relationship. Though my friends during that time told me that, for almost half a year, they didn't see much of my smile after that long-distance relationship had ended. I decided to put love aside and focus only on academics. After all, if I wasn't loving myself during that time, how could I expect another person to love me?

I wasn't hopeful that I'd find love after that. I did date a little when opportunities were presented to me, but dating wasn't a priority, nor did I try to make it one. I knew many factors had to fall into place for both parties: the right person, the right place, and the right time in life.

Years passed, and I focused on things I needed to do first: get my degrees, find a job, invest, save up, get a backup green card, have a social life, build must-have survival skills at work and life, and so on.

A huge milestone was when I made peace with my polio leg on the century ride. I loved and accepted all parts of myself, even the part that some people thought was "broken." That was 2005, and I was twenty-nine years old. I finally knew who I was and accepted my complete self. I was independent, felt comfortable physically and financially, and learned how to be happy in life just by myself. Love was not a necessity; it was that cherry on top. My desire for love was to have my own family, just like what my parents had. That desire for love was pure, and I was ready to face any bruises coming out of it because I was so strong inside by then. In the past, I was just waiting for love to show up. I figured that if there was any opportunity to come my way, I would take it. This time, though, I was ready to be proactive and take the initiative instead.

To find the man I wanted to spend the rest of my life with, I made a commitment and a plan: to not give up until I dated one hundred men in the following three years. If I reached that number and still hadn't found him, I would allow myself to put that desire to the side. I would still live a happy and fulfilled life, alone but without any regret since I'd tried hard enough already.

Why one hundred? Honestly, I don't know. I just needed an impossibly high target to show my determination. I don't know where my courage came from, but I knew that it must be treated seriously at that stage in my life. Before that time, I'd dated the way I knew how: a boy asked me if I wanted to be his girlfriend, I said yes, and then the relationship lasted until it ended...mostly when he wanted it to end.

I'd never dated without an initial commitment to a formal relationship. Finally, I realized what "dating" should really be like. After all, how can you commit to a relationship before you even know the other person in that relationship?

The question then switched from "if" to "how."

I thought of posting classified ads, just like I had done for a job posting during immigration times. Instead of using newspaper classifieds, though, I thought I'd use Craigslist, which I'd used for almost all my moving needs and had a great experience with the platform. It was the most popular classified ads website back in 2005, I figured, so why couldn't I just post classified ads for myself?

(Big mistake.)

One Friday night, I posted a very simple post in the dating section. It was short and simple: A twenty-nine-year-old single Asian woman in the Silicon Valley Bay Area looking for someone local for a potential long-term relationship. I kept an open mind and only asked that the other party be independent, relatively close to me in age, and have a good personality. I expected one or two replies in the first week or so.

Instead, within the first couple of hours, I received fifty—if not one hundred—replies. Of course, after weeding through those overwhelming replies (including some uninvited nudity), I realized there were only about one or two who appeared worth replying to. I picked those who, in their initial emails to me, sounded genuine, listed their basic info, and had decent pictures attached. I carefully selected the first one I wanted to meet and replied with my photo and an invite for coffee as the next step.

I was absolutely traumatized by the first set of people I met off Craigslist's dating category. Even though I wrote clearly who I was and what I was looking for, not everyone was as honest, or they didn't tell the whole truth.

When my first Craigslist date showed up at the coffee shop, I could tell he was at least thirty years older than the man in the photo he had shared. I politely asked if he'd sent the wrong photo, and he replied that it *was* his photo...just that it had been taken thirty years ago. Some dates after that were dealing with big issues in their lives: addiction, anger, being in the middle of a divorce...I didn't think there was anything wrong with them dating. At least they were honest with me! But the problem remained: we were just not at the same stage in life, and their priorities didn't align with mine.

Around this time, I started learning real-life language. For example, I recall in earlier responses when someone asked me if I was "420 friendly," I would reply "not sure where the 420 code is, but I am '408 friendly' and OK with any Bay Area code." Eventually, someone explained to me that "420" was referring to marijuana, instead of the area code in phone numbers that I thought it was. When people asked me if I was a "SAF," I had no clue that in terms of dating, that refers to "Single Asian Female." I learned to constantly google what something really meant before I responded, realizing what terms were off the table for me if they described something I wouldn't accept.

I also learned to read between the lines in dating profiles. The men who were "in between jobs" often had no ambition or could not hold down a job. Guys who were supposedly "taking care of parents" turned out to live in the basements of those perfectly healthy parents, unwilling to make it on their own. The men who needed to "go to bed early" were almost always married. (What grown man can't take a call after 9:00 p.m. because he's sleeping?). The guys who kept accidentally forgetting their wallets didn't believe in equality as much as mooching meals from unsuspecting dates…

One of the worst experiences happened at 2:00 a.m. when my phone rang, waking me up. Earlier that night, I had a great first date with a gentleman (let's call him Mr. J), and we'd said our goodbyes only a few hours before that call. As I answered the unknown number, rubbing my eyes, I didn't understand the phone vibrating at first. The woman on the other side kept asking me who I was. It took a while for me to figure out that she was the wife of Mr. J—the same man who, at dinner that night, had told me how important family was to him and that he wanted to have kids and a dog with the right woman. At the moment, I connected with his values and plan for his life, even though I had a feeling that he said what he thought women wanted to hear. Now I was listening to his sobbing wife who told me that he already had all those things *with her*: a marriage of seven years, three kids, and a dog. I spent an hour comforting her before I finally hung up the phone, only to get another call an hour later. This time it was Mr. J, who said it wasn't "cool" for me to tell his wife about what happened because he believed every man needed multiple women. He could make us both happy! He asked if he could see me again. I told him where to go and how to get there.

And that's how I realized that using Craigslist to find true love wasn't going to cut it.

I also realized that dating wasn't like achieving a goal at work or learning a new skill. Determination alone would not cut it. It was dangerous to assume that I could do it right without hurting myself or hurting others.

At that point, I'd rejected a few, and a few others had rejected me just after a first date. To avoid hurting myself or others in the dating endeavor, I decided to lay some ground rules:

To Avoid Hurting Myself:

Ground Rule No. 1: Understand That I WILL Be Judged, and That's Expected and OK.

I know who I am. The people I would meet did not (yet), nor did they have to. Their opinions and judgments about me were theirs alone and would not change me. Through those experiences, I could learn how to be a better person if there was any constructive criticism or feedback. I would remove my personal ego from the experience and understand that I would always be judged—some of those judgments might be right, and some might be wrong.

Ground Rule No. 2: Don't Judge Others Too Soon. Give It More Time When There Are Good Fundamentals and No Red Flags.

If there were no red flags and the fundamentals were there—i.e., a good personality, a similar view of the world, alignment in expectations about life and family, and so on—it was important to give *time*. Spending more time together allows more communication and builds more trust. Time would allow deeper conversations to happen honestly and organically. To achieve my goal, efficiency mattered, but it was equally important to not miss the right one due to a hasty decision.

Ground Rule No. 3: Nobody *Has* to Like Me, and Odds for Even a Second Date Are Statistically Small.

Other than our parents (if we are lucky), people can only like us to a certain degree, for certain aspects, and for a certain period. That's the way life works. That's the reality. Look at the data: if my samples were large enough and human decisions were binary enough, there was about a 50 percent chance that the other party would like me. Out of that 50 percent, I had a 50 percent chance to like them back. That meant the odds of two people both liking each other were no more than 25 percent. Even if mutual likeness happened, odds were that we wouldn't like *everything* about each other. Other than good fundamentals, there were many other factors in deciding if it was worth moving on to the next date: having chemistry, making time, seeing the potential, being at the right stage in life, etc. If I considered all those factors, I would have just a few percent of chances to have a second date within the total sample population, regardless of if I tried my best or not.

To Avoid Hurting Others:

Ground Rule No. 1: Always Be Honest, and Don't Try to Sell Myself for What I Am Not.

If dressing up in pretty clothes and having nice makeup was not what I did most of the time, I wouldn't try too hard and do those things on the first couple of dates. That would just set up the wrong expectation. I tried to be the median value (most of the values) of myself on appearances and laid out the facts of that median value of my hobbies, my character, and good/bad habits.

I did have a dilemma, though: *do I state that I have polio and am disabled before, during, or after the first date?* I wondered.

I decided to inform my respective partner(s) about my polio at the end of the first date *if* I decided to see them again. Then, I'd tell them and leave the decision up to them of whether or not to go on a second date. I wasn't sure if this was the most honest approach, but it was what I landed on. There was no rule book I found on dating with a disability. But because I strongly believed what defined me most was my spiritual attributes instead of physical attributes, I stuck to that plan.

Ground Rule No. 2: Always Be Respectful in All Aspects.

I would respect others' time by never being late, or at least communicating if I *had* to be for any extenuating circumstances. I would respect others' money by splitting the bill or taking turns. I'd respect others' lifestyles, characters, and beliefs... regardless of how different they might be from mine. I'd stay open-minded. In general, I'd treat others the way I would want to be treated.

Ground Rule No. 3: Set the Right Expectations with Clear Communication.

I decided to make sure I let others know that I was still new at dating in this Western world. I'd explain that if there were any certain unspoken rules or dating routines they liked to keep, I might not meet those expectations. I would be very upfront about that to avoid wasting their time (and mine). Also, I'd be clear about my timeline: I only wanted to have coffee or a meal and some good conversation at first. If things went well, maybe we'd have more dates to get to know each other and try to develop further slowly. No other expectations anytime soon. Building something long term takes time.

After the ground rules were made and I was mentally prepared again,

I also adjusted my strategy and went with paid-service dating websites. I picked eHarmony first due to their claim of using a scientific approach to finding the right match. I was excited to get started and began filling out my profile, noting criteria for the type of man I was looking for. After hours of putting in those criteria, I clicked the button to ask the system to start searching for candidates.

The result?

"We found 0 matches for you."

I stared at the screen for several minutes, scratching my head and trying to crack their algorithm. I realized then that I'd have to relax my constraints in the model: increase the distance to me, relax the age range, any race, any build, and more career choices.

After I did that, voila! I got matches.

Dates from paid services weren't as crazy as the ones from Craigslist. I felt like being a paid service raised the bar. I was also able to keep my sanity after many failed dates, thanks to the ground rules I had made. I could only hope I didn't accidentally hurt anyone else during the process. If I did, I didn't mean to, and you have my sincere apologies. I assumed that saying "Let's keep in touch" was just a polite way to end a first date without any further expectations from either party.

In the end, I didn't make it through all one hundred dates. I ended up going on dates with eighty men in a period of half a year. They were mostly one date only, including some speed dating, where you meet ten to twenty men in one night. In late 2005, I ended up with one serious long-term relationship for over a year with my eighty-first date. We both cherished our time together, but we ended up splitting after he moved away from our area, chasing his dream of becoming a doctor at age forty, and I chose to stick to my own career in Silicon Valley instead of moving with him. We also wanted many different things in life and couldn't imagine ourselves spending the rest of our lives together with those differences. When that ended, I was exhausted and bruised. I had to pause for a long time just to heal.

I understood that although love is not logical, I must be logical in looking for it. I wanted another independent soul just like mine—someone who desired similar things in life, and with whom we could make each other laugh. It sounds simple, but it's so hard to find just that *one*.

In late 2007, I decided to move on with Mr. Number 82. I couldn't give up yet! I did a mental reset, thinking clearly about whom I was looking for and revisiting my failures from the past. At some point earlier, as a woman who had received intensive advanced education in STEM (Science, Technology, Engineering, and Math), I decided to sit down and build a complex mathematical model to solve my problem and crack the code of success in the dating world. I'd built many complex mathematical models in my life, and my PhD dissertation included dynamic modeling of complex systems. If I could predict all the complex component residues at any given point of time inside a vacuum-sealed chamber after an initial chemical explosion, I reasoned, why couldn't I build a math model to predict the perfect man whom I could spend the rest of my life with? After all, many of the math modeling contests I had experienced in school were to solve real-world problems.

And this was a real-world problem. I just happened to have it, too.

A great math model can take a set of inputs and predict the right output. I could simply use people's dating profile descriptions as the input, extract keywords and sentences, feed them into the model, and have the model calculate the odds of success. Back in 2007, models that could be built with natural language processing (NLP) were statistical methods instead of the neural networks that became popular after 2010 due to deep learning. But even the old-fashioned statistical models can converge quickly for a dating prediction. There are many ways to build the model that works for you, even without the need for programming. For example, if you identify a set of key features of a man as input layer (age, career, location, chemistry, hobbies, habits, etc.), then you convert them into values and assign each a weight. Your prediction, then, can be the total score for that candidate, which can also represent the probability of your success rate.

It was interesting that I initially had a long list of attributes for people I'd date, which included many common things people care about. But very quickly, it became hard to comprehend many dimensions of people's attributes. I then used an unsupervised machine-learning algorithm like principal component analysis (PCA) to reduce all those dimensions to the top three dimensions, based on how the dating samples were clustered. After deeper analysis, my final top three dimensions for a date surprisingly became: passion, ethics, and cognitive skills.

Passion was a dimension I had never thought of at the very beginning. My initial laundry list included: job status, stability, independence, financial status, etc. I was looking for people who had a job, a stable career, and independence, but I also found some great people who didn't have a job, were not making much money, and even lived with their parents. What, then, was the hidden component? I stared at all my past samples, looking for that common factor in those I was attracted to. I landed on "passion." It turned out that I really clicked with those who had a passion for something. It had nothing to do with their job status. When people have a passion for something, they become attractive to me due to their focus and obsessiveness over something they love.

Ethics defines how one sees things as morally right or wrong. Morally, I knew I needed to have some alignment, especially on important qualities like treating others with kindness, respect, and equality. This dimension was manifested in my initial massive list as kind, nice/polite, respectful, etc. Grouping all of those into ethics simplified the model as a second principal component dimension.

Cognitive skills define how I could have a healthy and logical conversation or debate with someone over any subject. This dimension was buried under my list of attributes with traits like logical, comprehensive, scientific, worldview, etc. In the end, I realized that if the other person had the right level of cognitive skills, we would be able to enjoy productive conversations. Even with conflicts or different points of view, we would be able to list out data and facts, explain our reasoning, come up with logical counterarguments, and respect different opinions if we couldn't reach the same conclusion.

I'd taken another close look at my model and refined it before I dipped my toe back into the dating world. I signed up for Match.com and read through at least one hundred men's profiles on the first night. Among all those profiles, I identified one that scored really high from my model.

I don't know if you have gambled using slot machines, but each time you win, it emits a *ding* sound. That man's profile felt like hitting a slot machine jackpot: *ding, ding, ding, ding, ding* all over the place. I was excited and sent him a wink (to show interest). He winked back, and we decided to meet in person the next day.

It turns out, he was the one.

8.2. THE EIGHTY-SECOND'S THE CHARM (2007–2009)

How did I know to pick him? Well, all those previous dates had helped my prediction algorithm to converge to the most optimum values. Once I saw his profile, I knew right away. Curt didn't have one of those stuck-up professional headshots. Instead, he posted a casual picture taken with his computer. I liked that he didn't care about the lighting and presented himself exactly the way he was, with the boy-next-door look and smile. I didn't care for the polished profiles who were trying to make a hard sell. Curt was a "what you see is what you get" kind of man. He looked both boyish and nerdy, and the first sentence of his profile read: "I can fix anything." I knew he was my guy. His profile was short, sweet, and simple; he mentioned that for fun he'd "fix cars and build robots," which I knew—if it were true—came with hard-core engineering skills and deep expertise in mechanical and electrical design, hardware engineering, battery and sensor technology, and software engineering. His smile was pure, warm, and nice, as a potentially good indicator of his ethics. All the flags I saw were green.

On our first date, at lunch, our conversation was effortless and comfortable. I first validated my assumption that he was very technical. Not only did he "build robots"—as he'd casually mentioned in his dating profile—but he'd also competed in DARPA grand challenges and BattleBots, which were both very serious competitions.[20] And that was only what he did in his spare time just for fun! Curt was also kind and funny, and I knew right away I wanted to see him again. We ended up talking for several hours about anything, finishing each other's sentences, smiling, and laughing non-stop. But then he looked at me and said, "Libo, you sound perfect and unreal," and my heart dropped. We'd been sitting the entire time, having a wonderful conversation, but I dreaded Curt seeing my limp once I got up to walk. I told him that while sitting, it was hard for him to see how imperfect I really was. Remembering all the times people had asked me to walk in front of them to assess me physically, I told Curt I was a polio

---

[20] https://www.darpa.mil/; https://battlebots.com/.

survivor who walked with a limp, and I looked into his eyes and said, "I can and am *willing to* walk for you if you want to see for yourself."

He looked at me, smiling brightly, relieved instead of disappointed. "Oh, then I also have a confession to make," he said sincerely. "I have a bad nose that's allergic to many things. I am glad we are both more real now."

I found it endearing that my disability was a complete nonissue for Curt. He genuinely felt his allergies and my polio were on par. Nobody's perfect. Who cares what the specific imperfections are? It was the first time in my life that I had a totally new perspective on my disability. My disability was neither something shameful to ignore and hide, nor something so important it eclipsed everything else about me. It was a simple fact that had no bearing on my connection to this world.

We talked for much longer. Reluctantly, we had to leave our lunch when people started showing up for early dinners. We walked together to our cars in the parking lot and gave each other a hug goodbye. After the high of that first date that was almost too good to be true, I stared at my phone for hours. Ring, stupid phone! I doubted myself. *The conversation was wonderful, so something bad was going to happen*, I thought. If the date went well, he would at least send a text or call after. Right? But he didn't. I was convinced he wouldn't call, so I didn't call either. I grew more disappointed with every passing hour. That night, he finally sent a message via Match.com and invited me to dinner two days later. I was relieved. At least we mutually wanted to see each other again.

At the end of the second date, when he walked me to my car in the parking garage, Curt pointed out I had a low tire that I hadn't noticed I had been driving with. "Lucky you, I'm a handyman," he said, before rolling up his sleeves and crawling under my car to inspect the low tire. Curt found a big screw stuck in the tire that had caused the leakage, so the backup tire needed to be replaced. He asked me if I knew how to do that. I didn't.

Curt found the jack in my trunk—I had no idea where it had come from—and he started looking for the spot he could put the jack under to lift the car up. As he was looking for that spot, he asked, "How did you survive all those years without knowing how to change a tire?"

"Well, this is the first flat tire I've had in my life," I answered shamelessly. "When the car feels strange to me or some warning lights start to come on, I just take it to a shop and let them deal with it."

Curt laughed. "Well, your days of being ripped off by other men at the shops are over. Starting now, I am your personal mechanic!"

His words warmed my heart. Somehow, I trusted him at that very moment. We made plans to see each other again for a third date.

On the day of our third date in the same week, I called Curt from work, telling him I couldn't leave to meet him. One of my other tires had blown up, and my car sat in the parking lot, undrivable. "Stay where you are and send me your location," Curt said over the phone. Twenty minutes later, he showed up in the parking lot with his toolbox, ready to patch the tire. "This is too easy," he said, winking. "If you're trying to test me, you need to come up with something harder."

While watching him patch my tire right there in the parking lot, I thought to myself, *This one might be a keeper*. At the same time, after failing so many times, I wasn't naïve enough to think things would always go as planned. I knew time would tell everything, but I had a great feeling about him. We spent a perfect third date together as well.

Time flies. Curt and I spent a lot of time getting to know each other, and everything about him felt just right. It still felt unreal and too good to be true. I kept wondering: *What is he hiding? There must be something wrong with him, right? OMG, what if he is already married and just faking it all? Then I'll just be left with another broken heart.*

I shared my crazy thoughts with him. He laughed and said I could visit his house if I was comfortable with it. I could then see for myself how he lived a simple and single life—and that there wasn't a family hiding anywhere.

I decided to take him up on the offer and see his daily life with my own eyes. When I walked into his house, I felt one primary emotion: relief.

It was such a regular single guy's house. Comfortable yet distasteful furniture, no color-matching scheme . . . and there was a giant motor in the middle of his living room. His excuse was "I was going to fix that!"

"Really?" I asked, smiling. "How long has it been there?"

"About a month," he smiled back, a bit embarrassed.

I also noticed his garage was full of heavy machinery equipment: several lathes, two CNC (computerized numerical control) metal milling machines, many other machines I couldn't even name, and many heavy-weight robotics parts he was in the process of building and assembling. His fully packed garage was a true paradise, of which any serious robot maker would be jealous. This made it very apparent to me that he truly *did* spend his spare time "fixing cars or building robots!"

A true professional! I thought. *Also, there is no evidence of any woman living with him, no family hiding in the basement, and I can help bring some taste to this place if he allows me.* We had a very comfortable evening cooking together and talking like we'd known each other for years. I was so comfortable with him that I invited him to see where I live next.

When he visited me at my apartment, he saw a giant TV sitting on my living room floor.

My excuse was "I was going to install that!"

"How long has that TV been sitting there?" he asked.

"About a year..." I answered, with a lot more embarrassment than his.

We both laughed. I really didn't have any time to watch TV, and it turned out the cable I had thought was missing was right in that box, amongst many other cables. Curt helped me install my TV, and while I was fixing dinner, he also fixed my shower door, sliding door to the patio, and a leak in the sink.

Everything after that was simple, easy, natural, and comfortable.

I must admit I remained paranoid for a few months after that. *This is too easy*, I kept thinking. *It's too good. It feels too right.*

One day, I told him I wasn't going to consider him my boyfriend until we had our first real fight. All my previous relationships had included some arguments or some fundamental differences that I knew just wouldn't work for the long term. Curt and I hadn't even had the tiniest spat in many months of dating. I was worried that I hadn't seen the worst of Curt, the ugliness that only comes out in fights. He told me that seemed like a very strange condition for becoming my boyfriend. Spoiler alert: he's now my husband, and I'm still waiting for our first serious fight—the kind like in the movies, where people don't talk for days after. I'm starting to think that's not going to happen.

Curt responded to my worries not only with words but with actions that let me know how important I was to him. When he told me he wanted to visit my family in China after half a year of dating, I thought it was strange at first. He showed a great interest in where I came from. He said he wanted to know where I grew up. "I know we are still in the early stages of dating, but I want to meet your parents and extended family. I want to understand the culture you came from." My Cao family heritage is precious to me, and being with a man who wanted to honor my culture and family this way only made me more convinced Curt was the right one.

And yet, I was nervous about the visit and so were my parents. They only knew of Americans from movies and TV shows. My parents asked me a million questions before his visit. Some were serious, asking if Curt was treating me kindly. Some were more lighthearted, like wondering if their stereotypes about American men smelling worse than Asian men due to being much hairier, were true. I was glad I could assure my family that Curt treated me well and smelled great. (Well, most of the time.)

Our time in China together was a milestone in our relationship. Curt won over my parents easily, not only because he fixed everything he could get his hands on in my parents' house. My parents also saw the kindness and attention with which Curt treated me. When we'd go out together, Curt always held my hand, and when my legs got too tired from walking, he would carry me on his back. His actions spoke loud and clear to my parents who could now see with their own eyes that Curt would always take care of me when they were not around.

My parents gave their blessing for our relationship, and Curt was so excited during our stay in China that he didn't want to leave. He loved going out with me at night to the town squares that were always full of people laughing, dancing, and eating. Curt had never seen this many people in his life, and it was impossible to drag him home. Back when I had first moved to Ohio during that long, lonely, dark winter, I ached for this place full of color and life. I couldn't have imagined then that I would meet Curt and share these experiences with him.

For his trip to China with me, he not only brought himself, but he also brought a very long, in-depth letter from his parents. His parents asked me to translate their letter into Chinese and read it to my parents. They introduced Curt to my parents, with many pictures throughout different stages of his life: the day he was born, first birthday, first Christmas, first day at school, first robotic awards in school, all the skills he had learned (including how to water-ski and so on), how he could fix anything we could ever imagine, his first job, first house...

It took me hours to get through the letter, reading it to my parents, and they were deeply touched by the time Curt's parents had spent writing this letter to them. I saw them start hiding in their bedroom to plan for a reply. Only a few minutes later, they came to Curt and me and said, "There are less than ten pictures taken of Libo before she was in middle school, and then she only studied in schools before going abroad. No hobbies, just piles of academic awards and technical certificates. There's nothing else we could put in a letter that can match what Curt's parents did. We really hope you don't regret choosing her because she is not refundable by now." Of course, Curt laughed and confirmed to my parents that he was very serious about me, and he didn't plan for any return.

After meeting Curt, my parents totally changed. They'd started by not being sure about him, but then they thought I might not be good enough for him and were afraid things would go south. There was a strong cultural element at play. My parents are very humble and always taught me not to be a peacock, encouraging me to be better. In this case, Mom pulled me aside multiple times and tried to coach me on how to do laundry properly, how to cook better, and how to have better manners when I'd someday meet his parents. Dad tried to prepare me for the possibility that if the relationship were to end, it totally wouldn't be the end of the world, since they would still love me. We all felt that Curt was too good to be true and all wanted to make sure that when it ended, we were ready for it. Dad always makes sure I know how to prepare for rainy days.

Back in the US, Curt asked me to spend Christmas with his family. I was terrified that they wouldn't like me. I begged Curt to give his parents a heads up about my disability, but he refused. "It won't matter to them," he said, "and even if it did, it wouldn't change how I feel about you." When we arrived, I was overwhelmed by Curt's parents showering me with attention and praise. Curt's mom presented me with a beautiful bouquet of flowers, and his dad told me how much he enjoyed reading my dissertation.

"What? You found my dissertation and read it?" I was shocked.

"That's right. I looked you up, and I read your dissertation, though I couldn't understand most of it," he said. "I know you are super smart. What did Curt do to deserve you?"

I tried to tell them how lucky I was to be with their son, and they laughed. "Curt is the lucky one, having won your heart!" Curt's dad replied.

Curt's mother was very considerate and kind. Not only did she set up our room nicely with everything I would need (including my own personal slippers and robe), but she also tried to figure out the Chinese food I would like. She did everything she could to ensure I felt at home.

We had a wonderful Christmas break together at his home with all his family and friends. After that milestone, we had both met each other's families and gained formal acceptance from our parents. The rest of the relationship would be totally on us to figure out.

Curt and I are quite different in terms of our personalities and character. I think and move very fast, like a rabbit, without the patience to dwell on things. Curt is conservative in his decision-making. He is careful and takes his time, like a turtle. So, we bumped against each other's expectations many times, but we learned each other's ways and grew together.

One day while we were dating, he asked about my day. I told him that day I'd flown to a different state, bought a house there, and flew back before dinner. Curt was very surprised I hadn't told him about it before and that I could make such a big decision so quickly. Why would I tell him, though? I didn't understand initially. It was my money, my decision, and it was a great cash-positive deal. We were dating but had separate finances, and it never occurred to me to discuss my investment decisions with him. Curt wasn't trying to tell me what to do. He considered us partners and wanted to openly discuss big decisions as a couple. It was one of the first times I reflected on what it meant to be partners in every way, including financially.

When Curt got a great deal on a car during the 2008 financial crisis, he called me to ask my opinion. He said it was a great Cadillac sports car edition that used to cost more than $60,000, but he could now get a cash deal for only $30,000. I said sure, but why would it matter if I liked his car? He explained that since I'd be riding in it, too, he wanted to include my preferences in his decision-making. My heart melted when I heard his answer, and I started to understand how great it could feel when you are in the picture for another's decision-making. After that, I changed my behavior of not discussing big financial decisions with him—but I set that "big" limit to be high so that we both have the freedom to make decisions financially without having to consult the other. It's a good compromise.

Undeniably, Curt and I were raised in a totally different environment and see many things differently, especially in the sense of "security." I had made much progress in creating safety nets for myself and overcoming old doom-and-gloom thought patterns, but they still occasionally reared their heads.

I felt a sense of instability in my childhood, having spent years moving from place to place and living in hospitals or with relatives. That's why, as an adult, the first thing I do when I get to a new place is establish a sense of security. For example, I stock up on lots of food wherever I am, even if I am surrounded by grocery stores. Somehow deep inside, I feel like it's me against this world, and I must always be prepared and ready to tackle any crisis that comes my way, alone.

One night, I tried to explain to Curt how important "security" was to me. He was in the garage working on a giant robot part. With his boyish smile, he proudly held up a giant wrench he'd just made. "Does this make you feel secure?" he asked. "My killer robot can beat anyone who breaks into our house, which by the way is also level-eight earthquake-proof. You don't need to worry about security."

I wasn't talking about physical security from intruders or natural disasters. I was concerned with economic and financial security, that a significant economic downturn could cut my net worth in half. I always aim to make my financial net bigger, stronger, and even bulletproof. I wanted to be financially settled and secure for life. Curt grew up in a family that was already financially secure when he came along. He never had to worry about money. His critical life decisions were not dependent on whether he could afford something. Our different upbringings heavily impacted our decision-making.

Curt worked for a legendary Silicon Valley startup called Willow Garage at that time. Since he was the very first employee at the company—hired by the founder, Scott Hassan, after a DARPA contest in which Curt had competed—he owned plenty of pre-IPO shares. The company had developed a robotics middleware suite called Robot Operating System (ROS), which became the most popular and widely adopted middleware for robots. The company was valued at an extremely high price that could potentially make every employee in that company very wealthy if the company were to be sold or went for IPO, but the founder decided to offer ROS as open-source software. This means it would be public domain and free to use for anyone. Curt agreed with the founder that if they didn't offer their technology in the public domain, only a small market would adopt it. Only very large corporations would be able to buy and use their invention. They believed the industry and the world would be better served with unlimited access. I was impressed with this decision because I considered it selfless and admirable. At the same time, I also knew the head of the company, like Curt, was able to make this decision because they wanted to do the best for the world instead of themselves. Money wasn't the highest priority, though undeniably very important. Their ambition was something I had never thought of: changing the world.

Curt had the privilege of living his life without money being a big factor. I was the exact opposite. For a long time, I was envious of his abundance mindset versus my scarcity mindset. I've since realized that it's just part of my story, and part of his story. Neither of us asked to be born in the specific circumstances we were brought up in. All we can do now is to be mindful of each other's experiences and learn from one another.

One important thing I learned from Curt and his family was that not all worthwhile experiences are goal-oriented. Growing up, I had to focus on the activities that would have the biggest impact on my life and career. I had little time or resources and needed to use them efficiently. Anything that didn't have a specific purpose and demonstrably positive impact on me directly had to fall by the wayside. But now I was in a different place in my life. I had an education, a good job, and a secure financial foundation. And still, I felt like I always had to worry about my future and carried a sense of insecurity, wondering if something bad was going to happen. It is true that Curt grew up very comfortably, but his parents also taught him the value of volunteering and giving back to the community. His mom, after her retirement, volunteers at her local charity organization several times a week to read to the children and prepare meals. As a retired physician, Curt's dad volunteered his medical and teaching services during the pandemic. During COVID-19 time, he soon began volunteering for the COVID-19 vaccine clinics at the local hospital. Watching the Meyers family give freely of their time taught me that there is true joy in giving to the community. I had felt a burst of that joy myself during my century ride for leukemia patients. Their example inspired me to continue finding ways to contribute my time and resources. Later in my life, I also became a board member so that I could influence the community and help create a better future.

On Labor Day of 2009, Curt proposed to me at the same restaurant where we'd met for our first date. Everything felt right: Curt cried; I jumped as high as I could. The sun was shining, and so was my ring. We decided to hold our wedding in his hometown during the winter holiday season that same year. My parents and friends would all fly to Curt's home to join us.

The night before our wedding, Curt showed me all the paperwork for his assets, his house, his savings, and his stock portfolio. It made me feel like he now understood what I had meant by needing to feel secure. "These are all I have," he'd told me, shuffling through the papers. "But don't tell me how much you owe now. Let's deal with it together after our wedding." His face was serious then, and he walked out with firm determination—as if even if I could have caused him to be bankrupt, he would have still married me.

We didn't have joint accounts before getting married, and Curt thought I was always broke. I asked him to lend me a few thousand dollars a couple of times, which I would pay back a few days later after I moved money around. What he didn't know was that I had little liquid cash because I had poured everything into my investments, and it always took several days to take money out when I needed it.

It meant a lot to me to know that Curt was in it with me for better or worse and that he wanted to help me carry the load. I laughed to myself after that conversation the night before our wedding because I knew how surprised Curt would be when I told him the next day that I had zero debt. In fact, I owned several houses, among other investments, and was quite well off on my own. As it turned out, we both brought many assets to our relationship and marriage.

During the time Curt visited China with me for my brother's wedding, he saw my brother giving a red envelope to the bride's mother. He asked me what that was about, and I told him that it was customary to give the bride's family a red envelope filled with a particular amount: ¥10,001.[21] In our culture, this specifically symbolizes that you've found "the one out of many." On our wedding day, Curt gave Mom the same type of envelope with the same amount. Gestures like these confirmed to me that Curt carefully observed what was important to me and honored my heritage and my parents every step of the way.

Our wedding was hosted in Curt's hometown in Indiana. It was small, intimate, and lovely. My mother-in-law did most of the arrangements for the wedding. Curt and I made a few key decisions, then just sat back and enjoyed the ride. We had rehearsal dinner at the best Chinese restaurant in town, and on the wedding day, I wore both a Western white dress and a traditional Chinese red qipao. We had a Western ceremony and exchanged vows, with Curt's cousin as the officiant. We also had a traditional Chinese ceremony where we both served tea to our parents for the first time. I had my best friend from college, Hongmei, as my bridesmaid, as well as my

---

[21] ¥ is the symbol for the basic unit of Chinese currency, also called yuan. One dollar equals about seven yuan.

dear friends Charlotte and George from California. Many of Curt's child-hood friends were in attendance as well. At the dinner after the ceremony, everyone from Curt's side shared a story about how he'd fixed their stuff: cars, auditorium equipment, computers, and so on. Curt's brother shared a particularly funny story about the time Curt had found a broken stun gun on the side of the road, fixed it up, and tested it on him without any warning. Those who spoke from my side shared my journey of growing up in China and how I'd found my way here after many challenges, and they honored all the precious moments Curt and I had created together. That day, we danced until we all dropped.

After that, life felt like a movie in fast-forward: we bought our dream house together in 2010 and made it our own beautiful home. That story represents one adventure of many: we put in a cash offer the second day the listing came up, and it was off the market by the third day. It was a foreclosure and needed quite a few repairs. We had two months until our first baby was born, and we were committed to fixing it up ourselves—well, Curt mostly. Every night after work, Curt headed to the new house to fix things until 2:00 a.m. Sometimes I would join him for a few hours, with my very pregnant body, handing him a wrench or some other tool to fix some sort of problem: the plumbing, the drywall, the electrical panels, you name it. We were able to move into our beautiful new home before the birth of our first son. Our families, in more ways than one, also came together to help make the dream happen. From day one, we've been a team. We each represent a thread that, when combined, makes a stronger rope.

It has been over fifteen years since we first met and fell in love, and that love still hasn't faded a bit. If you've ever thought *I'll never find the one*, keep going. You never know...the eighty-second time could be the charm.

8.3. THE DIFFERENT AND THE SAME FAMILIES

People say when you marry someone, you marry their family as well. There is some truth in that. I married into the Meyers family, and Curt married into the Cao family. Our families are different in many ways, yet we're alike in more ways than you might think.

Just Be Yourself

My first visit to Curt's home to spend Christmas with his family showed that how Mom viewed the dynamic was quite different from how Curt's mom viewed it.

The way I was brought up in China, I needed to demonstrate my usefulness and work ethic to be accepted by my potential future in-laws. So I got up early the first morning to cook for the whole family like Mom had advised me to do. As you know by now, cooking is not my strong suit. But what was I supposed to do? I had to prove my worth to Curt's parents somehow. My mother-in-law wouldn't have any of it. She was already in the kitchen cooking and shooed me out. "Go back to bed, Libo," she said, waving me off. "When you guys are here, just be kids. Go relax! I'm cooking for you all!"

It was such a relief that I didn't have to pretend to be someone I wasn't and that I didn't have to earn my in-laws' love by showing how much I could contribute to the household. I was relieved that they seemed to genuinely like me for who I am already.

I called Mom with the good news and needled her a little about lying to me for years. "Mom, you were wrong! You said nobody would marry me if I couldn't cook, and no mother-in-law would accept me if I don't get up early to cook for the whole family. Curt's parents don't want me to do anything!" Mom drew a big breath, and I knew I had it coming. "It was a test, Libo, and you failed it!" Through the phone I could hear her exasperation. "Now they know you're lazy at doing housework because you didn't insist on cooking for them! What have you done?"

My mother-in-law assured me that I hadn't failed any test, and I could just be me and enjoy the time with them.

When Curt visited my family in China, Mom did the same thing: just let Curt be like Curt. He wasn't asked to taste the food he wasn't comfortable tasting (like chicken feet and preserved eggs). At the dinner table, while my own family enjoyed traditional Chinese food, he'd enjoy a steak cooked the American way. To this day, it feels great that we can just be ourselves, even after marrying into another family and another culture.

The Tools and Approaches in the Kitchen

When Mom cooks, she uses a single butcher knife for everything: chopping, opening, smashing, grinding, and more. She always finds a way to make that single big butcher knife work. She also taught me that a great cook needs to clean up *while* cooking. That means no matter how many dishes she cooks, she's cleaning up as she goes along. By the time she's done, the kitchen is always spotless—like nothing had happened. Mom also doesn't use many recipes. Even when trying something new, she just takes a quick look at the recipe and moves on without minding the precise quantity of the ingredients. However, somehow everything always turns out great, as if there is an internal scale in her head.

The first time I saw Curt or my mother-in-law cooking, I was so amazed at how many specialized tools they used: can openers, rollers, grinders, noodle makers, choppers, pizza cutters, etc. It seemed that every task must have its own tool. They also treated the recipe like a rule book and relied on precise measurements. When they'd sit down to enjoy the fruits of their labor, the kitchen usually resembled a war scene—kitchen tools in the sink, gadgets on the counters. But to them, food must be enjoyed fully before any cleaning makes it on the agenda.

I find it amazing how different we are. I realized that when Mom started to run her kitchen while taking care of me and my brother back in the 1980s, she had to do everything on her own. That often meant minimalism. It took a one-person army to get everything done efficiently. At a young age, I saw her running back home during lunchtime, riding her oversized, clunky bike. She would hold a giant butcher knife to prepare meals for me and my brother. While we were eating, she would take that knife outside to cut grasses and vegetables, chop them, and mix them with other things to feed all the animals in our yard. Sometimes she also had to wash our clothes by hand during that period. After all that work, she would put a bun in her mouth, hop on her bike, and race back to work. There was no time for her to clean up the kitchen, which is why all the cleaning had to be completed during her cooking time.

In the Western world, while Curt grew up, it was totally different. Tools were commercialized to boost the economy, and various utilities (like dishwashers) were invented to improve efficiency.

I became the type of person who adopted both cultures. I will use many tools in the kitchen like my Western family—after all, opening a can with a can opener is easier than doing it with a knife. But by the time I finish cooking, my kitchen is spotless—just as efficient as Mom.

What Mom, my mother-in-law, and I now share is, however, the same philosophy: whoever is dominating the kitchen, the others need to get out of there. There is only one strong woman allowed in our kitchen so that she can do things her own way.

I Am on Your Side as Well as His/Her Side

Both sides of our family try to see the other's perspectives. Those moments of making others feel like "I am on your side as well" help build stronger relationships.

Shortly after we moved into our new house, I really wanted to get the backyard fence redone. Curt didn't think it was a priority and dragged his feet on the project for years. Even though it's not a great idea to complain to your mother-in-law about her son, I found myself talking to her about the fence one day. My mother-in-law, the sweet, soft-spoken woman, told me that if she were in my shoes, she would put on a vulnerable face and "get" Curt this way:

"Libo, you just pretend to cry a little and say, 'Curt, you know we soon will have our boy running in the backyard, and I am just *so scared* that without a solid fence, he could be bitten by any neighbor's dog that could get into our yard!'" My mother-in-law exaggeratedly acted out how I might deliver this speech: teary eyes, pouty mouth.

I laughed out loud seeing my mother-in-law trying to help me trick her own son into doing what I wanted. I thanked her but told her that I just didn't know how to "fake cry" while keeping a straight face. Crying and begging for mercy just isn't me, so I'd have to find another way to get it done and have Curt come around.

We both had a good laugh at that. While our personalities are very different and I ended up dealing with the fence issue another way, I deeply appreciated her efforts to listen and help me problem-solve. Both of Curt's parents have been nothing but kind to me and never take Curt's side by default in any argument. They truly care about us and our families and offer genuine support and care without any blame.

My parents have done the same thing, even though they don't speak the same language as Curt. If I ever have the slightest complaint about my husband, my parents are always on Curt's side. They make a point to make sure I see things from all perspectives and aren't afraid to say that when a problem occurs, it is just as much mine as it is his.

Family Is Everything, but We Express It Differently

The Meyers treat holidays and special occasions very seriously.

One Meyers family Christmas when our older son was about six, he told everyone that Santa wasn't real. Most adults figured it was normal to grow out of this belief, but Grandpa Meyers wouldn't have it. "He's too young! He should get a few more years of Christmas magic before growing up!"

Grandpa Meyers came up with an elaborate plan to prove that Santa was real. He set up a camera in the living room, explaining to the kiddo that if Santa was real, there would be proof on camera the next morning. Grandpa rented a Santa suit and got up in the middle of the night, crawling on the floor as if popping out of the chimney and into view of the camera. He arranged the gifts under the tree. He drank the milk. He ate the cookies. He waved hi to the camera.

That was his mistake right there.

The next morning, when our son suspiciously reviewed the footage, a very tired Grandpa felt triumphant: "See! I told you Santa was real!"

"Nope," my son remarked unimpressed. "That's you, Grandpa."

The outcome really didn't matter to me. It was the thought, effort, and willingness to go out of his way to make magic for our kids that I found endearing.

And that never stopped—not with Grandma Meyers either.

Every birthday, Valentine's Day, Halloween, and Thanksgiving, little goodies arrive from Grandma Meyers. One Valentine's Day, the boys opened musical cards that played silly songs for them to dance to while eating their chocolate. Sometimes it's a little package with small toys or a special treat. Those little touchpoints and kindnesses add to the close bonds in our family. And even though I'm a grown-up and no longer care about my birthday, my mother-in-law still sends me a card and gift every year, just like every other kid in the family. I am loved and included in the same way. I matter to her, and she shows it in a million little ways that add up to a close and loving relationship.

The Cao family treats holidays and special occasions in the opposite way: not seriously at all. The only holiday the Cao family used to spend together was the Spring Festival. Growing up, we never celebrated birthdays together. Our tradition was just to have a bowl of noodles, indicating a long thread of life. Sometimes the bowl of noodles had an egg in it, indicating a full circle of satisfaction, or whatever meaning you can find for an egg. Mom and Dad never celebrated their anniversary, but they always talked about how on their wedding night, all they had were two wooden boxes made into a bed, wildflowers, and a warmed-up tent. They made us feel like every day was a special day.

To describe how the difference feels to me, holidays in Western culture are like a series of waterfalls: a burst of energy that is beautiful and lasts a short period of time. But my family's attitude toward celebrating each day is more like the drizzle of a water spring: it's slow, ongoing, and always there.

With each approach, it's clear that family is everything to us all. Unlike the Meyers grandparents who could visit us every few months and during the holidays, the Cao grandparents can only visit us every couple of years since it's not that easy for them to travel overseas. My boys can communicate in simple Chinese with the Cao grandparents. What matters is that their grandparents from both families are a steady presence in their lives and that they grow in tremendous amounts of love.

Stay Open-Minded and Be Explorative

After the Meyers family got a Chinese daughter-in-law, they started to learn a lot about Asian culture. My mother-in-law started to learn some Chinese language, playing mahjong (a tile-based game created in China in the nineteenth century) with her friends, and even wore the traditional qipao I gifted her for the Chinese New Year celebration. My father-in-law started reading and watching material about China and often sends me snippets to seek my point of view. They've tried to learn as much as possible about this different culture, explore things they have never experienced, and stay open-minded.

My parents have done the same with Western culture. Upon knowing I would be married to an American, they asked for etiquette lessons before traveling to the USA to make sure they weren't impolite by accident. They started carrying enough bills to tip in restaurants, which is unusual in China since waiters work on salary without tips. They tried their hardest, with limited success, to stop slurping their noodles. I had explained to them that while it might be a compliment to the cook in China, it was considered rude in America. Whenever we went out to eat noodles, my parents tried their hardest to eat as quietly as possible. Then we'd take the leftovers home, heat them up, and sit around the kitchen island, slurping noodles as loud as possible and giggling together. If Curt walked in, we'd look at each other, laugh, and immediately quiet the slurping noises.

Not only did my parents adopt the American culture, but Mom even single-handedly changed the culture around her in this country.

Mom is the social butterfly of our family. The very first time she came to visit, she met almost every single family in my neighborhood, even those who didn't speak Chinese. My parents would go for walks every night, greet people in Chinese, and strike up conversations. I was perplexed. "How do you do this, Mom? You have nothing in common with these people, and now you are friends with half my neighborhood?"

After only a few weeks in this country, she was able to make herself comfortable with the environment and begin navigating it by her own rules. She got busy doing things with neighbors she made friends with, and every few days, she would make homemade dumplings or bao and bring them to her friends. I told her that we usually don't do that in this country; she can't just show up at someone's door and bring them homemade food. We usually make appointments and only bring food when we are invited to a party someone is hosting. But somehow everyone around her accepted her rule and even started showing up at our front door with *their* homemade food, unannounced.

"We are not that different, after all. We are all humans, and humans all love yummy food!" Mom proudly announced to me.

Sometimes I wonder if my parents are getting more energetic and curious as they get older. I don't see them slowing down. Dad, especially, seems to be aging in reverse. He's always waiting at the top of the mountain for me as I'm struggling to keep up with his pace. Twice I took my parents alone to Hawaii for vacation, while Curt took the kids with his parents to Disney. We went kayaking, and Dad found it hilarious when both of us fell into the water repeatedly, struggling to get back on. The three of us went snorkeling together, and Dad was always the one who first identified a turtle close by or something interesting. When Mom and I were both exhausted, Dad kept going until we dragged him out of the water—he was about eighty years old but played like a little kid.

The two families are so different in terms of the food we eat, our living habits, and our background, yet they are so similar in many ways. They are all tireless people who have kept moving, exploring, and finding their own ways to contribute and influence people around them. All the grandparents enjoy learning new things in life, different cultures included. Neither family judges the other culture. In fact, they are all very open-minded and embrace differences. Or, in Mom's words, "We are not that different; we are all humans!"

The Frugality in All of Us

Even though my parents were very open to learning new customs, they couldn't change all their ways. Mom, frugal to a fault, unplugged every device powered by electricity as soon as she came to my house for the first time. Then she followed us around and turned off the lights whenever we left the room. Growing up with few resources, she couldn't believe how wasteful we were, leaving on all the lights in the house and every device always plugged in. We explained that repeatedly turning the lights on and off costs more energy than leaving them on, but only after a very long period, she stopped doing that (though I could still see her trying to not switch the light off the minute we left the room).

We ended up installing a solar system for the entire house, so we are net neutral and Mom doesn't have to worry about our waste electricity.

The Meyers family is frugal in another way. At that time, the installation fee for the solar panels was as much as the material cost. Curt dismissed the installation cost immediately. "I don't need help with that." He came up with an installation design, put up all the panels with his forklift, and wired everything up to code. He read the entire city code book, designed the electrical panel, and passed the permit inspection flawlessly. That frugality is in the Meyers' blood. Uncle Meyers, who owned countless real estate properties and had a big net worth, would drive around to three different stores buying a gadget for five dollars at the last store, rather than spending ten dollars at the first store. When I asked him why, he said, "I'm not going to be ripped off. If I know what something should cost, I'm not going to pay anyone double for it." I respect how principled and stubborn the Meyers are about money.

Both families have accumulated wealth through not only deep expertise in their own domain but also by being very savvy financially over many years. Both families are also very generous as well when it comes to gifts for their friends and family and donating to causes that are important to them. At the same time, neither the Meyers nor the Cao will overpay or be ripped off. Each penny we spend must have a purpose.

Debate and Grow Together

The Meyers family has two medical doctors. My father-in-law, after finishing his postgraduate degree in family medicine, fulfilled his military obligation in the Air Force. Two years later, he transitioned into private practice and remained there for the next forty-seven years until he retired. Curt's brother is a physician who is double board-certified in critical care and emergency medicine. He later served as the division director of emergency critical care at a major New York City hospital. Both have given generously of their time in teaching at the local medical schools and residency training programs in their specialties.

During my first visit to Curt's hometown, I was able to see what the Meyers family dinners were like—when father-and-son doctors are at the same table. Once, before I knew any better, I asked them both a medical question. After hearing that, Curt put his hand over his face, sighed, and shook his head. "You don't know what you just started," he muttered.

And he was right, because nobody would be able to leave the table until the two doctors reached the same medical opinion. Research papers would be quoted, laptops would be pulled out, and there goes the rest of the night with tireless debates... without noticing that the people who'd asked the question in the first place had left the table already.

But more often, the two doctors would start discussing a specific medical field and exchanging tips and learnings, like father and son—that is, if they didn't get into another debate on different treatment approaches. It was all in good fun, of course, and highly entertaining for me to watch at times. Even though nobody in my family had a medical degree and I was often lost in the jargon, I very much enjoyed that Curt's family members were smart and educated with strong opinions and not scared to have an intense and spirited debate.

My family's debating style was a lot less intense, likely because nobody in my family is in the same domain of expertise. Our debate mostly happened around the dinner table as well, but for the Cao family, enjoying food was usually more important than winning a conversation. Nothing was serious enough to waste a table full of the yummy feast that Mom had put together.

The most important thing for all of us is that, outside of work, we spend time together. It's the time we all grow together that makes family so dear and precious to all our hearts.

The Cao family and the Meyers family grew up in totally different environments, had different beliefs, lived different lifestyles, ate different food, and spoke different languages. Yet they are so similar! Both sets of grandparents have been happily married for about fifty years; they are all caring and love their family more than anything else in the world; each one of them loves to learn new things and enjoy exploring the world at their age; and they are all very open-minded and accept people who are different from themselves. I am fortunate to have the love from both the Cao family and Meyers family. The love and appreciation we have for each other make it easier to deal with any cultural difference that otherwise might drive us apart.

Race or anything else couldn't separate us, and I wish this world could experience what I have experienced. Love has no boundaries.

8.4. BUILDING MY OWN FAMILY (2010–2014)

"Do you have to leave a single sip of Coke in every can you drink? Why can't you rinse it out and put it in the recycling?" I looked at Curt, slightly annoyed.

"I wasn't done with it yet!"

It used to be cute that Curt would leave all his nearly empty Coke cans on the counters for me to pick up. It got old somehow after we got married. If I didn't throw it away, the can would remain stuck to the counter for eternity. When I pointed this out to him self-righteously, he was quick to come back: "You leave every door open behind you, the closets, the cabinets! I always know where you've been because the door will be left open."

I defended myself weakly. "I was coming right back!" But I knew he had a point.

Marriage means your husband still loves you after banging his head into hard cabinet doors because you have a habit of not closing them right after. And it means you accept that he will never ever finish a Coke in his entire life, and you will oversee the recycling until the end of time.

Like every couple, we had to navigate how to transition into a new phase of our relationship when we got married. Things that used to be cute in the beginning were starting to become annoying in daily life. Sometimes those pet peeves and petty arguments can sour a love that was once sweet. We decided early on that we would not let these little things fester but discuss them instead. Once they were out in the open, we both realized that the things we found irritating about each other were too small to fight over. We are also equally and mutually flawed in our own ways, just like when we first started dating—nobody is perfect, and my biggest flaw is not my polio, nor his allergies. We both accepted that we would need to let these small irritations go and focus on the fundamentals instead. Do we love each other? Do we trust each other? Do we respect each other? Do we still laugh at each other's jokes? Our marriage is founded on resounding yeses to these questions and a commitment to be honest with each other. You would think that if you love each other, you would change for the other, but most likely neither of you would change. What you change is how you deal with it. After fifteen years of being together, we developed this tacit agreement that I clean up the last-sip cans on the kitchen counter and he closes the cabinet doors.

I was already thirty-three when we got married, so I wanted to have children right away. We got pregnant quickly with our first son, and I kept working right up until he was born. During pregnancy, I wasn't careful with what I ate and added fifty pounds to my small frame of one hundred pounds. A 50 percent increase in overall weight would be a lot for anyone, but for me, it felt like a repeat from my college days when Wendy's hamburgers helped me pack on so many pounds that it caused excruciating leg pain. Because of my polio, any extra weight makes it much harder for me to walk. During the second trimester, I slipped and fell, resulting in a broken tailbone and bed rest for two weeks before going back to work again. During the third trimester, it was getting extremely hard for me to move around. Simply getting up off the couch to go to the bathroom made it feel like a part of my body was going to fall off at any second. After the birth of my first son in November 2010, I was still thirty-five pounds over my original weight. I blamed my constant pain and exhaustion on those excess pounds. After maternity leave, I went back to work. Working all day and then taking care of a baby at night was enough to keep me in this state of bone-tiredness that I couldn't seem to shake. Curt was an equal partner in everything... but still, I was completely drained of energy.

In late 2011, I joined Apple and began a very challenging and demanding job. The initial ramp-up in *any* company is tough, but this was the best technology company—a place where the smartest and most talented people gather. I felt like a top, spinning through work during the day, and I just kept on spinning at home throughout the night. Even with a full-time live-in nanny at home and a very helpful husband, I couldn't find a moment to rest. Or, if there were such moments, I hadn't yet learned how to take a break.

Curt's work was demanding, too. We'd usually leave early for work and come home for dinner after 7:00 p.m. Leaving our son alone with the nanny the whole day made me feel terrible, so we would spend all our time with him playing before bedtime. I felt so guilty that I overcompensated in other aspects of his life. For example, every time I heard him make the tiniest noise on the baby monitor at night, I would jump out of bed and rush to his side. I nursed him or rocked him until he was asleep, then tried to tiptoe out of the room . . . but if you have kids, you know how babies are. Right as you have peeled their sweaty little limbs off you to put them back in their crib, they stir awake again. Sure enough, the whole dance would start again and would repeat several times every night. I got no sleep. Still, I needed to show up at work energetically the next morning as the strong leader and strong woman I was.

That state lasted until our son was one and a half years old. At that point, I realized I couldn't do it anymore. I was so sleep-deprived that I didn't have the energy I needed to keep going daily. The fix? Sleep training had to happen. The first night, my little boy screamed for three hours. I stood outside his door, crying along with him the entire time, forcing myself not to give in and run to him. It was a special kind of torture. The next night, he cried for an hour. The third night, a miracle happened: he slept through the night, and so did I.

I'm not advocating for sleep training, but I *am* advocating for finding the solutions that work for you regardless of what the mommy bloggers and parenting experts say. Every parent is different. Every child is an individual. Every family has unique needs. Don't let the guilt get to you.

In late 2012, I felt like I'd gotten the hang of work and motherhood and was ready to do it all over again with another baby. This time I was smarter and managed to only put on an extra twenty-five pounds at the end of my second trimester. However, even that was too much on me. To make it worse, I would often forget that I was pregnant and still walk at a very fast pace. One day I was running to a café on campus to grab a quick bite in between meetings. I didn't notice there was a spill on the floor and walked right into it.

I'd done it again! Another slip and fall. To make matters worse, I hadn't learned from the first time, landing again on my tailbone and causing another crack. I still remember that fall vividly because it was during lunch hour, and the café was packed. After the fall, I couldn't move any part of my body for a long time, and so many people surrounded me to see if I was OK. I tried to get up but couldn't, and people were scared to lift me due to my very pregnant situation. Lying there in embarrassment, I remember wondering if it would be too awkward to just cover my face so nobody could identify me (or if it was too late). Within a few minutes, security arrived. I told them I could get up and walk again, that I just needed a minute. They, on the other hand, believed I needed an ambulance instead. That was both the first time I'd ridden in an ambulance and the first time I had ever had so many people taking care of me all at once. I had to call my teams and cancel all my afternoon meetings that day. Sure enough, as I'd predicted, I had another broken tailbone that resulted in one week of bed rest before going back to work again.

In March 2013, my second son was born. The recovery was much worse than the first time, although I only had fifteen pounds to lose after the delivery. I was thirty-six years old at that time, but somehow, I felt my body had reached its end-of-life. Every morning I would wake up feeling extremely exhausted, like I had just run a marathon, even after a very good night's sleep. I didn't understand what was going on with my body, nor did I have time to think about it. I just kept going: work and home, work and home. The show had to go on.

When my younger son was one, I made a big change. Our live-in nanny was wonderful, but the guilt was getting to me: they were closer to her than they were to me. I felt like I wasn't spending enough time with my children, and part of me felt like I'd failed as their mother. So, I let the nanny go and decided to send both to the same daycare, which was a bilingual school where they both could learn Chinese growing up. As part of that change in routine, I decided to send them to school every morning before 8:00 a.m. and pick them up around 6:00 p.m., committing to spending all my spare time with them.

Somewhere along the way, I noticed I was acting out of character. I would spend time with family with a smile and ensure I was energetic and charged at work, but I felt very sad inside when I was alone, seemingly for no reason. I would show up and go through the motions daily. I lost my curiosity and ambition. I was sleepwalking through my life. I felt extreme fatigue all the time, especially waking up in the morning. I would be angry with Curt for no reason. I started to be angrier with myself and felt like a failure, also for no reason. I felt like my body was falling apart, and the only activity I could do was to soak in a very hot bath, as if the steamy water would take all the exhaustion away. After we sent the kids to bed after a long day, I would lock myself in the bathroom for hours. Then, I would lie in the hot bath staring at the ceiling, the sadness pressing down on me.

I didn't understand what was going on. It seemed that I had it all by that time: two smart and healthy sons, a supportive husband, a great career, and a beautiful home of our own. I was financially secure and had loving family and friends. All the boxes that signal success? Check, check, check. Why, then, did I feel like a failure more than at any other time in my life? Why, after I got everything I'd ever wanted in life, did I feel sad and worthless instead of happy and grateful?

Maybe I'm just tired, I told myself repeatedly.

But if that is true, why am I so tired? I used to train for three or four hours riding bikes and didn't feel tired, and I don't even have time to work out now with two toddlers around. Is my polio finally getting worse? Is it the post-polio syndrome that finally got to me? But if it's just that my physical condition is getting worse, why is that impacting my character? Why am I feeling sad about that?

A million questions and thoughts raced through my mind, but I kept all those to myself because I didn't want to appear ungrateful.

It's pointless to talk about my sadness because I have no right to feel sad about anything! How can I complain when I have it all? There are people living in this world who must deal with real hardship, and they just keep going. I refuse to become an ungrateful person who lives a privileged life and complains about her nonexistent problems.

I kept moving through my life like that, upholding outward appearances while spiraling inwardly...until one day the dam broke.

Life looks perfect—this is what we put on social media (2015)

Life behind the scenes—this is the reality we hide from people (2015)

9.

EXPERIENCING
THIS WONDERFUL LIFE
(2015–PRESENT)

The Master said, "At fifteen, my heart was set upon learning; at thirty,
I had become established; at forty, I was no longer perplexed; at fifty,
I knew what's ordained by Heaven; at sixty, I obeyed; at seventy,
I could follow my heart's desires without transgressing the line."[22]

(子曰: "吾十有五，而志于学，三十而立，四十而不惑，
五十而知天命，六十而耳顺，七十而从心所欲，不逾矩。)

Confucius (551–479 BC) was a teacher from ancient China.
Many of his lectures were recorded in the book Confusion Analects,
which contains the above wisdom.

Thousands of years ago, this great thinker shared how at a different age,
our focus and experience in life evolves. I learned this saying at a
very young age but didn't fully understand it until I grew older.

At fifteen, I had my mind set on learning; at thirty, I stood firm
by being independent; only at forty, I was less confused about
life itself and started to learn how to experience it with joy.

I hope you, too, can navigate the ups and downs. Good or bad...
all our experiences are part of life's beauty.

---

[22]   "Primary Source Document with Questions (DBQs): Selections from the Confucian Analects:
On Confucius as Teacher and Person," Asia for Educators, Columbia University, accessed
February 14, 2023, 1, http://afe.easia.columbia.edu/ps/cup/confucius_teacher.pdf.

9.1. DEPRESSION AND RECOVERY (2015–2017)

"Did you bring the ball today?" my son asked from the back seat as I drove him to daycare one morning.

"What ball?"

"You forgot?" he yelled, upset. "Today is 'bring a ball day,' and I don't have a ball! It's not fair!"

Then, it hit me: suddenly I remembered that it was the week when, *every single day*, parents were supposed to bring a picked item to preschool for their kids to share with the others. Monday, for example, was "bring a ball day." I'd read the note from the school and even put the various dates on the family calendar: bring a ball day, bring a toy day, bring a book day… That weekend before, though, I'd had to spend a lot of time at work and wasn't able to go through my routine to prepare for the week ahead. I didn't have an excuse, nor was it the first time something like that had happened.

"You forgot the ball. You forgot my Huggy. You forget everything. You are the *worst* mom ever!" the sad kid announced.

That hurt, even though it came from a four-year-old. How did I drop my performance from being the "best mom ever" the night before when he kissed me goodnight to being the "worst mom" the next morning? I felt horrible and tried to figure out what I could do to fix the emergency.

If I drop him off before 8:00 a.m., my first meeting isn't until 9:00 a.m. I'll have time to make it to the store and back.

I recall running up and down Walmart's aisles, murmuring, "Ball, ball, where are the damn balls?" After I'd finally found one and checked out, I remembered I'd forgotten to send diapers to daycare for my younger son. I raced back into the store again, checked out again, and dropped off the ball and diapers to their classrooms, apologizing to their teachers for my mistakes. Once I arrived at work, I realized my 9:00 a.m. meeting was at another campus.

How did I miss that?

I blamed myself and raced back to my car to drive over. By the time I arrived at the correct location, I was sweating, panting, and exhausted...just in time to start the workday: ready, set, charge.

This example doesn't even describe a particularly bad morning. Who knew there were so many things little kids needed? It wasn't just time-consuming; it was also nerve-racking. I feared daily that I might leave my kids in the back seat and forget about them. I feared that someday I would be too busy working and forget to pick them up at night. I had time and location-based reminders made for things like: "check back seat for kids," "Friday is PJ Day for daycare," and so on.

Once, I got a call from daycare informing me that our kids somehow had lice. *What?* Only then, I realized Curt and I had forgotten to bathe them for four days at that point, and many families at daycare had just taken vacations the week before, including us. Regardless of our busy schedules, one of us needed to pick up the kids right away and do a lice treatment at home.

One of the worst experiences of daycare was when our younger son, at around two years old, bit another child. After being warned twice, he got kicked out. Neither Curt nor I saw that coming. At the first warning, we'd talked to him, and he'd seemed to understand that biting was bad. The second day, he bit again, and we had a longer talk with him. The third day, he was told to leave that daycare, *forever*. We had no clue because he was only biting one little girl, but that didn't matter at the time: someone had to go get him, and I was the closest.

I hustled to pick him up, panicking and trying to get him into another daycare. I was lucky to get him transferred to a new daycare the same week, thankfully, and he never bit again. Every day, I was just trying to get through without making any mistakes, both at home and at work.

If you could hear my brain at that time, this is what it would've sounded like driving to work every morning, with my kids in the back seat:

The slide I did last week still needs some work. I've got to find some time to polish it. Did I pack their favorite blankies? I hope no kids get into trouble today. They both looked upset at daycare yesterday. How did our friend Mark handle their seven kids and we can't even do two? Did I get all the action items aligned with partner teams and project managers synced for the feature planning? What else could I do to solve the resource issue? Oh, I forgot to tell Curt he has to pick up kids this week; remember to text him later. I need to practice the speech I need to deliver at WWDC [Worldwide Developers Conference]. Why did I agree to be on the big stage talking? Did I order allergy medicine for the kids? Their noses are all stuffed. Why are my back and tailbone still bothering me; it's been so long…

It went on like that, and the world kept spinning.

I found myself overwhelmed, and I couldn't understand why. I'd done harder things before, but why did I feel so hopeless, sad, and out of strength constantly? Every day at work, people would come to me for answers and solutions, but I had no answer or solution for myself.

It must be just a phase, and it will be over once the kids are bigger, I told myself, trying to bring comfort.

Somewhere around 2016, I was at a doctor's exam due to my abnormal daily physical exhaustion. The nurse asked me to fill out a questionnaire. I didn't know why I'd gotten that questionnaire, but I filled it out anyway, like a zombie. When she reviewed it, she plainly refused to let me leave. "You have shown very obvious signs of depression," she said.

"I don't think so," I countered, slightly irritated. I was tired. It was perfectly normal.

The nurse gently explained to me that I had responded "yes" to one of the questions screenings for suicidal ideation and depression: "Do you sometimes think the world is better off without you?"

"Well, the question said 'sometimes,'" I said. "Doesn't everyone 'sometimes' think that way? But don't worry; I'm too busy to be sad or to kill myself."

My attempt at a joke fell flat.

I was taken to a quiet room to wait for another doctor to talk to me. I was very annoyed because that changed my whole afternoon schedule. I decided to just tell them that they had made a mistake so I could quickly get out of there. A female doctor came in and asked me follow-up questions. How's your work? *Fantastic.* How is your family, your husband? *Couldn't be better!* How is your financial situation? *I never have to worry about it.* But then she looked at me and asked:

"How are *you?*"

My throat started burning, my eyes welled up with tears, and I knew if I opened my mouth to answer, only sobs would escape. But it was too late. The floodgates gave way to what felt like all the tears I'd suppressed in my entire lifetime.

I sat in that office and cried for three hours. *Three hours.* I'd never cried that much in my life. Or since. What cracked me wide open was not only that simple question ("How are *you?*") but also the way she had delivered it, looking deeply into my eyes.

The staff was kind. I forgot about time, and she didn't look at the clock either, as if she knew before walking in that it wasn't going to be quick. She sat with me and let me cry and talk, even though I wasn't making much sense. I kept saying, "I don't know why I'm crying. My life is great. I have no reason to be sad, no reason to cry. I am so sorry. I don't know what's wrong with me. My kids think I am a terrible mother. I need to get back to work. You know the more time I spend here, the more time tonight I must spend catching up with work? But I can't stop crying. What's wrong with me?"

My doctor just listened to me, let me keep rambling. When it was quiet, she asked, "When is the last time you took some time off for yourself?"

Myself?

I realized that I hadn't spent any time taking care of myself since my first son was born. I was always thinking of the kids, work, things around the house, my parents in China, and more work. Even during family vacations, it wasn't relaxing to drag two toddlers around. When I was alone, my brain just spun with to-dos.

"Do parents really do that, take time for themselves? And if they do, do I deserve it?"

My doctor assured me that yes, every parent deserves to take some time off for themselves. She recommended that I take some time off for my mental health and to give my body and mind a break. I realized that other than the week that I'd broken my tailbone, I hadn't taken any sick days for many years. Even during that week, I was having remote meetings, lying down on my couch. Faced with the question of how I felt, I discovered I *did* feel sick, mentally and physically.

I asked the doctor if my issues were caused by PPS from polio. Unfortunately, my doctor didn't know anything about PPS, and I couldn't find any other hospitals around that specialized in polio patients. But the doctor recommended that I start working out at least three times a week. I thought chasing two boys around at home was enough of a workout, but she said it wasn't the same. She also suggested yoga and meditation to help me relax and clear my mind.

They took my blood for a comprehensive testing panel and put together a follow-up plan. I don't remember everything the doctor said to me, but I do remember this: "It's not your fault. You didn't do anything wrong. Sometimes brain chemicals get out of whack and cause these difficult emotions and feelings of deep sadness. There is nothing wrong with you as a person. It's a chemical reaction in your brain that you have no control over."

I would remind myself of her explanation during that phase. "It's the *chemicals* in my body, not a personal failure, that's making me feel this way." I said it to myself, over and over, like a mantra.

I didn't want to talk about the situation with anyone, but I did tell Curt that I may have depression and needed to have some time to myself to heal. Curt understood what I was going through and gave me the personal space that I needed. Since I was going through depression without showing it outwardly, I wondered if Curt might be experiencing something similar. I asked him if he was OK, and he confirmed that he was. He knew I was collapsing inside and assured me he would hold down the fort for me. He took care of the kids and was as supportive as possible.

I spent all my alone time doing workouts then soaking in the hot tub to relax my body, but my brain wouldn't stop.

I am nothing. I am worthless. The loop in my head was relentless, and sometimes I had scary thoughts. *What if I just sink slowly into this tub and end it all?*

Sometimes, the tiniest spark of hope, my doctor's voice, broke through. "It's not your fault, Libo. It's the chemicals messing you up. We'll figure it out and get you feeling better."

Once I felt that tiny glimmer of hope that I would get myself back, I'd climb out of the tub and put on a smile. I'd go out into the living room and spend time with my little family, pushing it all down until the next night.

I took some medication and vitamin D for the significant deficiencies detected in my blood. I worked out almost daily for thirty minutes until I sweated. I gradually felt better, and that phase of physical exhaustion and mental stress was gone within a year. I started to feel energetic and upbeat again. The specifics of my diagnosis and what my treatments were are not important.

What is important is that if this sounds familiar to you, please go to the doctor. You are not weak. You are not at fault. You deserve help. The world is *not* better off without you. The sooner you realize that, the better your chances for recovery. Don't let the darkness drag too long and swallow you like what it almost did to me.

I was lucky and grateful that the nurse noticed something about me, gave me that questionnaire, and stopped me from going back to work and home that day. Without that nurse and doctor, I could have developed severe depression without even knowing that I was sick. The chemicals in my body got balanced quickly, and I am glad I could leave that awful phase behind.

I slowly learned to take better care of myself. I learned that sleep, nutrition, exercise, relaxation, and stress management are all important, as is asking for help from others. I used to rely on myself only when anything would go wrong, but I learned to seek help from the doctors and others when I needed it. Lots of things can be improved or alleviated with lifestyle changes, but there are some that can't and require medication. It's OK to ask doctors to do what they're here to do: help us. You're not weak for taking medication. You are brave for seeking help.

Also, during my recovery, I did a task categorization for my life and employed a system of ranking things based on importance and urgency. I decided that I'd only keep urgent things in my brain—no more than three from life, and no more than four from work. I looked at my mental capacity like a queue that only held seven items: when something new came in at the top, something nonurgent had to go from the bottom. At work, I decided I would focus on growing better leaders in my organization so I could delegate more and refocus on critical tasks in my core competency areas. In life, I decided that the quality of time spent with my family mattered as much as, if not more than, the quantity. For example, I would spend dinnertime with my family and read the boys bedtime stories, but I would not try picking them up from school nor cleaning the house.

We found a professional service to pick up the kids so both of us could get home without a rush or stay late for work if needed. We hired a professional cleaner to come weekly to our home. For a while, we even tried to have our laundry outsourced, which turned out to be more work for us. Curt decided to take that on because he was very specific about how laundry should be done, and we all helped getting it ready for him. Whatever helped Curt and me stay sane at our work and at home is what we tried.

I recognized we were privileged and lucky to be able to afford getting help from professional services. But I didn't feel guilty about it from a household perspective anymore because those tasks were on my nonimportant list. If I trusted my teams at work to do their jobs correctly, in life, I must trust someone to drive my kids safely between school and home. It wasn't easy, but we had to let go. Something had to give. I realized I was not a supermom or superwoman who could do everything on her own...and more than that, I didn't have to be.

As for the kids, I made sure they started taking on their own responsibilities. It's not the mother's job to remember every single day-care activity. They needed to learn how to be prepared for the next day, as age allowed. If they forgot, it was as much their fault as it was mine. Both boys started dressing themselves in the morning, following their own routines, and getting ready for daycare or preschool. During the weekend, we would do family chores together, teaching the kids more about responsibility. They learned how to clean up after themselves quickly. Also, our kids understand that it's not acceptable to call me the "worst mom ever," even if they are super mad. I made them aware that I am the best and the *only* mother they've got! Ever since then, they've never used that language toward me or others again.

Curt and I made plans together and executed as a team. Gradually, I got my life back, and we were happy again as a family.

I know I might not win the "best mother" award, but lowering expectations is sometimes the right thing to do. We are all healthy, together, telling each other "I love you" every day. What else is better than that?

It's of course difficult for all new parents, but it is still much harder for moms. It seemed like I was always the one getting called at work when one of the boys misbehaved or got sick at school. Even when Curt was happy to deal with the issue. I was also expected to volunteer much more than Curt, even though we had equally demanding jobs. Though there are certainly exceptions, society places substantial default responsibility on mothers. I've seen fathers lauded as superheroes, receiving public praise for doing less than an everyday mom.

These issues of equality in parenting are real, even in families like ours, where we are equal partners who respect each other. We discussed if one of us should become a stay-at-home parent. I wasn't the default choice.

In the end, both of us wanted to continue working—we couldn't deny our passion for technology and our love for working with brilliant people to build things. I hope when this type of conversation happens for other parents, women do not have to make sacrifices by default.

Today, I strive to be a better mom, wife, daughter, sister, and many other roles. I focus some energy on things that I didn't find important enough when I was younger, like cooking healthy meals or making a beautiful home. I work out every day, not until I'm about to pass out, but enough to be called "making a great effort." That's a fitting metaphor for my entire life right now. I don't torture myself, but I still push my limits.

This experience made me realize that success is more about what you feel inside than how your life looks from the outside. Only *you* know if you are truly happy inside. When you are not, find the reason for it, and figure out how to get that back in your life. This life is too beautiful to not enjoy every minute of it and too short to fake it just for others.

Lastly but most importantly, learn how to take care of yourself, and don't ever forget to love yourself! The best person who knows you is *you.*

Libo on stage for Worldwide Developers Conference (WWDC) (June 2015).

Libo in Town Hall for tech talk at Apple (March 2015).

9.2. GROWING WITH THE NEXT GENERATION

One of the reasons that your kids can drive you crazy is that they come with their own built-in personalities, which are not decided by you. My sons are, in many ways, totally different. We chose our first son's middle name, Cao, so we wouldn't lose my family heritage, so he is referred to as "Little C" in this book. Our second son's middle name is from the Meyers side, and he will be referred to as "Little M." Coincidentally, Little C's personality is a lot like mine: he likes to challenge everything, loves to debate, and has a hard time following rules. Little M, on the other hand, is very much like Curt: kind, helpful, and good at keeping himself out of trouble. Below is a typical example of how Little C and Little M deal with things totally differently.

Me: Hi, Little C. Can you help bring your laundry basket to the laundry room?

Little C: Why do you want to do that now?

Me: Because Saturday is our laundry day, and now is a good time.

Little C: But now it's not a good time for me.

Me: You are just playing video games; please help.

Little C: Why do I have to help? Why not ask M to help you?

Me: Because you are older than him, so you need to do more work than him.

Little C: So older people are supposed to do a lot more?

Me: Yes!

Little C: But you are much older than me, so you can just do a lot more and get that for yourself then?

Me (frustrated, exhausted, and giving up): Hi, Little M. Can you bring the basket to the laundry room?

Little M: OK, Mom!

Regardless of their different personalities, they both have to meet their parents' high expectations to earn any privileges in life. They both must do their chores inside the household as well as the backyard. Since the boys were young, Curt and I decided to each pick one extra activity for them. I picked Chinese, and he picked piano, initially. We did that for years: every Saturday, the kids would attend Chinese school in the morning and do homework in the afternoon. Every week, Curt would take them to piano lessons. Eventually, the kids protested to drop the piano, and we replaced it with VEX Robotics as Curt's pick. At a young age, of course, the boys hated all the extra work we asked them to do outside of school. They wanted to at least have one day off during the weekends, so we gave them each Sunday off. They named it "Do Nothing Day," or "Lazy Sunday."

In a strange way, these Lazy Sundays became a teaching moment for me, too. Curt and our boys showed me through their example that it is good and healthy to drop everything sometimes and be in the moment. They value my spending time with them just the way I am. I don't have to be useful or productive; I only need to be there and be present. I had grown up with the understanding that every minute of my life mattered and that I'd better not waste one. I didn't divide my daily schedule into hours, but down to ten-minute intervals.

If you are used to having your days planned out in ten-minute chunks, it's very hard to deviate from the plan and feel OK about it. When Curt and I dated, he'd ask me to cuddle sometimes. I'd put five minutes on the timer and say, "You can hold me until the alarm goes off, then I have to get moving and get things done." It sounds ridiculous, but I simply couldn't handle sitting still. As soon as I wasn't productive, I felt immense guilt creeping in.

For Lazy Sunday, the boys play lots of video games. When they ask me to play with them, I always decline. I tell them it's a waste of time because two hours of playing games gets me nowhere. "But Mom!" they explain, "It's for *fun*, and you don't have to get anywhere!" I eventually learned from the boys how to have some fun, but I also want the boys to learn perseverance by pushing themselves to achieve hard goals, including dealing with failures along the way. So, I've kept challenging my kids, and they have challenged me back.

Many years ago, I asked Little C to learn how to solve a Rubik's Cube. He said, "If you can't solve it, why ask me to learn it?" So I did. I told him I was able to solve it and showed him my approach. Within two hours, he'd learned how to solve it as well and even beat me speed-wise by the end of that day.

Another challenge I want both boys to achieve is to practice Karate. They both resisted and asked me, again, why I was putting some expectation on them when I couldn't even do it myself.

So, I signed up myself too.

Ever since then, I have been training with my boys, all starting as white belts. The scene during that early stage looks a bit funny: I was the only adult training with five- to twelve-year-old kids, while all the other parents watched. I am glad that phase didn't last long, since I practiced harder and got into more advanced belt color and started to train with only other adults at night.

In 2022, my boys are ten and twelve, and they have been growing into little adults who occasionally teach me a lesson. One day, I was asking Little C to do something, and he kept negotiating with me to avoid the work.

"But WHY do I have to do it?" he kept asking.

"Because I said so, and I am older and wiser." I got impatient and wished to end this conversation.

"Wow, that's ageism!"

"What? Ageism?"

"Yes, you are an ageist! You just discriminated against me based on my age. You think by default, older people are wiser. Young people can be just as wise!"

I realized he was right; I shouldn't use my age as the reason to convince him to listen to me. Of course, I had to use the "because I am your mother" card. As you can imagine, that was equally unconvincing to him, but at least he couldn't call me an ageist.

We grew up with different circumstances, and while I'm glad they don't have it as difficult as I did, I don't want them to get obsessed with video games or social media. Just when I think we've planted enough seeds in their brains for them to desire to be the best engineers or scientists, they still think being a YouTuber is the coolest career on Earth!

I try to remember that they are growing up in a completely different world than I did. I am glad they can have fun and be silly. At the same time, I wish to instill a solid work ethic in them and secretly hope they'll change their job aspirations. I ask them if they maybe want to create technology to help society instead of making YouTube content. So far, it's a no. But I have a few more years to keep working on that, or else I guess I will be the first subscriber to their channel when they are old enough to have one.

It's not easy for me to influence them. On the other hand, it's not easy for me to change either. On our Lazy Sundays, I must force myself to relax like everyone else. My default is to get dinner cooking in the Crock-Pot, pack up the boys' school bags with supplies for the next day while catching up on a TED Talk, then do a workout session while waiting. It feels impossible for me to keep myself from multitasking. If we watch a movie together, I'm usually off to the side, working out while watching or at least doing some yoga. Now I use my Lazy Sunday to digitize Dad's handwritten manuscripts for his book or write my own. I also try to practice martial arts by myself as much as possible when my brain or eyes need a break. I can convince myself that those are Lazy Sunday activities because I truly do them for my own enjoyment, and they're fun.

But still, it's an accomplishment for me that I learned to sit and drink a cup of coffee occasionally without giving in to any guilt. It is an achievement that I no longer set a timer when cuddling with my husband. These may be small things to other people, but they symbolize a larger internal shift to me. I don't always have to perform. I don't always have to be productive. I don't always have to be moving on to the next step. I can take a minute, breathe, and be with myself and with the people I love the most.

This represents work, just a different kind of work.

"What's the hardest thing you've ever done?" I was asked by someone at a professional development forum, where people try to seek answers from leaders who they think are "successful" and have "figured it out."

I paused for a while, but my answer did not involve technical challenges nor projects at work. "Honestly, raising kids is the hardest thing I've had to do!"

Undeniably, I've experienced many tough projects, harsh deadlines, and impossible missions during my professional career. However, I've always had a sense of being in control dealing with professional challenges because I believe that—when you put a great team together, set a clear goal, and have the right collaboration, focus, and innovation—we can solve any challenge in front of us. Raising kids, however, is a different game. It's the first time I experienced that no matter how hard I try, the control is, in many ways, out of our hands. All we can do as parents is to be there for them, love them, try to steer them into the right direction, and sometimes see them fail or succeed in their own ways in life, just like what I've done for myself.

Curt and I try to be their friends at times, but we never forget that at the end of the day, we are still their parents. I don't know how my parents were able to pass down their family values to me, but they certainly did. To this day, I'm not sure if I am able to pass down those same values to my own boys. Maybe it's too early to tell. Maybe I just need to wait patiently until they start to tackle this world themselves. Maybe then, we will all realize that they've been carrying the family values all along.

9.3. BLACK BELT IN KARATE

As far as I can remember, I have always been very physically active. Even during the years I had to go through surgeries and ended up with casts on my polio leg, I would still either hop around with my only good leg (or use crutches or a wheelchair) to keep moving. The only few years when I forgot to work out and take care of my body were when the kids were little, and I experienced the worst time of my life. Being physically active is now a habit of how I live my life. Taking care of my body is as important as taking care of my mind. There is no reason for us not to continue to grow our minds and bodies. After all, we only get one mind and one body in this life!

To take care of my body, it's very important to know my own limitations. Of course, there are scientific approaches to training, but we are all built differently. Only you know how your body reacts to various activities. Before I was twenty-eight years old, I don't recall experiencing any pain in my leg (when there was no surgery), just extreme exhaustion when I used it too much. But during that brutal hundred-mile bike ride against the wind that took me eleven and a half hours, I started experiencing pain. At some point, I started to notice there was a pivot point of the polio leg. After I reached that threshold, I'd experience sharp pain from the inside of my bone. It was so deep that it almost felt like my bone marrow was being poked at. I would lie in bed, and that pain would come and go every few minutes. Luckily, I have a high pain tolerance, so this wasn't my biggest problem associated with the leg.

My biggest problem is that sometimes my polio leg becomes totally nonfunctional after that certain pivot point of usage. It means I can't even use that leg as a stick to hold my body for even a moment. Once the polio leg reaches the ground and has just the tiniest pressure on it, the sharpest pain starts occurring throughout my leg, hip, and even some portion of my spine. The good thing is that when that happens, I only need to stop using the leg for about a day or two, and it will just recover on its own. I started to design experiments to figure out when I'd reach the pivot point with certain types of activities. As a result of those experiments, at age forty, I know that it's safe for me to ride on the bike for about sixty miles if I don't try to use any strength in my polio leg. For walking, it's safe to take 10,000 steps a day, but I will be in trouble the next day if I am above 12,000 steps. For jumping on a trampoline, one hour a day should be fine if I only use the polio leg for occasional balancing. For different activities, I know clearly where my limit is (and how to avoid pushing it) so I can keep being functional after a long workout session. I also see that the pivot point changes over age—as I grow older, that point comes earlier.

After I learned my body and its limits before pain occurred, I came up with ways to push for more without getting myself in trouble. Curt set up a sit-down elliptical for me in our bedroom. This way, if I reach my polio leg usage quota by the end of the day, I can switch to the elliptical and only work out with the other three limbs. Curt also got me an arcade basketball game after I complained that I didn't like any of his pinball machine collections. For the basketball arcade game, I simply use my good leg to hold myself up and shoot hoops to exercise my upper body until I sweat. That game is the only game in our household where I've ranked the highest score. I also became good at doing weighted Hula-Hoops, which allow me to exercise my whole waist, standing on only the good leg. I can work out for thirty minutes with a three-pound Hula-Hoop, supported with only one leg, without much sweat, which I do a few times a week while reading a book or watching something.

Karate, though, was something I never thought I'd try. For one, I can't have good balance and control of my body with one weak leg. Also, I can't kick effectively. I can swing the polio leg to the side, but I can't kick with it. If I tried to kick with my good leg, I would fall easily because I'd be using the weak leg to stand and balance.

Still, I wanted my boys to be able to enjoy the fun of practicing karate while learning the skills to defend themselves if needed. When they challenged me to join them, I agreed. Why? Because if I want to teach my boys to gain confidence and believe in themselves, how can I not even believe in myself? I know it will be extremely hard for me to become a black belt, but nothing is preventing me from trying. I can't let my mind limit myself before my body does.

I was very curious to know if any polio survivor had ever earned a black belt. After some research, I found one: Bjorn Rasmussen, who wrote a book called *From Polio to Ironman: Thoughts about Life and Overcoming*. It's a tiny self-published book with only fifty-three pages that recorded how he conquered multiple ironman races and earned a black-belt distinction. His polio leg is more functional than mine based on what he described, but I am currently younger. He started training at age fifty-two and got his black belt seven years later. Also, while researching, I discovered that many others with disabilities had earned their black belts, too. I found a seventy-three-year-old woman in a wheelchair who was able to break two boards during her test.[23] I even found a sixth-degree-black-belt wheelchair karate teacher.[24]

---

[23] Mary Sturgill, "73-Year-Old Woman With Disabilities Earns Black Belt in Tae Kwon Do," News19, March 13, 2016, https://www.wltx.com/article/news/73-year-old-woman-with-disabilities-earns-black-belt-in-tae-kwon-do/101-79781103.

[24] Attitude, "6th Dan Black Belt Wheelchair Karate Teacher (Being Me: John)," November 27, 2021, YouTube video, 23:05, https://www.youtube.com/watch?v=KUtAjpWLruQ.

I am inspired and encouraged by those pioneers who have made me believe I could do it too. Though I am a smaller woman who is five foot two, I am only in my midforties, and I do have one fully functional leg. There is no excuse for me if someone has already shown it's possible. That's the power of role models. So, I marked the date and set a goal: my boys and I will achieve our respective black belts before I reach age fifty and before they get to college. Only after that belt color can we choose to stop or continue with our own training journey next. I am glad that my boys challenged me, and I am glad that I didn't back down from such a challenge.

"A black belt is just a white belt who will never quit." This is a quote I particularly liked when I started learning about karate. Though I am aiming to earn a black belt, I also understand that the color of the belt doesn't fully reflect someone's skill in karate. However, getting a black belt does require lots of dedicated effort, and normally it takes many years of training before getting to that level. Based on the type of karate you practice, a decent organization may award you a black belt in five to ten years. I have talked to some black belts, and many of them don't think it's a huge accomplishment because it merely marks the beginning of another journey for them. Undeniably, though, it's not a small deal either because most people give up along the way as the training gets harder. To me, my goals for becoming a black belt are many: to find out where my physical limitation is in martial arts; to share the learnings with others who have similar or different disabilities; to appreciate and enjoy a sport that can be practiced in a supportive community; to build the confidence that I, as a little tiny woman, can and will be able to defend myself with skills when such scenario occurs; to experience the same journey with my sons so I can feel their struggle, pain, and joy during this period of their lives; and more.

The type of karate I picked for our training is called kenpo, which is "an all-inclusive system of martial arts based on ancient martial arts methods applied to solve modern-day violent scenarios using logic and practicality to survive nonconsensual, violent altercations." I picked a local family studio that's headed by a professor who is a seventh-degree black belt and has been practicing karate for over fifty years. I consulted with my professor to see if, with my condition, he could train me. He was very encouraging and believed in me—and my boys were watching—so I kept training. We started with many basic forms and techniques, and my professor has allowed me to adjust my moves based on what my body will allow. For many things, I can compensate with my upper body strength and adjust accordingly. I train harder than my boys because they have nothing to prove, but I do. I started training several nights a week and practicing on my own when possible. I absolutely love the culture of the studio, where not only the professors but also many black belts training there teach new students like me, lending us their skill, time, and patience.

After a long day working in the high-tech world, dragging my weary body at night to the training studio where I can punch, kick, and practice sparring has become a habit I've begun to enjoy. I believe that joy comes from my curiosity and desire to learn things that are new and challenging. Even in my midforties, I am still that little girl who stays hungry and foolish, who just keeps limping forward toward any goal I set out for myself. So far, I have been earning higher ranks gradually along with my boys. I don't know where life will take me after this journey of karate, but I am sure this won't be the last challenge I try to tackle. There are too many unique and exciting things in life worth experiencing. I plan to take on as many challenges as possible, until the day I stop breathing. It's a crime not to take advantage of the opportunities life presents to you, and it's a shame if we don't chase after things that are hard but worth having.

For now, I envision a black-belt martial artist gazing at me from the top of the mountain, waiting for me to join. I can see that when I finally arrive there, the Yoda-like master will have a calm smile and say to me: "Arrived, I see you! Much to learn, you still have."

9.4. EXOSKELETON AND RUNNING

When I first got into the college that wasn't of my own choice, there were times I just needed to let all my negative feelings out—I wanted to scream at the top of my lungs, I wanted to punch something with all my strength, and I wanted to run until I couldn't any longer. I couldn't do any of those things with others around me because I felt the need to hide outbursts from others, especially those who loved and cared about me. It felt as if I was constantly holding my breath in front of people, making the need for that breath to come out much greater when I was alone.

That meant sometimes I got up early in the morning, before anyone else in the dorm woke up, to scream. Specifically, I would go to a close-by mountain, climb all the way to the top, and scream there alone as loud as I could, letting it all out. That felt good for a short period of time—that is, when I was able to do it at all. Unfortunately, most of the sadness and anger arrived at nighttime, and I was afraid to go out alone to the trails. That left only one close place for letting it out...in a quieter way this time: the school running track next to the dorm. I would wait until it was completely dark, when nobody could see me even up close (we had no light around the track). In that total darkness, I attempted running. However, what I could achieve was more of a fast limp instead of a run because my polio leg doesn't have the strength to push the ground for each step. "Running" with only one leg plus a stick-like lower limb never lasted long, and I usually had to stop after less than two hundred meters. That was around the time the pounding impact on my polio leg turned into full-blown exhaustion.

I remember the moment when I watched *Forrest Gump* and he started running. I watched as his leg braces began to fall off, and my heart pounded harder as he continued to run, unleashed. People asked him why he ran, and he said he just felt like running. That scene pulled me in! I *understood* why he ran—he needed something to clear his mind, and the focus of running helped to get those complex emotions out of his system. What I've always admired about running is that it's an activity where you spend time with yourself, no matter who else is around and no matter what the outside environment is: it's your own time with this world. Just you, your heartbeat, and your pace.

Later in life, I accepted myself and made peace with my polio leg. Part of that acceptance was vowing not to let it be a limiting factor for anything I wanted to achieve. *It's part of me*, I thought. *But if I have been trying to get better in all aspects of my life, the polio better keep up as well. I refuse to let my disability be the bottleneck for anything I want to experience in this wonderful life.*

After I started karate, I was frustrated that I couldn't do certain kicks with firm control. So I started investigating if there was any device that could help me gain the strength to kick effectively. It was a lengthy process since neither I nor my doctors knew what could help me. After researching modern medical devices that could improve my mobility, I began asking my doctors for their professional opinions. They recommended I take some trials, but I found the general movement-assisting devices to be too bulky for me, actually making movement more difficult. My requirements are totally different from others who mostly just want to be able to walk. I want to be able to kick and do karate effectively. My doctor kept asking me if my work would require me to use such a device, reminding me that was the only way insurance would cover it. I told her I could move around just fine for work, but I wanted more than that—much more. Specifically, to kick like a black belt in karate! The doctor reiterated that I would have to pay for the device fully and that it would take a great deal of effort to find one that works for me. I accepted all those conditions because, while my work matters a great deal to me, so does my experience of life. Eventually, I was referred to a clinic that used to make US Army medical products and has helped many severely injured veterans to be redeployed. I was so thrilled to hear that! *If this device can help injured veterans to fight again, it must be hard-core enough for me,* I thought. *A soldier must be able to kick and run, right? Does that mean I could potentially run as well?*

The facility is called Hanger Clinic, located in Gig Harbor, Washington. The clinic's CPO, Ryan Blanck, designed the Intrepid Dynamic Exoskeletal Orthosis (IDEO) while working at an army medical center in 2009. The device I would try is called ExoSym, which is an evolution of the IDEO, designed for wider use. Ryan first talked with me over the phone to ensure that I understood all aspects of this device, the process, and the effort involved in it. I committed to anything needed on my side to make it happen, including two trips to their clinic for feasibility testing and device usage training, followed by various self-training afterward. The device adaptation process can take months, even years.

The first visit to the Hanger Clinic was eye opening for me. Under the sign of Hanger Clinic was their mission statement: *Empowering Human Potential,* which got my blood pumping right away. At the entrance, there was a US flag reminding people of the original mission of this clinic—to help veterans gain their power back. On the walls, there were posters of many inspiring human beings with their prosthetic limbs, playing the sports or the activities they love. There was a world map with location pins all over it, indicating those whom Ryan and the Clinic have helped to reach their potential postinjury. Ryan took me around to tour the facility with the workshops where my future device would be made, and he assured me that he would do whatever he needed to help me to achieve my goals. He took the 3D cast of my leg and all the measurements needed to make the device fit perfectly to my body. He examined me carefully, watching how I walk and use my body, before giving me a testing device the next day. During those conversations and tests, what really surprised me was the misunderstanding I had about my own body. I had always thought my polio leg would remain weak and that there was not much I could do with those damaged nerves. Ryan watched me walking back and forth thoughtfully before saying something that was mind-blowing to me: "Libo, do you know you have a very strong glute on the polio side?"

"My polio butt muscles?" I was surprised.

"Yes, the muscle surrounding your hip joint—your glute is strong enough to make this work." Ryan was very certain that muscle was going to help me leverage this device.

I never knew my butt could play a big part in walking and other motions. Ryan spent a lot of time training me to walk consciously using my glute, which I call "butt walking." Instead of dragging my polio leg while walking as a habit, I need to consciously tighten my right butt muscles to move each step forward so that my body won't swing so much as a result of over-compensation. If I don't use my glute properly, the device could become a burden to me instead of helping me get stronger. While he was trying to figure out how to make me kick better, I asked if there is a potential for me to run as well.

"That's possible," he said. "But you might need two devices—one for running, and one for kicking."

I was very excited to hear that potential, even though that means before I head out every day, I must decide carefully if that day I want to run or kick someone's ass—a tradeoff I must make, I suppose. But it is better than no choices.

I waited patiently for my second trial a month later, when a real carbon-fiber material device would be made to fit me perfectly. The night before the trial, I was so excited that I stayed up the whole night thinking about all the things I could do with this device. I got up many times, just to "butt walk" around so I could exercise my glute even more before the morning came.

When I finally arrived there, instead of letting me put on the device to start running and kicking (as I had imagined), Ryan asked me to use only the bottom part of the device and have Rebecca, one of their trainers, teach me to walk correctly instead.

"Trust the process," Ryan said. "You must learn how to walk with this properly before running."

For two days, Rebecca and I did various activities so that I would "wake up the muscles" that I didn't know existed in me. We did various physical activity tests with my polio leg. When I thought there wasn't any strength in there, Rebecca would identify a tiny motion and point out that I had a piece of muscle there, just waiting for me to "wake it up." She kept reminding me to "recruit all the muscles" and "don't let your core and glute go." Without the device, though I was limping with weakness, it felt easier to move around because my body had already learned how to compensate for the weak leg without me having to think about it. But with the device, my body still tried to compensate (out of habit, not need), and I still walked by swinging my hip around. Now, the trainers helped me see why each step must be "intentional and purposeful." In order to do that, I must build the necessary strength in my core and glutes so that I can better leverage the exoskeleton and improve my posture.

In karate, to punch with maximum power, you must move your hip and torso in the right direction along with the direction of your fist—and that's how I felt about the process. I must make the rest of my body stronger so that I can come out stronger with this leg, and the foundation must be built correctly before piling layers on top. I must trust the process and build up my confidence for more capabilities over time. Belief is a strange thing—I never thought I had active muscles in my polio leg, but once Rebecca told me they are there and they can get stronger if I start recruiting them for usage, I started to feel their existence. Overnight, I felt lots of spasms coming from the polio leg, and Ryan told me that it's the reaction from the muscle exhaustion. I woke them up!

It's a powerful feeling knowing that there is some potential in me I hadn't yet tapped into. I began to research things I never thought I would research before, like "people with polio running in Olympics," and I couldn't believe a result popped up. At the 1960 Rome Olympics, Wilma Rudolph, a polio survivor, became the first American woman to win three gold medals in a single Olympic Games.[25] She used to wear a leg brace, and her family took turns massaging her leg for years. Along with physical therapy and training, she eventually had the leg brace removed and won Olympic races. That story blew my mind! It takes only one example to see what is possible,

---

[25] Arlisha R. Norwood, "Wilma Rudolph," National Women's History Museum, 2017, https://www.womenshistory.org/education-resources/biographies/wilma-rudolph.

and she is that example. I know that her condition might've been different from mine, and it might be too late for me to race in the Olympic Games. But at least I learned that this disease is something that *could* evolve into recovery instead of only becoming worse over time.

After my time with Rebecca, I was so excited to return the following day for more training. My confidence was high! Ryan designed a running knee piece and another piece attempting to combine both running and kicking functionality. I felt stronger with both pieces, but nobody can master these devices on day one—or two. I must change years' worth of walking habits to make this device feel like a natural part of my movement instead of a contraption going against it. We trained for hours in each of the following days, and I was walking, jumping, running, going up and down stairs, and using various gym equipment, including a standing elliptical that I could never do before without the device. Rebecca would observe my initial form and teach me the proper position for each workout session, ensuring my core and glutes were being put to work.

At the end of the training, Ryan believed I was at 30 percent of my potential and would need about six months to gain the other 70 percent. I love the fact that this device requires me to get stronger over time instead of only assisting me. The more I gain core strength, the better the device will work for me. As of this writing, I need to follow the training routine at home after the trial session and work hard with it. Comfort and growth don't go together; people grow when they face challenges, and I love this challenge that demands me to be stronger.

There was one poster on the wall for the Hanger Clinic, written by someone who had gotten an ExoSym device in the past: "Six months from now, you can be in a completely different place mentally, spiritually, and physically. Keep working and believing in yourself. You got this!"

I got this! Though I am not running or kicking like a pro yet, only one month after training with this device, I can already work out on the elliptical for at least one and a half hours, and it's just the beginning. This technology will empower me to tap into all the potential that I didn't know I had before. If you have anything in your life that's limiting you, go find your own Ryan and the support that can help you to unleash your potential. Don't give up! You got this as well!

This marks the halftime of my life, which could be the pivot point where I could start to *leap* forward instead of *limp* forward.

I could never have gotten to this point alone. That's why, now that you have read my stories, I would like to take you back 3,000 years: to the stories of my roots, the Cao family. The reason I have been able to climb mountains today is because of the various mountains my ancestors climbed before me. The rich history of the Cao family reveals the origin of my family's spirit and perseverance century after century, generation after generation...

Libo with her exoskeleton leg that enables her to
practice karate and run (Dec. 2022).

10

THE STORIES FROM GENERATIONS BEFORE ME

曹氏家乘叙

人本乎祖如水之有源木之有本由来尚矣我曹氏定姓以来相传有两派其一曹安在夏为诸侯赐姓曹于春秋为邾战国为邹汉曹参其苗裔也其一曹叔振铎之后以国为氏居曹州之定陶己乃迁居嘉祥南来范李金元间又迁汶阳曹庄自时尚彦达荣德至义赠嘉议大夫礼部尚书上轻车都尉追封东平郡侯越七世凡十一世我支始祖只嘉公复于前明年间又迁梁宝寺之西南十八里

As I am still learning and growing, I continue to ask
the question, "Where am I coming from?"

That is not a question that can merely be answered by
geography alone. It is so much more than that.

My ancestors who came before us, regardless of
what those individual journeys looked like, made choices
and sacrifices that they ultimately hoped would
benefit the generations who came later.

Our great-great-great-grandparents. Our great-grandparents.
Our grandparents. Our parents. You and me.
They lived—and so we must live—not only for ourselves,
but for the good of future generations.

The legacy of my family is such that each generation takes the
family to a higher and better place than the one prior, being kind
to others along the way. We always prepare, awaiting and creating
opportunities, and grit our teeth through difficult moments—
times of war, disease, and starvation. Sometimes those moments last
years, even decades, and sometimes they last seconds. We do not falter.

We know actions are greater than words. We take the right action,
time after time, and know that the sun will come.

10.1. THE 3,000 YEARS OF CAO FAMILY TREE

As poet and author Maya Angelou famously said, "If you don't know where you've come from, you don't know where you are going."

China has the longest continuous civilization in history. Its first dynasty, Xia, began in 2070 BC, setting the stage for about 4,100 years (and counting) of history. Even before Xia, there were a few mythological kingdoms, and China's civilization and legends can be traced back up to around 5,000 years.

Growing up, I kept hearing that "China has about 5,000 years of history," but I never thought much of it until I started asking myself one question: *Where do I come from?*

The earliest known written records of the history of China date from as early as 1250 BC, from the Shang dynasty (1600–1046 BC). *Book of Origins* (世本) was the earliest Chinese encyclopedia, which recorded imperial genealogies and explained the origins of Chinese clan names. It was written during the second century BC at the time of the Han Dynasty (202 BC–AD 220).

Book of Origins recorded that as early as the third millennium BC, the legendary Chinese Yellow Emperor is said to have ordered people to adopt hereditary family names. Our first ancestor of the Cao family, *Cao, (Shu) Zhenduo* (曹叔振铎) (?–1053 BC), is the sixth son of King *Wen of Zhou*, who reigned from about 1041 BC to 1016 BC. If we assume our first ancestor got the Cao family name granted by his dad at the end of that kingdom (1016 BC), we could estimate the Cao family has lasted for over 3,000 years (about 1016 BC–AD 2022). However, though rooted from about 3,000 years ago, the Cao family book was only first recorded during the early Qin Dynasty (221–207 BC). Since then, many family-branch books have been recorded, especially during the Tang Dynasty (618–907).

These books are all handwritten and can likely only be found in museums and family heritages. However, during the Song Dynasty (960–1279), movable-type printing was invented around the Qingli period (1041–1048). I assume some family books have been in printed format since then, though I couldn't locate any based on the resources to which I have access.

Most of the Cao family-tree books that can be printed are kept by each branch organization that maintains them. Each branch organization includes an elected committee of the most well-respected men from Cao families. Since the Song Dynasty, the unwritten rule is to make a new revision of the family book at least each thirty years, while most Cao families make a revision every twenty years. It's considered to be heartless (不仁) if a family-tree book is not renewed every twenty years, and it's heartless and disobedient (不孝) if a revision hasn't been made for over thirty years. For every sixty years, each of the Cao family books that are managed by each branch are supposed to create a joint-lineage book together. However, due to war and turmoil in the last few hundreds of years, such a task is often hard to achieve.

In the Qing Dynasty (1636–1912), the organization or group that oversaw making a revision of a family-tree book was very comprehensive and complicated—It was generally composed of: the patriarch (the head of the branch), the chief of the ancestral hall (the reviewers), and those who set up management, correction, division, and cocultivation; besides those functionalities, there are also endorsers (those who pay the most money), writers (those who are literate), and editors (those with the highest culture); on top of that, there are also staff who make and supervise repairs and those who provide financial management, such as prime ministers.

For hundreds of years, it was considered a family glory if someone was chosen as a part of the organization that oversees family-tree book revisions, and only men are allowed to be on that committee. Not only that, but daughters of the family are not listed in family-tree books, either. If a man does not have a son, his branch is marked as "extinct" in the family-tree book, which was considered to be a moral crime.

I did not fully understand where the cultural bias against girls came from until I learned about all those ancient rules for family-tree books. To this day, when I watch the various versions of the movie *Mulan*, I can feel the deep emotion woven into the plot: a girl who wants to represent that family glory but must disguise herself as a man to achieve her goal.

There are many controversial discussions about the value of a family-tree book and whether some rules should change to "keep pace with the times," so that daughters are recorded in the book as well. Personally, I see tremendous value in looking back in history to understand our roots. But at the same time, when rules don't make sense anymore, we must adapt and change.

The Cao family-tree book I have is one out of many series of books for different ancestor branches, recording the last five hundred years (around 1522–2022) of names of our Cao family branch. This Cao branch all lived in the Cao village in which Dad was born, about eighteen miles to the southwest of Liangbao Temple, Jiaxiang, Jining, Shandong Province, China. Based on the Cao family book, the Cao village was started by the seventy-first generation of Cao about five hundred years ago, during Jiajing, Ming Dynasty. It was hard for me to imagine that someone just moved to an empty ground, built a house without any modern technology, and gradually expanded that into a big village that now holds thousands of households.

The Cao family book started with ancestor history as described in the Introduction, followed by each revision after the seventy-first generation: the 1845 revision was done by the eighty-fourth generation; the 1940 revision was done by the eighty-sixth generation; the 1982 revision is the first one done during the People's Republic of China by many people from the eighty-fourth to eighty-seventh generation; then these are followed by revisions in 1990 and 2005. The last revision was made in 2016, for which Dad and I insisted that daughters' names deserved to be there as much as sons and advocated that *this* daughter be rooted in the Cao family book. We succeeded and changed history that has stuck with us for thousands of years for the Cao family tree.

10.2. STORIES FOR GREAT-GREAT-GRANDPA, GREAT-GRANDPA, AND GRANDPA CAO (1760–1947)

In the Cao village, *every* family has the surname of Cao. Dad couldn't know what happened for the first few hundred years, but he was able to tell the stories passed down to him from his great-grandpa and grandpa's generation.

My great-great-grandpa, Weiqin Cao (1760–1820), who lived in the mid Qing Dynasty (1636–1912), was a thrifty farmer. He inherited some land from his ancestors, and through hard work and careful management, the family business developed rapidly in his hands. During his late years in the Jiaqing period (1796–1820), he both worked hard and took careful care of his family. Upon his death, his two sons, my great-grandpa (Zhaoxiu Cao) and his elder brother (Chengxiu Cao) each inherited over a hundred acres of land with several house sets.[26]

During the first twenty years after great-great-grandpa's death (1820–1840), opium imports into China significantly increased, and many families were destroyed due to its consumption. Both brothers—great-grandpa and

---

[26] A house set is called a siheyuan, which is a square circle of houses, which include four rooms on each side.

great-uncle—became addicted to opium and started selling family assets away little by little.

My great-grandma came from a wealthy family, and she watched my great-grandpa closely. Even so, my great-grandpa was able to sell off two of their house sets and about eighty acres of land. They had three sons, and the family was able to live off the leftover ten acres of land, a series of houses, and a barn. Around the Republic of China (ROC) period (1930s), my great-grandpa owed substantial debt due to opium consumption. He was eventually killed by his creditors by a javelin head while sleeping outside during a summer night. Those were chaotic times; nobody bothered to chase down the killers, but his sons remembered who killed their dad and started their planning of revenge.

In 1937, Grandpa Cao—who had made lots of friends over the years in his preparation for revenge—finally set his plan into action. One night, there was a Peking opera in the village—a big show that would bring a big crowd. Grandpa knew the killers would be in the audience, and he asked his friends to help him kill the two people who killed my great-grandpa —which they did. China in the 1930s functioned differently than our society today, and people were settled in their ways. Grandpa just paid for the two coffins, and they called it even.

Upon Great-Grandpa's death, his three sons split the assets: each son inherited three acres of land. Based on the number of heads in each household, Grandpa Cao got four north rooms and two west-side rooms in the house set.

In 1938, most of the Cao village was destroyed by flood, and everyone moved to a small middle-high-ground section to avoid flooding. People's lives were saved, but that year, no crops survived. So began a year of starvation. As hunger grew around the country, so did the people's desperation.

Great-Grandma wasn't particularly fond of Grandma because they were not blood related. Her son, Grandpa Cao, was away a lot looking for work. Grandma was told to take her kids and leave, forcing them into a situation without stability. They had to beg for food and became part of a small band of outcasts from the village. There were about thirty people who had been rejected by their families for different reasons. It sounds cruel, and it was. But it was also a time of such hardship that it is difficult to fathom for us today. People were dying of starvation every day. Everyone was in survival mode, trying to keep themselves and their closest family alive. Blood outweighed marriage.

For four months, the pack of outcasts kept hunting and begging for food on the road. Luckily, they met the People's Army, the head of which came from the same Cao family (Shangzhi Cao). They took in the starved Cao village people and fed them with whatever they could. After the army fed that pack of outcasts, they provided some more food and made sure a leader of the pack was picked so that they could safely travel back to Cao village. Dad told me to never forget about this piece of history: without the People's Army (currently serving the government of People's Republic of China), Grandma Cao would have died from starvation along with her two elder sons, and Dad would never have been born. That was how Grandma survived until Grandpa Cao came back from trying to find work. Once Grandpa Cao was back in the village, Great Grandma let her daughter-in-law and grandchildren move back in.

Before 1946, Dad's family only got three acres of land to farm on— which is not enough for a family of five. Later that year, Grandpa Cao got more good land from some of his friends as well as from gambling. By the end of 1946, the family had twenty-two acres of good land to farm, which was considered middle-class wealth.

While World War II was raging, China was also waging an internal war. China's two main parties, the Communist Party and the KMT (Kuomintang), were fighting for dominance domestically. Sometimes the two parties cooperated with each other to fight Japan—which invaded China at that time—and sometimes they fought each other. World War II ended in 1945. Japan surrendered, but China's Civil War ramped up. It was a very dangerous time because party affiliation could mean life or death based on the day and who had a temporary upper hand in the power struggle. Dad's village was often caught in the crosshairs of the warring factions, as it was in no-man's land that both parties used to rest or stage attacks on the others. Dad told me stories of the Eighth Route Army (People's Army of the Communist Party) coming to his village to camp there for a few days. They kept mostly to themselves and didn't bother the villagers. However, when the KMT (a.k.a. the Nationalist Party, who is residing in Taiwan, China, currently) came through their village, things were much different. The village was often plundered, and there was nothing the people could do to defend themselves against an army. Dad's family had some gold and jewelry they'd buried under a tree in the village to keep it safe and hidden from plunderers. Unfortunately, they were found out, and all their possessions were taken away from them. Much worse than taking the villagers earthly possessions and most of their food, the KMT would force many boys, barely teenagers, to join their army at the threat of death. These boys had to leave their families at a moment's notice and become soldiers for a cause they didn't believe in.

At that time, Grandpa's brother was the leader of the army force for several nearby villages and served the Communist Party, and Grandpa also wanted to join the Communist Party. But one day, a man from the nearby village came and found him.

"Look at the situation now," he said. "You never know who will eventually win. Since your brother serves the Communist Party, you should join KMT. That way, no matter who wins in the end, someone from the Cao family will belong to the winning team."

That sounded like a good plan; in that way, they hoped to form allegiances to each party so they'd have leverage to save family members regardless of which party would ultimately succeed. Grandpa Cao didn't think much of it, and he joined KMT.

Two months later, during a night attack from the Communist Party, Grandpa Cao was killed. Ahead of the attack, Grandpa's brother (who was in the Communist Party) had tried to warn Grandpa, but unfortunately got there too late. All the captives were executed before their arrival. The second day, Grandpa's friend carried his body back to the Cao village and buried him on his own land. After that, Grandma was left to raise three sons alone; Dad was the youngest, just seven years old.

In late 1947, civil war ended in a victory for the Communist Party for the Cao village. After the liberation, the Communist Party implemented "land reform" so every family could have land to farm on. Based on this system, each family was assigned a *class* based on how much land they owned. All the big landlords would lose their massive amount of land because they had to give it away to those in the lower class. Luckily, based on the policy, only land owned before 1945 was counted as a family asset (they are considered to have benefited from being a landlord before 1945). That meant the nineteen acres of land that Grandpa had acquired during 1946 from gambling and friends didn't count. Instead, Dad's family only counted the three acres that they inherited from his great-grandpa. Based on that, under the new system, Dad's family was classified as "poor and lower-middle peasants' class."

Great-Grandpa's opium addiction—the one that made him lose most of the fortune—ended up saving the family years later. If they'd still owned lots of land in 1947, they would've been classified as "landlord" status, which would have been a serious political issue at that time and would have had catastrophic consequences to the entire family during the later Cultural Revolution years (1966–1976).

After the land reform, peace returned to the Cao village. The young men started joining the Eighth Route Army to fight the Civil War to liberate the rest of the country. Over thirty young men were sent off to join the war of "Huaihai" in 1948. In the winter of 1948, the Cao village donated thirty big-wheel and fifty single-wheel wagons—along with food and a team of people—to send to the front line of the war. Dad's eldest brother joined that long, hard trip as well. This was excruciating work: the winter in North China was cold enough to turn dripping water into ice instantly, and the team from the Cao village had to carry food to the front line of the war. Though they were barely fed themselves, they didn't touch any food that was supposed to be given to the army. Many people died due to starvation and the freezing weather, some of whom Dad still remembers. Luckily, Dad's elder brother was one amongst those who returned to the village safely. A year later, the People's Republic of China was founded, on October 1, 1949.

Those were the bits of stories left from generations before Dad. Through those stories, I was able to see a glimpse of China's history of the last few hundred years. I see China symbolized as a giant dragon that went through dynasty after dynasty, war after war, only able to heal slowly in the last seventy years during peace. I ached deeply as I studied this history, learning how this dragon got beaten up repeatedly through the last 5,000 years, many times leaving it near death. But the dragon kept breathing, determined to fight through. Though bruised, it persevered and kept limping forward. That's the country I came from, and I am extremely proud of my heritage.

10.3. PERSEVERANCE, PERSONIFIED: DAD'S STORY (1940–PRESENT)

Dad was born in 1940. That means he is older than the People's Republic of China, which was only founded in 1949.

Before 2020, he traveled around the world every year. During the COVID-19 pandemic, Dad—then eighty years old—started writing a book about his life. His goal is to pass it down to his children so that those stories are not lost. Every week or so, I would receive pages from his handwritten manuscript in the form of photos, and I would convert them into electronic forms during my weekends. After writing about five hundred pages, more than 150,000 Chinese characters, and continuing, I've gotten a first-hand view through Dad's eyes of eighty-two years of China's formative history.

One thing that has surprised me about this project is Dad's amazing memory. As I read his words, it's as if I haven't known him my entire life. In his manuscript, he remembers things that happened when he was a young boy, even five years old, down to details: dates, what he ate, how much he spent on what food, and so on. His book also covers two generations before him, including stories told by his elders during his childhood. As I read his book, I feel like I am reliving his life, sometimes with joy and sometimes with tears. I've taken a small portion of those stories from his book and included them here so that you may understand how my previous generation lived their lives, and how that heritage was formed.

10.3.1. Childhood with Wars and Hunger
(1940–1948)

Due to endless wars, Dad grew up during a very tumultuous time in China's history. When he was born, the Cao village at that time was invaded and occupied by the Japanese. Japanese invaders killed inhabitants of his remote villages. Though they didn't outright kill people in the Cao village, they were unpredictable and often violent. You can only imagine the amount of terror and pain people lived through during that time. Dad has shared little bits of memories, starting from when he was five years old, before World War II ended in August 1945.

Dad told me the story of how one of his elderly family members almost got beaten to death by the Japanese. Nobody in the Village spoke or understood Japanese, so they had to communicate with gestures. The Japanese soldiers grabbed this village elder and patted his behind. He thought, "Oh, they want to know where the bathrooms are." So, he led them to the area in the village with the holes in the ground for defecating. The soldiers got angry and beat him viciously. Then they made their hand-gesture request again, and he realized they were talking about chickens laying eggs. They were hungry. They wanted to know where the villagers kept the chicken eggs. The village elder tried to explain to them that these very soldiers had already stolen all the chickens. There were no eggs anywhere in the Village. The soldiers beat him so badly a second time that he barely survived.

All the families in the Cao village made a pact to stand against the Japanese invaders. They had no weapons and couldn't fight nor physically defend themselves. They could not keep any army from plundering their village repeatedly. But they could make a sacred pact with each other to never betray their country or each other, to never give up any information about which villagers were members of the Communist Party or the whereabouts of the People's Army.

Of course, people were starving, and hunger made them desperate. Sometimes, individuals or whole families would try to bargain with the Japanese—trading information for food, secrets for necessities. If the village head found out, the traitors were killed immediately or cast out of the village—it was better for them to die than to bring shame to our country. Standing up for China and protecting our values and way of life runs through Dad's veins. Even though I have lived in the US for decades now, I'm deeply rooted in my Chinese heritage. Dad has instilled in me that no matter where I live, I will never bring shame to China, or else I will no longer be a Cao.

Even though there was suffering, political disturbance, and natural disasters impacting many parts of the country, Dad has many fond memories of his childhood. In his memory, the Cao village was beautiful, surrounded on four sides by big walls and guarded by a river that afforded villagers self-defense during times of war. The village was separated into east, west, south, north, and middle villages. Kids would run around the village, and everyone knew everyone—all in the Cao family.

In 1946, after the war ended, when Dad was six, the village started a school. Dad was in the same class with about fifty other children, ranging from six to ten years old. He didn't care much about school. He was much more interested in playing by the village's river. One day, he told his teacher that he wasn't feeling well. The teacher excused him to go home. Instead, Dad went straight to the dam at the river and played while all his friends were studying. He was so engrossed in his play that he forgot time. The day turned to evening, and when he didn't return from school, his family got scared. The entire village started searching for him. When Dad saw and heard the villagers looking for him and yelling his name, he hid himself under the crops that had been harvested. He didn't know everyone was scared he was dead. He was just a six-year-old kid who had lied about being sick, skipped school, and didn't want to get in trouble (so he hid)!

For hours, hundreds of people searched for him. Villagers dove into the river to search for a drowned little boy. Soon, night fell, but they didn't give up. They carried lanterns to illuminate their path, never giving up on finding Dad. Once it was pitch-black, he got scared and started crying. It was his crying that alerted the search party, and he was finally found safe and returned to his family. Customarily, Dad would have been whipped for his disobedience. But the joy over finding him alive and Dad's little body shaking with uncontrollable sobs convinced his family otherwise. He was never punished. He was fed two precious chicken eggs instead. And he never skipped school again.

In 1947, Dad was seven years old. He remembers that one day, he caught many fish himself and carried them, pole in hand, to his maternal grandpa, who lived about twelve miles away. Each time he visited, he would check on an apricot tree that belonged to their neighbor. When he delivered the fish, he knew it was almost time for those apricots to be ready to be picked and identified six apricots that were turning yellow. After the darkness, he snuck out of his maternal grandpa's house, climbed quickly, and—based on his memory of the location of those six apricots—he picked exactly the six that were ready to be eaten. He ate four of them and left two for his grandpa. He wrote at length in his book about that story, and I laughed so hard reading it.

Dad remembered each year helping the family to farm. Since there wasn't much he could do as a young child, his duty was to guard their field during harvest times. On the side, he would make money by getting a little lamb, spending half a year feeding it, and then selling it. He was able to make a profit of five silver dollars with half a year of labor raising that lamb.

During wartime, many kids didn't get the opportunity to go to school, so everyone got bundled together for the same education after the war ended. There were only one or two girls in the class at the time because it was commonly viewed as "a waste" for girls to receive education back then. Instead, a woman's default destiny was to get married, have children, and take care of everything around the house for the rest of their lives. Women with more education were considered more trouble; it was widely believed that having too many thoughts would only cause damage, dampening the family-first values they were supposed to hold.

In class, there were seven or eight young men older than sixteen, and Dad was the youngest. Those elder ones sat in the back, and occasionally, someone would disappear and never come back, having gotten married. In that time, education stopped after marriage for young men, as they became the head of the household. Their duties were not to study but to provide for their family after that point.

Dad saw his fellow classmates drop from class and, understanding the dynamic, was determined that he wouldn't get married until he completed college. Nowadays people would say that's just common sense; however, that was a decision he made when he was only eight years old. When everyone else around him was following an identical path, he channeled courage and wisdom in deciding that his path would be different.

Though well-intentioned, that new path wasn't an easy one. By the time he reached fifteen, many matchmakers started to visit his family, trying to convince him to wed girls from nearby villages, some of whom were beautiful and came from wealthy families. Dad resisted those temptations, instead burying his head in books.

10.3.2. The People's Republic of China was Born
(1949–1951)

In 1949, the Chinese Communist Revolution culminated with Chairman Mao's proclamation of the People's Republic of China. Westerners view Communism largely as a negative. And yet, for Dad and his family, the Communist Party and the People's Army were what kept them alive during the worst parts of his life. This was a critical turning point for China because the country was under the control of Chinese people again. The Japanese and other invaders had been defeated and got out of China. The Chinese people had suffered through unspeakable tragedies, poverty, hunger, violence, and unrest for so long, and China was still standing. This kind of endurance and perseverance cannot be taught.

In 1950, after the People's Republic of China was founded, a new school granted by the education department opened. There, students would learn Western modern science instead of only "Four Books and Five Classics," which is the traditional Chinese education model that focuses on values. This meant that at age ten, Dad, in a way, started his education all over again. They had a five-year elementary system for that period, meaning kids could complete elementary by 1955, follow with three years of middle and two years of high school, and be college-ready by 1960. This structure is the reason Dad was able to become what is widely considered the first generation of modern college-educated people in China.

Dad's education looked very different than it does for today's generation. He started at 6:00 a.m. for morning self-study. Then, at 7:30 a.m., they would each go back home for breakfast and return by 8:30 a.m. Morning classes ran from 8:30 a.m.–12:00 p.m., and after a one-hour break, afternoon school resumed from 1:00–4:00 p.m. Then, they had another one-hour break for dinner, followed by study time from 6:00–8:00 p.m.

This was the cadence of his days throughout each of his grades. Since there was no electricity in the village, they leveraged the early morning daylight. After 6:00 p.m., they would light a kerosene lamp in the middle of the desk, and several students would circle around that desk to read together.

Dad recalls that his writing skills were the best in his class. Many of his early writings were about his brothers' business ventures. He described the ways in which they used to make money for the family, including getting up early to catch fish (sometimes spending a whole night somewhere else to fish and selling them at the market); buying seasonal new-year pictures and selling door to door before the new year; making steamed buns and selling at the county fair; getting wholesale kerosene and matches and selling them at the open market; and so on. Whatever it took. Dad always followed his elder brothers around to help whenever he was not in school. Though Grandma Cao was with them, it was still too early for people to accept a woman trying to make money for her family, so Dad's elder brothers primarily bore that responsibility.

10.3.3. Korean War, Locust War, and the Great Leap Forward (1952–1960)

In July of 1952—just as everyone thought the war was over—the Korean War started. The armies from the Communist Party were sent away to fight, so KMT started using this opportunity to bomb many places in mainland China. One memory stands out for Dad: one day, he was watching a big show in a nearby village when sirens began ringing out suddenly. Everyone started running, and Dad hid with his friends under a table. From his vantage point, he saw airplanes with machine guns shooting into the crowds of people. Many citizens were killed that day, including the mother of Dad's classmate. After an agonizing year of events like this one, in July 1953, the Korean War ended, bringing peace back to the Cao village.

Another war followed three years later, in January of 1956—only this war was one without humans. Warnings about locusts came from the government of Shandong Province: massive swarms were eating all the crops in the area. To defend their crops from the swarming, destructive locusts' clouds, thousands of students from schools of that area set up an army to protect the crops with their bare hands. Dad was one of them, spending three days waiting for the locusts to attack their crops. Then, they used giant nets to catch them and their own shoes to smash them. For many days, they would only take short breaks, smashing the insects until they were all dead. After what they called the Locust War, they would sweep up the dead locusts and take them home as feed for chickens, ducks, or even to fry for themselves.

For the period of 1950 to 1960, Dad had nearly every frame of a ten-year movie in his head, down to days...including what he ate that day, what happened at what time, and so on. To give you an example of the insane level of detail, in his book, he wrote about a basketball game he played in third grade, listing all ten players' names from each side, the play-by-play, a detailed breakdown of who scored and when, etc. Dad always said, "I only need to read the textbook once or twice to remember it and get an A." I had always believed Dad, but only when I read his book did I truly understand what he meant.

During those ten years, many significant political events and activities happened as well. China was trying to figure out the best way to move forward. In hindsight, many of those efforts were on the wrong track, though they were all approached with good intentions: to bring better lives for people. For example, many ways for farmers to work together were explored throughout those years: first were "mutual aid teams" of five to fifteen households, then "elementary agricultural cooperatives" in 1953 of twenty to forty households, then "higher cooperatives" of one hundred to three hundred families in 1956. By 1958, private ownership was abolished, and all households were formed into state-operated communes. That is considered the Great Leap Forward, during 1958–1960.

Dad lived through those events and observed many things that were confusing, though they seemed reasonable at that time. I can't elaborate on all those stories in this book, but I am glad Dad was able to pass those stories to me to remember how many sideways paths we took before arriving at the prosperous China the world sees now. Mistakes were made, then corrected. Another set of mistakes were made, then corrected again. Through those mistakes, China was able to learn and find its way forward to success.

Though he lived through those chaotic times, Dad always knew what he wanted in his own life. Since the farming endeavors weren't enough to feed the family, the Cao brothers started looking for ways to survive. Dad's oldest brother got a job at a coal mine and became a miner. Then, he got his second brother there to join him in earning more income for the family. Because Dad's brothers provided the means for his schooling, he felt very guilty. Dad tried to find any opportunity he could to help support his family outside of his school duties. On summer break in 1954, when Dad was fourteen years old, he would get up early in the morning, carry a few bags to the coal mine pit location, and climb down into the pit. Then, he would collect over one hundred pounds of coal, hoist the coal bag over his shoulder, and climb out of the mine pit. He did this over and over until all the bags were full, carrying each one a mile to home. Every day that summer, he worked two hours in the morning and two hours at night, using the rest of his time to study. That's how he spent a typical summer break as a teenager: trying to contribute to the family in some way during his continued education.

Dad wanted to be the most educated person in Cao village, so throughout his entire teenage years, he buried his head in books and was determined to see the outside world. In 1960, Dad became the first person in Cao village accepted by a university (Wuhan University of Surveying and Mapping Technology), presenting his family with a difficult choice: whether they should decide to support him for his college education instead of having him work after high school.

Dad was the youngest, and his two elder brothers decided they would sacrifice themselves to give Dad an opportunity at a higher education. That way, he could make a better life and carry on the Cao family name. The two elder Cao brothers would take turns paying for their little brother to go to university. This was extremely challenging at the time, considering the civil unrest, poverty, and starvation. One of my uncles had five kids to support, the other had four. Each month, one of the families would scrape together five yuan (about seventy cents) to support Dad's living expenses in college. One month the money didn't arrive. It was the depth of winter, and Dad sold his only winter jacket on the streets for five yuan so he could make it through the month.

10.3.4. College through the "Three-Year Famine" (1960–1965)

Between 1959 and 1961, China had three years of the hardest challenges it had faced since its founding in 1949—the three years of great famine. There wasn't enough food to feed everyone in the country.

Dad wasn't hungry; he was starving. For an entire year after he joined college in August 1960, most physical activities were canceled because people were too weak to move. When Dad walked to the dining hall in the university—that could only afford to feed porridge to those college kids for a long period of time—he saw that some people had to hold on to the walls of buildings to keep from falling. That's how weak their bodies were from the constant lack of food. Luckily, Dad's brain was still sharp, and he devised a plan to maximize his calorie intake. Most people tried to get their bowls filled all the way, but Dad asked for his bowl to be filled only two thirds of the way. Then he would slurp the porridge from the edge of the bowl as fast as possible, carefully rotating the bottom of the bowl, and then get back in line to get a second bowl, this time full to the brim. The people who had a full first bowl were always slower than Dad to finish their food, and not everyone would get a second bowl. Dad understood that taking less food up front would result in more food overall. Some people faltered during the famine, but Dad persevered, even when he was literally at times too weak to stand. To motivate his classmates, he said, "We should know that we must not give up on our own learning. This all shall pass, and things will get better!"

But famine wasn't his only worry. The college in Wuhan at the time allocated mosquito nets—a necessity, as the mosquitoes were overwhelming, and their bites could be quite serious. Dad was the league secretary of the class, and he saw the number of nets allocated to the students fall short; there weren't enough to go around, so he gave up his right to own one net for the good of others. At that time of year, the temperature was very high, yet he had to cover his body and head with sheets and clothing to protect himself from the bites. Sometimes, he'd sweat so profusely that he'd have to shower in the middle of the night, going right back to the sheet situation.

He then fashioned a makeshift net around his bed made of sheets, meaning he didn't have one to sleep on. The makeshift "net" worked for one night, but it did not hold back the insects. Still unwilling to request a net from the school because he knew there weren't enough for others, he wrote a letter to his uncle asking him to send a net that could save his life—which his uncle did, half a month and a lot of desperation later. As Dad says, he "suffered a bit" but found a solution to the problem, even if it meant putting the needs of others before his own.

This was not an uncommon theme for China in 1960. Once, upon returning to school from visiting family, Dad received a cloth bag containing fifteen *wotou* (like cornbread in the West) from a close grandpa from the Cao village—a gift more precious than perhaps any at the time. Dad calculated that he would consume nine for the next three days during his trip, after which he could share with his college friends after getting back. During the trip, he was hyperaware that he needed to be observant and protect his food from the many hands around him who were also facing starvation. At one train station, he managed to purchase a potato for dinner instead, opting to save the rest of the wotou and make the nutrition last the remainder of the trip. Before he could eat the potato, a man spat on it and snatched it out of his hand. That stealer did not eat it, though; instead, he ran and gave it to his small child who was hiding nearby.

Hours later, when Dad got on the train, he pulled out a wotou bun from the bag. He saw an elderly man in his seventies staring at him, his face thin and pitiful looking. The man explained he hadn't had anything to eat in a day and a half, so Dad gave him half of the wotou in his hand. Dad ate only a few mouthfuls at a time of the remaining half, quietly at night for the rest of the trip. People experiencing famine crowded the aisles, and he hid the bag squeezed between his feet like he was protecting gold. At that moment, Dad had mixed feelings about himself: he felt good that he had shared his food with someone else, when he was also in dire need of the food; he also felt selfish because he had no courage to share the rest of his precious food with more people on that train.

To survive through self-help, Dad and his classmates took it upon themselves to manage vegetable gardens for the university, supplying not only the individuals in the group but also the entire school via the canteen. In addition to the vegetable gardens, they also grew lotuses in a pound. Lotus root can provide enough precious carbohydrates and nutrition to be considered as a main course. By early 1961, their vegetable garden started to add cauliflower, water spinach, and cabbage to the school dining menu; by late 1961, all the lotus roots were harvested. They drained the pond to dig out all the roots from the mud, then used the front tip of the lotus roots to insert back into the pond so it would all grow back again the next year. Vegetables alone can make people half full. With the lotus root as the main course, many people at Dad's college were able to be nearly full. Thanks to this lotus-root approach, life appeared to come back to the university by late 1961. Students and teachers were laughing, physical education came back because students had the energy to move again, and there was a great camaraderie on campus. Dad recalls that one of the best parts of this rebirth was the depth of idea sharing that came back to his learning— as people became more nourished, they were able to think clearly and achieve more.

Another great thing happened around this time, too. For years when Dad was in college, he would write letters home where his mom and his brothers' families lived, but nobody from home could write back to him. They hadn't received the education that would have allowed them to read and write. Finally, the oldest son of Dad's elder brother got to first grade and was able to represent the whole family from home and write to Dad. Dad's nephew wrote:

Grandma and Dad speeches start:

Everyone at home is good and healthy, they are happy to hear that you are better now. Grandma was worried that you would be starving in college, so decided to make and sell popsicles, so that we could send you more money. Unfortunately, we couldn't sell much and everyday those popsicles melt into sugar water, so we kids drank them all every night.

Grandma and Dad speeches over

Dad chucked at the letter and replied, "Tell my mother that our school life has improved a lot, and we have added dishes to each meal, such as lotus-root cubes. Each person is given a small bowl, which is basically enough to eat. Please do not worry about me. I have devoted all my heart to my studies. Please take care of your grandma's health and the children in the home."

Dad stayed on campus that summer vacation, spending Monday through Saturday in the library studying engineering surveying, control surveying, astronomy, aerial photogrammetry, and more to prepare for his upcoming classes. Though the weather was especially hot in Wuhan in July, the library felt cool because it had five fans, and he spent many days and evenings there in the reading room.

The surveying courses were not merely theoretical. After years of studying, the first group of surveyors in China—of which Dad was a part—began their first internship, meaning they were to put their skills to use practically. The group was to cover an area of 1.25 square kilometers with five topographic maps. Each person in the group learned to physically run the ruler, measure the map, and draw; this was physical work, and both speed and accuracy were paramount. After days, they'd completed the task to the instructor's satisfaction—which wasn't always an easy task. Wuhan University was one of the best universities in China, and the instructors were often very strict and accomplished.

Time in Wuhan passed quickly for Dad, and to save money and focus on his studies, he didn't return home for two years. In the spring of 1965, it was time to write his thesis. For his topic, he chose an in-depth analysis on the accuracy of the evaluation and estimation of the measurement control network at Wuhan Iron and Steel Company Limited, and how that related to the practice of control surveying. He received good marks on the paper, as he had throughout school. In late May 1965, one thousand graduates filled the school auditorium for commencement. There, they heard a speech from Jianbai Xia, one of the most famous astronomers in the country. He called on all graduates to respond to the Party's call to go to the frontiers, to the most difficult places, and to "give their strength and build our motherland."

These are words Dad took to heart. Before graduation from college, each student needed to fill out a form to choose the locations they wanted to get assigned work from the country. Dad filled in his request-to-assign form with the five locations that are considered the toughest places in China to live, given their harsh weather and living conditions. The five locations were: Tibet, Xinjiang, Qinghai Province, Inner Mongolia, Heilongjiang Province (Daxing'anling). Back then, there wasn't an "I" focus. Everyone wanted to improve the country, and Dad was no exception.

In the end, Dad was assigned to be in Heilongjiang Province. Compared to the other locations, it was the closest to his family in North China. In August 1965, after five years of college, he became a geological survey engineer and started serving his country.

10.3.5. Working through Cultural Revolution
(1966–1976)

Dad was the first of his family, of his entire village, to get a college degree. Right after his graduation, what followed was a decade of sociopolitical moments known as the Chinese Cultural Revolution (1966–1976). China attempted to go back to its Communist roots and purge any remaining capitalist practices during those ten years. Most education and economic activity were halted for those chaotic ten years. Though some universities were still open and accepting students, learning knowledge wasn't the top priority for students anymore; people's energy was mostly consumed by political events. Dad was fortunate to graduate before 1966, and he got a government job to survey the country with a mission to locate rare mineral mines. Due to the nature of his job, he was traveling the mountains and forests, far away from the political unrest during most of that period. He was among the first batch of people who were college educated in science and technology after China was founded in 1949. Dad very quickly started leading teams during those years and made many first-time geological surveys and maps for China.

His first task was in Daxing'anling in Heilongjiang Province, the northernmost division in China. It's covered by endless forests with the coldest weather in China. The weather can reach -50°C to -40°C at night in wintertime. If you spit in that temperature, your spit will freeze before it hits the ground. He shared a four-person tent, keeping a bucket inside to pee in the night because walking outside could be deadly. Conditions were so cold that those on the team needed to take shifts to ensure the fire bucket set in the middle of the tent never went out. If it did, people could freeze to death by morning. His first assignment was supposed to last for only a month, but heavy snow hit at the end of their tasks. They were all trapped in the forested mountains for another whole month until the traffic line was back up again and the chest-high snow got cleared up from the roads. It was the first time in his life he'd endured such cold weather.

Other dangers lurked around every corner: black bears, especially, posed a risk to the team and their worksites. During his years of missions in the fields, many people's lives were taken as well. One of his teammates died when attempting to fight floodwaters to deliver goods from and to the campsite. Another died when rocks from the explosions they had to set up to remove obstacles hit him in the head.

Each year, Dad spent at least nine months in the field, where he surveyed many key infrastructures in China, such as tunnels, heavy industrial factories, and bridges, building many of the first maps of China's wildest forests. For example, in the construction of a double railway in cities A and B, the surveyors would conduct field surveys. Only by repeatedly comparing several routes could they select the best map line. From that recommendation, the railway department would understand the geologic conditions and various elevations and determine where to drill, etc. It is a very complex process, but geological surveys can provide detailed engineering guidance before the project. Ultimately, what I hope you take from this is an understanding that surveying and mapping work was an indispensable technical force in national construction.

Dad said that during those years, they didn't care much about themselves and primarily wanted to do something great for the country. Once, when they were doing a survey job around a river, the temperature was below zero, and there were small icicles in the river. Dad had to set a mark on one side of the river, followed by setting another across the river. To complete the task faster, he took off his clothes, swam across the frozen river with his equipment, and got the task done in time.

Dad's generation is extremely grateful for the Communist Party that founded the country in 1949, an era in which almost every infrastructure and system in the country needed to be rebuilt. They have lived through war, starvation, and the years before they could call the country their own again. It was the new China that provided everyone an opportunity to live a normal life. Though it was bumpy, the whole country kept learning and adapting to march forward. Dad wanted to be part of the force that built the country stronger and better so his next generation could flourish in a much better environment. He and his team traveled in the mountains, battling the elements, surveying the land for not just his future but the future of his country.

Dad understood how many people sacrificed for him to have these rare opportunities and he was determined to make the most of them. After Dad started to work, he earned a monthly salary of twenty yuan (about three dollars), and he sent half of that each month back home to his mother and two brothers as his gratitude to them. While he worked to provide stability and security, he was also decisive and assertive when needed, often taking risks for our family to improve our situation. As an engineer with excellent problem-solving skills, he was always looking for ways to improve situations, processes, and himself.

With a glimpse into Dad's early life, you may understand how he led the way for our family. You may also understand how—along with Mom—he influenced me to become the person I am today.

Parents taking a walk at the river in 1976,
Mom was five months pregnant with me (March 1976).

10.4. TENACITY IN ACTION: MOM'S STORY
(1952–PRESENT)

Mom was born in late April 1953 in a little tiny farming village in China. Mom's family name is Zhang, so Grandpa Zhang was later referred to as Mom's dad. For the first five years of her life, she lived happily with her parents and sister, who was four years older. Her memories from this time are fond ones, full of playing in the yard and enjoying family time.

Then, in 1959, the Great Leap Forward began in China. Farming was organized into people's communes, and the cultivation of privately owned plots was forbidden. Famine started occurring in their village, so Grandpa Zhang decided to leave their village to look for a better opportunity to feed his family.

On one dark night—afraid of being seen exiting through the front door—he jumped the fence of their house, taking with him only seven vegetable buns and one rice pancake as his food for the entire trip. There were many unknowns that night and the many nights after: to start, he was unsure where to go in the first place. So, he traveled north, barefooted, hopping on any wagon he could find. At times, he had to work for food before he was able to continue his journey.

Grandpa Zhang was gone for years, never sending a letter back home. Being able to afford buying stamps and sending letters was a luxury to a farmer who had leaped from the village. On her own and with two small children, Grandma Zhang had to start working as a farmer to survive. Sometimes Mom's elder sister would help Grandma in the field, leaving Mom home alone—even overnight. At the time, Mom didn't know what Grandma and Sis did every day or where they were; she just knew that she missed them very much.

One night, Mom decided she was going to find them. She knew that there was an old bullock cart that carried cornstalks back and forth from the field to the village. Even at such a young age, she reasoned that if she followed the bullock cart, she would find her mom. And she did, following that cart for miles and miles. Luckily, someone saw her while unloading cornstalks and started shouting, "Whose kid is this?"

Mom started to cry. Luckily, someone recognized her and told her mom to come get her. When they were reunited, Grandma Zhang held her tight, tearing up.

"How did you get here?" she asked. "And why did you come?"

"I missed you," Mom replied. "And I knew this cart would help me find you."

Grandma Zhang carried Mom home—all five miles—with her weary body. Then, she returned to the field that day for work. Mom was forbidden from coming back to the field where the adults were working, as it could be dangerous for young children.

Most of the time, Mom would eat yams for lunch and dinner. Once, when she didn't have enough cooked food, she decided to cook her own. Because she'd never cooked before, she simply mimicked what she'd seen Grandma Zhang do so many times before: fill the pot with yams, set the fire under the pot, and wait. To her surprise, smoke started to build, and a burning smell spread all the way to the neighbor's yard. Luckily, there was an old grandma next door who came and poured water into the pot to put out the smoke. Mom didn't know that to cook food, water is needed for the pot. The pot was destroyed. Unable to afford a replacement, they had to put a small pot into the big pot for cooking moving forward.

By early spring of 1960, before Mom turned seven years old and her sister was about to turn ten, Grandma Zhang got sick due to lack of nutrition and overwork. Mom didn't know what exact illness she had, but she recalled seeing Grandma Zhang coughing up blood. They didn't have money to see the doctor, nor could they afford for her to stop working. After all, there were two kids for her to feed at home. One day, as Grandma Zhang walked back from another day in the fields, she fell on the road and died. Her body was found and carried home by people from the village.

That night, many people came to their house to see Grandma Zhang for the last time. Mom remembers sitting outside of the house, staring inside at her mother's body. She couldn't cry. She couldn't believe it was real. Eventually, as night closed in, the people from the village went home. It was just the two girls, alone.

Grandma Zhang had an elder brother; Mom called him Big Uncle. He came to the house that night but would not come in, wary of his sister's body inside. He told the girls they needed to live with his family moving forward, but Mom refused. She insisted that they'd live alone until someday her dad returned.

Finally, Big Uncle ran inside, picked up the two sisters with each of his arms, and left the house. Mom remembers crying then—for the first time since learning her mom had died—as she realized she truly had no place to call home anymore. The next day when grandma was buried, they used three wooden boards as a coffin.

The image of dirt spreading over the wood as it covered her mother is one Mom could never get out of her head.

Big Uncle had a wife and four kids of his own. Taking in two more added a lot of stress to the household, especially in 1960 when the country faced famine. Food was incredibly scarce, and during the hardest times, Big Uncle made sure Mom and her sister were fed with what little food they had. Their own son was six—the same age as Mom—and he was so malnourished that he couldn't even walk. His name was Little Bean because every day, he could get limited beans as his food, and he would sit on a stool peeling those beans to eat. There was never one day he was full. One morning, after having cried out in the night for food, his parents found him lifeless in bed.

The day Little Bean died, everyone was too starved to have the energy to cry. Mom remembers that year there were many times they needed to all go to the field hunting for any food, even begging when there was nothing in the field to dig. It was not only the darkest and hardest moment of her life but the same situation for the rest of China, too. That was the same year when Dad was facing famine during his college time.

In the spring of 1961, the village was able to generate enough food from the field and receive enough help from the government, ending the famine that had plagued them for so long. Something else good happened, too: they received a letter from Grandpa Zhang, who'd been traveling a long time after leaving home, looking for food and opportunities.

He finally found a team of geologists looking for temporary workers to cook for their team. It was the team that, many years later, Dad started leading. They had a big team of hundreds of people who traversed the tallest mountains and went into the deepest recesses of the wilderness. Their mission? To build the first surveyed maps for China. In his letter, Grandpa Zhang said that he had to work in the wild a lot and couldn't visit home.

His letter provided more than just communication; it also had an address. Despite not knowing how to read, Mom and Big Uncle decided to find him in the North. They carried the envelope with them, asking strangers how to get to the next place on their ultimate journey of reaching the address.

After many days, the pair finally found Grandpa Zhang. But right after they met, he was notified that his team needed to travel to another location immediately, and no family members were permitted to travel with them.

Mom and Big Uncle were told that to follow the team, they'd need to follow a big river to the South. It took a whole day for them to catch the team. When they got hungry, Mom and Big Uncle would hunt for food themselves near the river, cooking over an open fire. Other times, Grandpa Zhang would sneak food away from the camp to help them. They stayed in that location for a month, until it was time to travel again. It was time for Big Uncle and Mom to return to the village. On the way home, they packed a few buns. When Mom was about to eat one of hers at the train station, someone grabbed it out of her hands and ran away with it. It was still a tough time for many people in early 1961.

In the winter of 1963, Grandpa Zhang was finally able to travel back to their village. When he returned, he saw Mom's elder sister holding the wall as she walked.

"Why do you walk that way?" he asked her.

She didn't recognize him. He soon learned that she'd given most of her food to Mom, losing her own strength in the process. She was so weak that she was unable to walk without holding on to something.

That winter, Grandpa Zhang got remarried to a woman who had a son. His reasoning was that when he was gone, there would be someone to take care of the kids. That way, he wouldn't have to rely on Big Uncle and his family any longer. Right after the marriage, Grandpa Zhang went back on the road with the survey team so that he could continue to make a salary and provide for the family while working in the North.

In 1965, when Mom was twelve years old, her elder sister told Grandpa Zhang that Mom must go to school. She said it was unfair that their step-mom's son got to go, but neither of the girls could. Grandpa Zhang agreed, though his wife thought it was useless for a girl to go to school. Mom was extremely appreciative of her sister for fighting for her to receive an education. Eventually, she was able to have five years of education in that village, which was critical and precious for a woman at that time. She was able to graduate from elementary school after the fifth grade and dropped out of education after that. It was generally received as a "waste of resources" for any woman to continue education after elementary because they were expected to start working and generate income for the family as early as they could, way before they reached sixteen.

Just that five years of education made Mom the most educated woman in the village, and she became a leader. She was recognized as the head of the publicity team in the village—one that wrote announcements for and kept communications among villagers—and even organized an opera team, taking the lead role on many operas for the villages around the area. She was popular and a star with her elementary diploma. Mom's sister, however, was never able to receive one day of education. To this day, she has never learned to read nor write—giving the precious opportunity for education to her little sister instead. Mom appreciated her deeply for that because, without the opportunities she had in those early years, she wouldn't have had the chance to pursue higher education later, eventually retiring as a high rank of government officer.

In 1970, when Mom was seventeen years old, she received a letter from Grandpa Zhang. There was a rare opening on the team he was with, he wrote, and she needed to join them for that opportunity. She did just that, traveling alone for three days to reach the team in the field to become the cook's helper. After doing that beginner job for a year, she became a cashier for the store that provided groceries for the team. While in this position, she met another woman on the team who recognized her desire to learn. The woman invited Mom to her office early every morning to read the newspaper with her. This helped Mom to keep learning—reading and writing—and to understand what was happening in the world at that time.

By 1975, Mom grew into someone who could assist all the geologists who were surveying in the field. Dad was the head of the team. They met and later got married in the summer of 1975. From there, their lives together began, and their entwined stories will be told through mine. But throughout her life, Mom never stopped developing herself.

In 1980, Mom became a clerk. By 1981, she became a trained CPA. I was five years old, and my brother was four years old, living with remote relatives at the time, while she traveled with Dad in the field. In 1983, Mom decided to stay in their base city instead of traveling with the team. That meant that she worked during the day, took care of two kids, and studied late at night. By the end of 1989—while keeping a full-time job and raising two kids mostly on her own—she was able to complete her college degree remotely and via night school. That's the year Dad decided not to go to the field anymore, moving our whole family to Dalian so that we could live a stable life as a family of four.

In 1993, Mom became the head of the finance department of one of the four divisions of the city. In 1995, she went through computer training, mastering typing and CPA work with all-electronic systems. In 1998, she went through months of full-time training to become an administrative cadre. During that time, she broke her knee trying to catch a bus but still went to daily study—cast and all. At the end of 2001, she retired as a deputy division-level government officer.

Mom said that she never had big ambitions, but she "couldn't stand to be left behind, with either old technology or old knowledge" in any circumstance. That's why she kept learning, kept improving, and kept making herself better. Her entire formal education started with those five years of elementary study, and every effort after that was inspired by her determination to not be any less than her peers.

She kept adapting to this world and does so even today. When I talk to her via FaceTime, she is as good as the young people in the latest technology trends. She will sometimes explain to me some new terms that I didn't even know! I admire her passion of learning, adapting, and always keeping an optimistic attitude toward life. Mom's story resembles that of many Chinese women who lived through the toughest times of China and who are living through the current prosperous China.

That was a glimpse into Mom's life. I bow to her and millions of women like her in China. I want to become like those women as well: women who are independent, keep battling hardships, keep learning, and keep adapting, all the while keeping their passion for and kindness to this world.

Despite their accomplishments, these women have almost always been invisible in family history books. Once I learned of this, I decided to change it.

Mom in Shandong Province, China, waiting for Libo's birth during her last trimester (March 1976).

10.5. LIBO: THE FIRST DAUGHTER ROOTED
IN THE CAO FAMILY TREE

My maiden name is Cao, Libo (曹力波). 力波 in Chinese means "strong tide." On the cover of this book, my middle name is represented by our family surname icon: 曹. It has two dragons circling an ancient writing of that family name. I look at it often, and each time, I feel like the dragons are like ancestors protecting me. At the same time, there are expectations from that icon, reminding me never to bring shame to our family name.

It wasn't until I felt I was settled—accomplished and able to stand on my own—that I started asking Dad about our ancestors. Dad visited Cao village many times after leaving it in his middle school time. After he got married and had kids, he wrote back to the person in the village in charge of making the family book, trying to ensure his family would be included.

Hearing from Dad too many times about this "family book," I started begging him to get me one.

In 2011, during a trip to visit me in the US, Dad finally brought the book. It was the first time I had seen the family icon. The Cao family tree book I have is one of many (hundreds or thousands?) of books containing all the names, professions, current residences, and family linkages to the rest for generations. Dad said that's the one including his "family branch" that recorded the last five hundred years of all the names of Cao and covered about the last twenty generations (seventy-first to ninety-first). Dad is the eighty-sixth generation of the Cao family, and I am the eighty-seventh. I flipped through that book and surprisingly noticed that my name wasn't in it, which is already covering up to the ninety-first generation.

"Why would you want this book anyway? You are not even in the book!"

"Wait, what? Why am I not in the book?" I asked with surprise.

"Well, since you are a daughter, your next generation won't carry the family name anymore. Only men carry their family name over to the next generation. You didn't know women are not included and never rooted in family books?"

That's the time I noticed that only women who married *into* the family were listed, but those daughters who needed to marry *out* of the family were either missed entirely or dropped off right after their marriage because, historically, they only belonged to the new family they married into. It seems that daughters don't matter to the family tree at all. Women from generations before Dad's didn't even have their own names. For example, if a wife's name is "XX Zhang" as a daughter of the Zhang family, after she married into a Cao family, her name would be recorded in the Cao family book once as "Mrs. Zhang, Cao." This indicates that she came from the Zhang family but married into the Cao family to carry their offspring. Her own name wouldn't be carried over nor recorded, since that didn't matter to a family tree. After marriage, a woman's only identity is a wife to a family without her own name, and her only mission is to give birth to a son who can carry their family name over. I saw so many identical entries for "Mrs. Zhang, Cao" in that book because they are the same in history: all women from the Zhang family married to the Cao family. If they didn't have a son later, their names weren't even included because that family branch stops there; there was no root created for another branch.

It was only around the 1950s (after the People's Republic of China was founded in 1949) that women started keeping their own names recorded in the book if they married in. For me, as a daughter to the Cao family, I didn't deserve a name there. That's simply how it was.

I was very mad and offended by not being included in the family book. How can that be "common knowledge" and acceptable today? Maybe that was the way accepted thousands and hundreds of years ago, but I can't accept it now. We are living in a modern age when women can contribute to society the same way as men, and equality is a basic right to us.

I am part of the Cao family, and my next generation must know they came from the Cao family as well. I was determined to fix this and become the first woman who is "rooted" in the book so that generations after mine could be recorded as well. I asked Dad to make a trip to the Cao village and provide very convincing points to have them add my name and my kids' names to that book. My points were: First, I am a very accomplished woman who has earned a PhD and am very successful professionally. Secondly, I married an American, who doesn't have a Chinese family name—which means my sons are carrying mine. They will forever carry the Cao family name forward. Lastly, I told Dad that if the village disapproved, I would set up a fund to buy the publishing rights of that book and insert my name in. If that's what it took, I was prepared to do it. I am passionate that women's names must appear in that book and be "rooted" with their own branch, from here forward.

A few years later, after Dad was able to make that trip back to Cao village again, I got my name, my husband's name, and my kids' names printed in that book. Dad was very happy that I became the first woman in the family who was "rooted," meaning my boys' names are listed with my rooted name, and the family tree goes on. The first revision of the book that he brought to me has a glued-on column that has our names added; it was before they were able to make a final printed version. Years later, Dad brought to me a well-printed book that contained the branch of Dad's family tree. There it was: my name and my whole family's names in formal print.

I am proud that I broke the rule that lasted for thousands of years. I know that even if I had stayed in China and married a Chinese man, I would still fight for my right to be included in a family book. Why? One simple reason: women can bring family glory just as much as men can, and we should have equal rights for our legacies to be seen, recorded, and passed down to future generations.

10.6. HERITAGE AND FAMILY VALUES

Both of my parents had a relentless drive to survive and thrive. They made the best of every circumstance they found themselves in, always looking for ways to improve themselves and our opportunities as a family. They stood deeply rooted in their families' heritage while making critical sacrifices to build a better future for all of us. Through it all, they supported each other in achieving their goals.

As I start learning more about my own heritage, my roots grow deeper to the ground. I feel myself growing like a tree. I may look tiny, tilted, and fragile from the outside. Any strong wind blowing might seem as though it would take me down and destroy me. However, with my deep roots, I grasp so strongly into the ground that no wind—just like no challenge or problem—can ever wipe me out. If a fire burned me down, the next fall, I would just grow back out again from my roots. My roots made me invincible, and it's a very powerful feeling that allows me to operate from a place of sturdiness and calm, even when times are difficult.

I treasure my heritage tremendously, for it's my fuel, my shield, and my strength—and the guiding star always points me in the right direction. I respect everyone else's heritage as well, for that's what makes this world so wonderful. We are all different, yet we are all very similar in many ways. Through everyone's heritage stories, no matter what race, gender, location, and time they are from, all I see is humanity. All the stories passed down from generation to generation have similar essential human virtues in them: wisdom, justice, fortitude, temperance, love, and so on. If only everyone in the world would realize that, hatred would fade away and peace and harmony would flourish.

My heritage became the family values I learned growing up. Those values became pillars of my own identity as a Cao. Through my family values, I see this world.

Self-reliance: I stand on my own feet, hold an independent soul, and make my own choices. I follow my individual will instead of conforming to social expectations. I focus on my internal compass rather than external praise or ridicule. I know who I am and where I came from.

Self-respect: I have my firm values in integrity and honesty and live true to them. I know my strength and am confident in what I do. I accept my weaknesses and know how to work around them. I don't look down on people, and I don't look up to people: I meet everyone at eye level. Regardless of status or background, I extend the same respect I have for myself to every person I meet.

Self-love: I love myself, which also allows me to love my family, friends, and the world more fully. I love myself regardless of my failures and successes. Self-love inspires me to take care of myself, physically, mentally, and emotionally.

Self-improvement: I work for what I want and persevere through difficulties. I focus on working on improving myself, rather than comparing myself to others. I value personal and professional growth achieved through effort and determination.

When interacting with others and dealing with the world, I can hear my parents' admonitions: stay positive, work hard, be honest, be kind, and be humble.

Stay Positive—
Remain Hopeful and Don't Give Up

When things are getting tough and hardship occurs, I never see my parents yield and give up. They always remain positive and hopeful, while trying to figure out every possible way to remove obstacles in front of them. During famine years in 1960, Dad remained hopeful and believed that "this too shall pass." He led others to grow lotus roots together for the next year to get more food, instead of quitting school. During 1993 when Dad started his own company, we lost our home and had to move several times a year to survive in the city. Mom and Dad kept smiles on their faces and believed that our family would get back on our feet again, and we did that together with huge success. There is always hope in any circumstance. If you don't give up, you are not losing.

Work Hard—
Grit Your Teeth and Don't Complain

Both of my parents have worked hard their entire life. Even during their retirement, they live a very active life; they never stop learning and growing. During the many years our family was apart, Dad had to stay in the mountains with harsh weather for months to accomplish the mission, battling the elements. Mom had to hold down a full-time job, raising two kids alone, and still used every bit of her time and resources to complete a college degree at the same time. They kept working hard and developing themselves for better opportunities. They prepared in every way they could to set me and my brother up for success. Their work ethic and mission-driven approach has impacted me significantly. During the hardest times in my life, I learned to lower my head, grit my teeth, dig deep, and never waste time complaining.

Be Honest–
Keep Your Integrity and Don't Take Shortcuts

Dad often says that if we are not honest and we take shortcuts in life, the consequences will always eventually get to us. Mom got removed from her CPA job during her career because she wouldn't cheat on the books to help the authorities. She doesn't regret her decision. She said, "I must be able to sleep at night, knowing I was honest." During high school, I tried once to cheat on my score by comparing my responses to a classmate's. In the end, I got the worst score ever for that year, and I carry the guilt from that dishonest act to this day. Being honest and relying on my own work often takes longer and requires more effort, but it's worthwhile so that I can always look at myself in the mirror.

Be Kind–
Act with Gratitude and Don't Take Advantage of People

Mom and Dad taught me to approach relationships by asking myself what I could contribute rather than what I could get out of the other person for myself. My parents are a living example of helping others without expecting anything in return—not because they felt obligated but because they lived through many struggles of their own. Relationships are not transactions, and the Cao family doesn't keep a tab on who's up or down. We give for the joy of giving, and we extend kindness to others because we're all struggling in some way and need a family and a community that has our back.

Be Humble—
Provide Value and Don't Be a Peacock

One day, I'd come home after dying my jet-black hair a lighter brown, as was the fashion in China at the time. Dad wasted no time telling me exactly how he felt about it. "Libo, you're a student! What is a student supposed to do? Study! Not spend time and money on your appearance. You're not a peacock! Don't use your appearance to beg for attention." Dad instilled in me a focus on substance rather than appearance, on garnering attention through my work rather than my looks. Dad insisted that I dye my hair back to black as an outward symbol of my inward dedication to what mattered in our family: substance over appearance, humility over conceit. Cultivating a quiet humility and inner strength that is unaffected by outside validation is the foundation for a strong sense of self.

Even though my heritage and family values gave me strong foundations to build on, it has taken me an entire lifetime to become myself, and I'm still becoming.

11.

CONCLUSIONS

"There is only one heroism in the world:
to see the world as it is and to love it."

–Romain Rolland, winner of the Nobel Prize in Literature

Our world is full of hope and despair,
bravery and fear, success and failure, excitement and
indifference, harmony and discord. To be able to navigate those
realities while sustaining one's inner peace requires courage
and a huge amount of cognitive understanding.
We all need our own guiding stars that can offer direction
in this life, philosophically and spiritually.

I here share my guiding stars with you: dealing with disability,
building perseverance, and viewing success.

Disability allowed me to see through our physical differences
and build compassion for others; perseverance is how I handle
challenges in this world, with confidence; successes are milestones of
personal growth, which fuel me to keep limping forward.

I hope you, too, can find the guiding stars that you
can follow to love and live this amazing life!

11.1. ABOUT DISABILITY

The world has made great progress to protect the rights of people with disabilities in the last couple of decades, but a lot more needs to be done for many decades to come.

Based on the United Nations organization, at present, there are more than 7 billion people in the world. More than 1 billion of them, or about 15 percent of the total population, have some form of disability. Eighty percent of them live in developing countries.[27] In the United States, according to the Centers of Disease Control and Prevention, 26 percent of the population (61 million) have some type of disability.[28]

The Convention on the Rights of Persons with Disabilities, with its Optional Protocol, was only adopted on December 13, 2006, and was opened for signature on March 30, 2007. It is the first international legal instrument to systematically protect the rights of persons with disabilities, and it has been signed by 164 countries and ratified by 185 countries by May 2022.[29] China's Standing Committee of the National People's Congress ratified the "Convention" in June 2008, and in September of the same year, the "Convention" entered into force in China. In 2012, the head of the Chinese delegation and secretary—general of the State Council's Committee on the Rights of Persons with Disabilities—pointed out that

---

[27] "Background, International Day of Persons with Disabilities, 3 December," United Nations, accessed February 14, 2023, https://www.un.org/en/observances/day-of-persons-with -disabilities/background.

[28] "Disability Impacts All of Us," Centers for Disease Control and Prevention, last reviewed January 5, 2023, https://www.cdc.gov/ncbddd/disabilityandhealth/infographic-disability -impacts-all.html.

[29] "Convention on the Rights of Persons with Disabilities (CRPD)," United Nations, accessed February 14, 2023, https://www.un.org/development/desa/disabilities/convention-on-the -rights-of-persons-with-disabilities.html.

China has more than 85 million disabled people, making it the developing country with the largest number of disabled people in the world.

Despite all that progress, we still have a long way to go. Not only should the rights of persons with disabilities be protected, but also, the acceptance and presence of the disabled community should be improved. We just learned that more than a billion people in the world have some sort of disability. Where are they, though? Statistically, one in every four Americans have a disability, and yet only about 3 percent of characters on screen are disabled. Even that number is a record high that only began in the last three years.[30] Children's television representation is even worse at less than 1 percent.

People with disabilities need to be represented more. Growing up, I met a few other people with disabilities in school, then they disappeared. They either dropped out from school, hid somewhere, or began working in a place that nobody would see them. In college and graduate school, I met only a couple of people with physical disabilities; at work, I can count them all with my fingers and toes. How is it that I rarely see people with physical disabilities represented on the stage or showing up in the media? Is it because of the belief that it was for our "own good" that we disappeared mostly from society, or is something significantly wrong with how we think of or see people with disabilities? I fought my way to a place where the world could see me if I chose to let it. However, most of those billion people still live in darkness and silence somewhere. It took me twenty-eight years to gain the courage and walk confidently in front of people with my limp, and that's because I was already embraced by love and care from everyone

---

30   Julia Stoll, "Broadcast Representation of Characters with Disabilities in the U.S. 2010–2022," Statista, March 1, 2022, https://www.statista.com/statistics/698132/tv-characters-with-disabilities/.

around me. I can't imagine how long it would take for someone to thrive with disabilities without that much-needed support system.

Where do we go from here, then? I advocate that people who have a stage or platform speak up more for the disability community. People with disabilities shouldn't be outliers.

On the other side of acceptance is something insidious: discrimination. As a disabled immigrant Asian American woman, I have had to face this on several fronts—and this is not only true in the two countries I've lived in. I believe discrimination can happen anywhere, partially due to our human nature. As human beings, we form opinions of this world based on our history, culture, and limited perceptions to which we were exposed. To make our opinions of the world easier to form, we put labels on other humans (or things) for simpler cognitive recognition while navigating complexities. When those labels are biased due to either limited knowledge or our different beliefs, discrimination can be formed. In both countries I've lived in, there have been times I've experienced discrimination from people—either total strangers or those who barely knew me—for my status as a disabled person, an immigrant, an Asian, and a woman. Undeniably, those are all my labels as part of my identity, but the problem is that those labels are *all* people could see of me. If we let only a few labels define our whole identity, the world wouldn't be as interesting, would it? Believing that a few labels should define a person would make the following equation true:

$$Libo = Disabled + Immigrant + Asian + Woman$$

How ridiculous a world would that be? Because if this were true, then the left side of this equation could be replaced by hundreds of millions of people's names and still stay true, but "Libo" isn't equal to the other hundreds of millions of people who also have the four labels—they are part of me but not *all* of me.

The more we fully appreciate another individual as a whole, the less labels will be put on us. Growing up in China, I remember when I first got into middle school, some people were very friendly to me while others kept a distance and looked at me differently. As time passed, very quickly, almost everyone in my class became my friends and started protecting me or helping me. So much so that for the second and third years of middle school, anyone who ran into me on the way to school in the morning would grab my bag and carry it for me. I've experienced extreme warmth from those around me who got to know me. I once asked one of the boys in my class what made the difference for him between keeping his distance from me and becoming a friend who treated me equally.

His answer?

"Well, when I first met you, I saw you as someone with polio. I noticed you were different from me. But after we got to know each other, I knew you as just Libo, and I like you as a friend. Your polio meant nothing to me, and I often forgot that you even had it. Remember that time I asked you to help me carry something heavy?"

I thought his answer had so much wisdom in it. Before he knew me, I was labeled as "someone with polio." But after he knew me, I became Libo, my own identity with my own characters and traits. That's how labels work: the more you get to know another human being, the fewer labels they start to carry with them. What replaced those old labels that include disability, looks, race, age, family status, etc. became more about character instead.

Unlike the obvious bullies I dealt with growing up, in adulthood, people's reactions to my disability have become more subtle. I am not even sure if that certain reaction can be called discrimination; it's something I just can't pinpoint. For example, there is one person I have interacted with for many years, and it happens that we frequently have to walk just a few minutes to the same destination. However, each time, he walks quickly past me—even if that means he must wait for me at the destination to get our activity started together anyway. Another friend who is from the same group, however, would always slow down and walk with me, matching my pace. Not only that, but when I spoke to him while walking, he'd lean his body toward me and tilt his head to listen to me (he was much taller than I). For many years, the one who slowed down for me became a friend, and we shared many fun moments while walking together... even if each time was just a few minutes. The one who didn't want to walk with me lost many of those moments when we could have built a better relationship. Both people are great, and I respect them both highly. However, I built a friendship with the one who slowed down for me, and I've never asked why the other person wouldn't walk with me. It's his choice. Whatever his reasons are, I respect them. I wish, though, that people would choose to walk a bit slower with company like me, instead of just passing by.

When it comes to immigrants, discrimination coupled with hatred can be pretty intense. During my time at Ohio University, I heard some international students—while just walking on the street—got blood poured on them from a car passing by. This act was later identified as a hate crime. Many years later, while I was just stopped at a red light in LA, a truck passed by me very quickly. As it did, the driver put his fist out and yelled, "Get the f*ck back to your country!" It happened so fast, and I really had no time to process it—not that I would've known how to respond in the first place. What I *do* know clearly is that I've earned my right to stay in this country—through huge effort instead of it being granted by default. Do I need to justify it to those random strangers though? Strangers who, at the end of the day, also likely descended from immigrants from other countries (maybe just earlier and several generations ago) and forgot about it?

I am not a domain expert in disability nor discrimination, and I don't want to represent anyone else other than myself. However, as someone who has been living with a disability and has dealt with discrimination, what I want is for people to treat me equally just like everyone else. I may be impaired from a mobility standpoint and need facilities or instruments to help me move better sometimes, but none of those change who I am, what I believe, or how I live my life. The assistance we require might be part of our identities, but it shouldn't define us entirely.

Due to my disability, accessibility is very dear to my heart, and I will continue to advocate to make this world a much more accessible place. On my first trip traveling abroad with heavy luggage in 2000, for example, I realized how privileged I was, even with my limited mobility. In some places, I struggled to climb stairs while dragging heavy suitcases along with me. It was at that moment that, for the first time, I realized people with wheelchairs couldn't make that trip on their own without having access to elevators. I was lucky to have one leg that could climb stairs, and I have eyes to see and a voice to communicate for my trip. How can people with less fortunate disabilities succeed when society doesn't provide the basic means for them to succeed?

I would encourage all architects to always validate their design by using a wheelchair to get from any random point A to point B. It would also be useful to blindfold themselves to see if a visually impaired person could traverse the same path easily. By doing so, they would unleash so much potential for those who needed it. I am sure things have improved significantly in the last twenty-some years, but providing accessibility in infrastructure is often not the first priority, and we still have a long way to go.

We also need to provide basic medical needs for those who are struggling with sicknesses that are preventing them from reaching their full potential in life. To this day, I still think about the other eighty children in the village who got polio at the same time I did. Were they able to eventually reach their full potential and live a great life? Did they have all the support they needed from their loved ones and society for them to thrive? I also think often about my dear friend Dongmei from my childhood, who died likely from tuberculosis due to a poverty-induced lack of medical treatment. China has a traditional festival called the Qingming Festival, in which we sweep tombs or burn fake money or messages to the dead. If I burn this book as my message to Dongmei, would she be able to read my book? Does she still remember those lonely days when only she and I were left aside, watching other kids doing PE classes? Would she be able to write in heaven with a smile and think of me as well?

I feel a responsibility to help more people with disabilities succeed. In 2020, I joined the board of the nonprofit organization Hope Services, which focuses on providing services to people with developmental disabilities and mental health needs.[31] The vision of the organization deeply resonates with mine. Only when we create a powerful community are we able to achieve bigger goals together.

The journey of dealing with my disability is a story of self-resurrection, and my story is both unique and common. Over the course of my life, I have often felt like that little kid during PE again. Navigating the world with a disability has left me feeling cast aside, different, and lonely. Always at the edge of the circle, I felt like an onlooker, an observer in my own life at times. When I realized my greatest dreams and aspirations would

---

[31]   https://www.hopeservices.org.

be denied because of my disability, I was devastated. The desperation I felt at seemingly having no control over my life was all-consuming. I was dependent on the help of others. And while many were kind enough to help, some were not. And some with power tried to keep me small, keep me quiet, keep me weak. But when the desperation turned into ambition, I could channel it. I learned how to become an advocate for myself. The fear of being barred from living the life I imagined mobilized energy stores I never thought I had. Slowly, over decades, I built my confidence. It was a painful road, dotted with sleepless nights and hours crying alone. I built confidence in my skills despite people telling me to give up, confidence in my body despite people judging me as inadequate and incapable, and confidence in my value despite some people dismissing me personally and professionally at times.

I am living this life with confidence, signing up for anything that brings great experience, and I *will* get that black belt in karate someday.

I don't doubt my capabilities anymore. I just give my best effort in anything I want to achieve, without hesitation or reservation. I want you to go live the heck out of this life as well: lift up your head with confidence, march and leap forward with all you've got, and live your life with meaning —until your last breath.

11.2. ABOUT PERSEVERANCE

The perseverance that ran in my parents' veins, their parents' veins, and their parents' veins also runs in mine. Cao, my family's storied surname, has been woven into the rich fabric of China's history for thousands of years. These dreamers and fighters are my role models. I am in awe of their strength and tenacity. They fought for a place to live, survived famines, endured civil wars, and sought every opportunity to create a better life for the generations to come.

Ultimately, they gave me the start in life that has led me to where I am today. And while I will never know all my ancestors personally, the Cao family values have been passed down through my father to me. In those values, I understand this world better over time, by observing those around me. I've built a certain set of characteristics that make perseverance a natural attribute in my own DNA. Some of my friends have asked where I get my drive and motivation from, so I would like to share a bit of what perseverance looks like for me (with the goal that, maybe, it will help *you* in the process).

Life May Not Be Fair, but Nobody's Life Is Easy

Have you ever reached a point where you felt like your life was just too hard to keep going? I've felt the same way before. Then, I discovered that everyone has some degree of hardship in their life. While some may have more material means than others (which certainly comes with its own set of privileges and financial ease), I believe I can see the hardship in everyone's life. You never know what someone is going through just by looking at them.

One summer break during my college years, I decided to lock myself up alone in a condo for several months to prepare for my graduate entrance exam. Every day, I got up around 5:00 a.m. to study, taking only short breaks to eat and walk around the room. I did this until well after midnight. I repeated that life daily in laser-sharp mode, without any interference from the outside world. At that time in my life, I thought I'd had it rough growing up with polio and that life hadn't been all that kind to me in the grand scheme of things.

Then, one night, I couldn't fall asleep and decided to walk the street around 3:00 a.m. I thought nobody would be out during that hour and the loneliness would be all mine. Surprisingly, I saw many people on the street during my walk. I realized at that moment that I wasn't alone, at least not in Dalian, China, that morning in 1998. I saw workers sweeping the street to get the city ready before everyone else got up. I saw some people walking with their briefcases and bags, either just getting off from work or beginning their days. I saw a mom with a baby strapped on her shoulder, setting up her morning breakfast stand and cooking on the side of the street.

Suddenly, I realized life is hard for *everyone*, as long as you start noticing it. Compared to those people I saw on the street at 3:00 a.m. in Dalian, I was the lucky one. I only needed to focus on one thing in life: to study and fight for my own future. But everyone else I saw that morning, not only were they living hard for themselves, but they also had bills to pay and family duties to fulfill. They didn't have the luxury to walk on the street aimlessly like me at all hours of the morning.

Though I'm not a religious person, I suddenly understood the meaning of the *Truth of Suffering* in Buddhism: that is, that all living beings are suffering.[32] Whether they are living in the heavens, roaming the Earth, or residing in hell, suffering is universal. Through my own realization, I believe our sufferings are not equal when compared through a subjective lens as a third-party observer. However, I also believe our sufferings *are* equal in some ways when looking through our *own* lens, since they are equally real and painful to ourselves.

---

[32] Joshua J. Mark, "Four Noble Truths, Definition," *World History Encyclopedia*, July 22, 2021, https://www.worldhistory.org/Four_Noble_Truths/.

I made a friend at my first job when I started working in Silicon Valley: Irina, a beautiful woman from Ukraine. Every day, she came to work with flawless makeup, an elegant dress, and high heels. We were so different in many ways. I joked with her that if we were all made by God, she must have been made in the morning when God was in a good mood, full of creativity, and I must've been created hours later when God just wanted to eagerly go home for the day.

Beauty aside, what made us great friends was her upbeat attitude toward life. She was always positive, carried her smile around, had a great work ethic, and kept learning new things. I always thought life had been very kind to her until I found out that she had her mother and daughter at home, both of whom relied solely on her to support. She'd been a victim of domestic violence and suffered through a nasty divorce. During the worst time of her life, she had to live in a homeless shelter with her mother and daughter. While staying there, she took on training to learn more skills, applied for jobs, and was eventually able to get her family out of that shelter. She bought her family a house all by herself, and she started investing in real estate. We spent a lot of time during those years talking about cash-flow real estate, and she was dreaming of buying at least ten houses, making great rent, then retiring early. She'd spend almost all her weekends hunting for investment houses or fixing them with her own hands. She ended up retiring in her early fifties with eleven investment houses providing consistent income. Her daughter went to a great university, and Irina took care of her mom while doing other activities like painting, writing, acting in shows, and traveling around the world.

Each time Irina and I get together, we can talk for hours (or even the whole night if we want to) without running out of things to talk about. We love each other because neither of us ever just complain about life when hardship happens. We acknowledge the challenges, we identify what we want, we come up with ways to achieve them, and we work tirelessly to make our dreams reality. I hope we can all learn something from Irina, the beautiful and elegant Ukrainian woman who took life into her own hands and lived life the way she wanted to be.

I hope this story and my example illustrate one main point: though the degrees of suffering vary, life is not easy for anyone. You may not see the suffering of others on the surface, but it's as real to them as yours is to you—and that's fairness on its own.

This Life Is Yours and Yours Only, So Be Confident about It

Irina isn't the only friend I've learned from in this life. I'd be remiss not to mention Preshious, from whom I learned how to be confident—no matter what life brings.

Preshious and I met during our graduate school years in Ohio. She was outgoing and confident, and her excitement and warmth drew me in right away. She is a Black woman and the first in her family to attend college, she told me. We couldn't have looked more different from the outside, and I believed neither of us looked like any of the women on magazine covers. But still, she carried herself with a grace and confidence I had only dreamed of. Life wasn't kind to her at that time; she had to deal with a type of blood disease during those years, and many people persuaded her to give up graduate school. She didn't back off, though, and she persevered...ultimately earning her PhD in the end.

What really amazed me was her confidence, which put a natural, beautiful glow around her. I recall once when we were both traveling for a conference, and she and I stayed in the same hotel room. One night, she laid out beautiful lingerie on the bed and asked me to pick out one for her to wear when she met her boyfriend. I blushed and picked up the black one. She respectfully declined and said red brought her color out better. She put them on with a beautiful, short dress and stood in front of the mirror, checking out the finished look. I admired her from the side.

"I've never worn a short skirt before in my life," I told her. "Because I have one really ugly leg."

She recoiled, almost mad!

"You're kidding me!" she cried out. "You have a beautiful figure, and it's almost a crime that you've never put one of those on."

"What if people think my leg is too ugly to be seen?"

"Then f*ck 'em!"

We both started to laugh then. When we caught our breath, she demanded I say those words out loud so I could practice building the courage to not give a damn about how others might judge me. I followed her lead and cursed for the first time, loudly. When she then asked me to curse in Chinese to show that same attitude, I became nervous.

"No way. I can't curse in Chinese! My ancestors are watching, and they would know what I said."

But ever since then, whenever I've wanted to wear a short skirt, I've worn a short skirt.

Confidence takes many years to build, but sometimes we just need a moment or someone to flip that switch. Preshious flipped that switch for me. I start to realize that this life is *mine* and I should live it the way I feel like it. Limiting myself in others' views is only going to cause long-term damage because that limitation will start to occur in many other places.

If I have the bravery to tackle two graduate degrees at the same time and become the first person who ever accomplished that in the two hundred years of history of that university, I wondered, *how can I not have the courage to show my leg?* My right leg and foot are tiny, deformed, and with many scars left from all the surgeries I went through. But those can be powerful statements: I have stories, I've survived, I am confident, and I am proud of what I have conquered.

I can't stress how important building confidence is to one's success. A few years ago, I was talking to one of my colleagues (who is one of the most famous deep-learning experts in technology), and I asked him how he achieved such success in the deep-learning world. I loved machine learning and built many models throughout my career, but I couldn't devote decades of my career to focusing on such a domain in which nobody knew when and if the hardest problems would be solved. There was too much uncertainty in the science of deep learning.

His answer was "confidence." He said he believes his intuition was right and his talent was there to lead him to accomplish amazing things in that field.

If you lack that confidence that's needed for your future success, find the people or knowledge you need to build it. When an opportunity presents itself, without confidence, I used to ask, "Why me?" Now, I ask "Why *not* me?"

Trust the 1 Percent Rule, and Persevere Until Goals Are Met

The 1 percent rule states that if we are only 1 percent better every day, a year later, we will be 37.78 times better than a year ago. If we are 1 percent worse every day, a year later we will be only at 0.03 of our original capability. It's the same as Warren Buffett's philosophy on the power of compounding to accumulate wealth: "Life is like a snowball. The important thing is finding wet snow and a really long hill." I believed in this 1 percent rule at a very early stage of my life. Though back then I didn't know the theory or math behind it, I firmly believed that if every day I just did *a little bit* more, over time I would become better than others. That belief made me build the habits of improving myself little by little through tiny efforts.

My life, in fact, has been a series of multiple tiny progresses. At any given time, I usually pick just two extra things to do on top of all the things I do regularly—including a full-time career, two boys and a family to run, extended family duties, and all the other things that go with my roles and responsibilities in this world.

The two extra things I added to do include one that consumes my leftover brain power, and another that consumes my leftover physical energy. I have long believed that over time, those efforts would pay off in life somehow.

To improve my brain power, one year, I decided to read twelve difficult books that could improve my cognitive understanding of the world and leadership skills. I am still benefiting deeply from those books. One year, I decided to listen to at least one hundred TED Talks; one year, I took on a Stanford Executive Education program; one year, I took many online classes to gain deeper understanding and knowledge in a technical domain. For the last two years, I've dedicated my spare brain power to this book as well as editing Dad's book in Chinese.

To make myself physically fit and strong, I always have at least one goal per year to chase after. You've read that one year, I tackled the one-hundred-mile bike ride, which I started before even knowing how to ride a bike. But once I made that goal, I just aimed at it and made sure that every day, I got a bit better than the previous one by building a little more endurance with strength. One year, I did hot yoga almost weekly so that I could relax my back pain. After a while, my body became quite flexible and energetic.

One year, I set a goal to have ab lines like what we see on very fit people, so I spent at least thirty to forty-five mins a day doing weighted Hula Hoops. (With a proper diet, I got two very visible ab lines after about six months). I've also tried many other varieties of physical activity to keep myself healthy and energetic, and I've had fun with them.

What works for me might not work for you, but the point is that I took small, consistent action to keep my brain and body fueled over time, little by little. I believe those little efforts have contributed to my current goals in publishing this book and becoming a black belt in karate. I don't believe in incidental success. For example, what enabled me to say yes to my boys and sign up for karate was the confidence I'd gleaned from years of little efforts before that moment: my habits of doing yoga and stretching before bedtime made it easier to perform falling, rolling, and other moves; the muscles I built from strength training allowed me punch, chop, and spar in this sport; the endurance training allowed me to survive five-plus hours a week of intense workout sessions; my constant pace of an active lifestyle makes me still energetic enough to go to training at night after a long day of work and family duties. No effort is ever wasted. If you think it is, maybe it's just not time yet.

Perseverance is all about that persistent effort over time. If you trust the 1 percent rule, many goals in life won't be that intimidating. You just keep at it. Even if it takes years of effort, eventually you are likely to reach that goal. And even if you don't—even if you fail in the middle—as long as you don't give up, that failure can be just a small pause in your journey. Life is a marathon; the ones who win at the end are the ones who keep moving forward with everyday effort.

If you don't accumulate little steps, you can't go thousands of miles; if you don't accumulate small streams, you can't make a river (不积跬步, 无

以至千里；不积小流，无以成江海), said by the Chinese philosopher Xunzi (313 BC–238 BC).

But … There Are So Many "Buts" in Life

In my experience, the only person who could ever stop me is me. I've failed in many things in my life as well—for example, being good at cooking or gardening. However, when I look at those failures, almost all of them are because I didn't want them that much. I had my eyes on other prizes, which is completely normal.

I am not saying that life does not come with obstacles or that those obstacles are dispersed evenly among all people. Neither of those things is true.

However, if we allow obstacles to become excuses, we can talk ourselves out of achieving our goals. For instance, I have been thinking about writing a book for at least ten years, if not longer. I wrote little articles to accumulate content as well as private journals to ensure details were not forgotten. But it wasn't until late 2020 (during COVID-19) that I truly became determined to have this book written and published. So, I made a list of all my excuses and was able to cross most of them out, one by one.

"But I don't have time."

I found evidence on my cell phone screen time that every week, I spent at least five hours reading random news at night or on weekends, so I called bull***t on myself and decided that I would cut my random internet surfing time and work on this book instead.

"But I don't want to lose my privacy and the peaceful life I have right now."

I am a very private person, to the extent that the only social presence I have is LinkedIn. I've often found social media overwhelming and distracting.

In working on this project, I've wondered if it's worth the risk of exposing myself to the media with this book. To find the answer, I had to go back to fundamentals. If by telling my stories, I can influence even one person's life in any positive way, this is all worth it.

"But English is not my first language."

Next to that, I wrote, "Then hire a very good editor, or write in Chinese."

"But what if it's a terrible book?"

I crossed that out, too, and wrote: "Then try your best to make it worthwhile!"

After moving through my list of excuses, I tackled this project formally and seriously. I hired a professional team to help me build a comprehensive end-to-end plan. I followed their guidance to execute the various stages of a book accordingly. I dedicated all my Lazy Sundays to this book by meeting with my editor early in the morning to discuss content and editing work, then writing draft after draft afterward. I worked hard from Monday until Saturday so I could fulfill all my professional and family duties by the end of Saturday night. Every Lazy Sunday, I tried to tackle 1 percent of the project. After two years and about a hundred weekends, the manuscript was completed—without impacting my full-time professional career or my family life. The rest I will leave to this world to judge and decide. I will move on to my next mission in life, whatever that is.

For me, unless that "but" is a life-threatening disease that can kill me, there really are no buts. If we want something badly enough, we can give it a priority, put in enough effort, and let time alone work its magic. Our paths are undoubtedly different, but I believe this approach could work for you, too, if you're reading this. Anything is possible. Just get it started, and never let yourself be the limiting factor.

11.3. ABOUT SUCCESS

When I was a little girl growing up in that village in North China, away from my parents, success to me was to be able to buy bubble gum anytime I wanted, as much as I wanted. I dreamed of the day that I could just chew two pieces of bubble gum at the same time. Oh boy, *how successful would I be if that could be true?* I thought in my dreams.

After I started my journey in hospitals, success to me was to be able to run like other kids someday. I dreamed of the day that I could join others in PE class, instead of watching from the side. *I would run so fast that nobody can even catch me, and I would be running every day with those healthy legs!* I often thought to myself.

When I had to deal with my best friend, Dongmei's, death, that little me swore in tears: *Someday I will be so rich and successful that I won't let any of my loved ones die from poverty and sickness, ever!*

In my school years, success to me was becoming number one in class in every academic subject. That's the only way I knew how to reach the top. I often got devastated and would cry for the whole night if I ever ranked number two. *If I can't be the best academically, what am I?* For many dark nights, I was trying to find my own identity.

In college and graduate school, success to me was controlling my own destiny in life. *Someday I will be so successful that I can study whatever I want, whenever I want, and in whatever way I want!* Success at that time meant something bigger: equal opportunities.

Once I started to work, success meant being fully financially secure, while knowing I deserved to be at a place by showing my values. *Someday I will be able to live anywhere I want and work or not work for anyone I want!* Success meant freedom of choice.

Then life became a blur after I got all the freedom of choice in life—a life that would be considered successful in others' eyes. *What's the meaning of life, what have I been chasing after, and why am I so tired?* During that blurry state, success to me meant obtaining an inner balance, a serenity in my mind, and a feeling of being content in life.

Finally, after all these years, I've found that inner balance and peace. *Veni, vidi, vici (I came, I saw, I conquered).* At current stage, I define success this way:

Success is the *ability* to live the life you want and to reach any goal you set for yourself.

When I thought success was related to financial or social status, I misunderstood what success really was. Now I know how to *not* let other people become the judge of my own so-called success. In fact, I define success in a much more comprehensive way instead of leaving it limited to what people can see from the outside (wealth, influence, fame, etc.). Now I understand that success is an inner ability, not an outward status.

When I mistakenly believed success was an outward status, I was proving something to others and to the world. Smart little me had a chip on her shoulder (for good reasons), and I decided I would prove the world wrong. If I planned to participate in something, I would be the best. I would outwork and outperform everyone. I would not let anyone tell me how to live my life. All that ambition and anger turned into motivation and led me to some high mountain tops and achievements that I am proud of. And yet, being at war with myself and the world also plunged me into the deepest valleys. Knowing that and redeeming myself got me out of those valleys, along with the help of my loved ones who supported me. Love was a big element that led me to the level of clarity I have today. The love of my family and friends has saved me many times over. They loved me until I learned to love myself.

Only when you are truly able to look at yourself in the mirror at eye level can you realize that this world and this life is *yours*. It has nothing to do with others. It's always that inner belief and strength that gets you through the realization and influences how you keep moving forward. Others are only there to either help or destroy that belief in yourself. Those who truly love you will love you no matter what happens to you—success or failure. Those who don't love you won't really change how they feel about you—success or failure. They may just be around you more when you are successful and leave you when you are not.

If you have a goal in life and wish to succeed in it, I will share my three-step recipe for this journey:

Define What Success Looks Like to You, and Make Sure You Really Want It

Success should be defined solely by you. That definition should have clarity so you know where to focus.

When I did the century ride, my first goal was just to learn how to ride a bike. Once I conquered that goal, I'd tasted what success felt like already. My ultimate goal was to complete the hundred-mile ride, and I did mentally prepare for my failure in case I couldn't finish it. To me, success meant trying all my best and pushing my own limits. I'd decided it was OK for me to fail at something that I'd worked hard at, but it was not OK to fail because things became hard. In short, only you know if you tried your best, so only you can define that success.

Once you've defined your own success and have clarity in your head that proves you really want it, you are off to a good start to get your journey started.

Make a Comprehensive Plan, Execute with Priority, and Don't Give Up Easily

For everything I want to achieve in life, especially the hard goals, I've always made a very comprehensive plan for it. The plan is a tree structure with choices and decision points. Once you have exhausted all the possibilities for anything that could happen, then it's comprehensive enough. If I don't write it down, I have it comprehensively built up in my head. Building that decision tree can help you cover all the best-case scenarios and worst-case scenarios. It can even get to the point that it's impossible for you not to succeed.

For example, if I have a goal to set or break a world record, then I would start by examining how many ways people can break world records (like the Olympics, Guinness World Records, etc.).

For the Olympics, I could start by splitting the categories into Paralympic, where I may have an advantage in both the "impaired muscle power" and "leg length difference" groups. Then, I would split the tree branch into sports I could participate in. For each category of the sport, I would evaluate my advantages in age/gender groups to make sure I fully leverage my strength and avoid my weaknesses.

For the *Guinness Book of World Records*, there are far more options. The key would be to come up with a new category or find one to compete in. I am certain that if I try hard, there is a high possibility I could beat the "most socks sorted in thirty seconds" record, for example, which is only eighteen pairs as of Sept 2022.[33]

This shows that making a comprehensive list can help you build the confidence that you can conquer your goal, one way or another.

On your journey, don't forget to build or find the community that can help you get there. I have a strong belief that for anything you want to achieve in life, there is a person or a group in this world who wants to and can help you—you just need to find them. Many goals are easier to achieve as a group, especially those long-term goals. We will all go through ups and downs in life, but in a group, odds are that someone will be upbeat when you are down. And you can always return the favor when you bounce back from it! When you lift up everyone around you, they lift you up as well.

The rest is easy: give it a priority, execute, and don't give up. It's cliché, but it truly is just that simple.

Once You Succeed or Fail, Keep It in the Past, and Move On

If you do fail after you have already used up all the strength you had, then find a quiet time and place, take your heart out, sew it up, pat it gently, put it back, then either start it all over again or move on with your life without any regret. If you succeed, treat it as a rest stop, enjoy it, celebrate it, then forget about it and move on to your next goal.

Once you realize success is that internal ability and understanding that you can achieve any goal you set in life, you won't feel that sense of insecurity

---

[33] "Most Socks Sorted in 30 Seconds," Guinness World Records, accessed February 14, 2023, https://www.guinnessworldrecords.com/world-records/most-socks-sorted-in-30-seconds.

any longer. As I get older, I don't even feel insecure about my age. I cherish my wrinkles as much as my scars. I embrace my full self.

Besides being a Silicon Valley executive who still wants to change the world with technology, I can be much more. There is no rule book about what we must do in life. I hope you can imagine your own success, find what brings you joy, then just go charge at it.

May success be with you all, and may failures be without regret!

AFTERWORD

I hope reading my story made you feel less alone. Maybe you found yourself in some of my stories. Maybe you learned something about a person, a culture, or a life very different from yours.

I know the stories in my book could be twisted to fit a rags-to-riches cliché or some platitude about how anyone can achieve anything if only they work hard enough. I don't believe that for a second, but I also know we are much more capable than we give ourselves credit for.

My approach to goal-setting and creating the life I've wanted isn't a guarantee for success. There is more than one way to do things. What helped me more than sticking to the minute details of a specific process was truly getting to know myself. Only self-awareness can tell us what we need to do as individuals regardless of what others say. I'm committed to taking the best ideas, wherever they may come from, and applying them to my life. Some will stick, and some won't. But I will make that decision for myself, and I hope you will make that decision for yourself as well.

When I think of all the different versions of myself I have been, that now make up my whole self, I am grateful. So many of my challenges have turned into treasures of self-discovery and self-realization. I have no doubt about who I am at the moment. At the same time, I have no doubt that I will continue to evolve until my last breath.

This journey of life has many twists and turns. If, along your journey, you begin to doubt yourself, I want to share with you this ancient yet timeless wisdom that has given me so much peace:

The supreme good is like water,

which nourishes all of creation,

without trying to compete with it.

It gathers in the low places unpopular with men.

Thus it is like the Tao.

Live in accordance with the nature of things.

In dwelling, live close to the ground.

In thinking, keep to the simple.

In dealing with others, be fair and generous.

In governing, do not try to control.

In work, do what you enjoy.

In family life, be completely present.

When you are content to be simply yourself,

and don't compare or compete,

everybody will respect you.

One who lives in accordance with nature

does not go against the way of things.

Who moves in harmony with the present moment,

always knowing the truth of just what to do.

—*Tao Te Ching*, Chapter 8, Laozi (around 400 BC)

Water is the representation of how I strive to live now. For so many years, I struggled with the question of whether I was good enough, always hoping other people would tell me that I was. Now, in my forties, I realize that I have always been enough. I see it now. I feel it in my bones. I am not perfect and never will be. But I am good, and I am enough.

And so are you.

ACKNOWLEDGMENTS

For the motivation and inspiration that got me to write this book, I dedicate this book to my closest friend during childhood, Dongmei, who died at age eleven from illness and poverty. She couldn't achieve her dream of becoming a writer. She gave me the strength to fight for chances to reach my own potential in this life, no matter how hard the journey is and no matter how many scars and bruises I've accumulated. Whenever it seems that I have lost all the strength in my body, I just tell myself that if I am still breathing, there is no reason for me to stop limping forward.

For all the love I've received that I can never repay, I thank everyone in the Cao family and the Meyers family who has supported me wholeheartedly. I hope you are all proud of me and this book.

For being great friends and reading the manuscript in its early stages to provide initial feedback, I would like to thank: Xiaoyun Huang, Hongmei Li, Guoxiang Chen, Lisa Zou, Irina Nanna, Charlotte and George Rogers, Fey Datu-Cocchi, Ean Houts, Matthew Allen, Håkan Borglund, Preshious Rearden, Lupita Garcia-Reilley, and many more friends, all of whom I couldn't possibly list here. You are all in my heart.

For my growth in the world of technology, I owe my greatest gratitude to: Isabel Ge Mahe, Bob Mansfield, Kevin Lynch, Doug Field, Mike Abbott, Mary Demby, Rolf Toft, Dr. Jamen Graves, Puneet Mishra, Brian Smartt, Mike Tzamaloukas, Prof. Peter de B. Harrington, and Prof. Howard D. Dewald.

For making this book a reality and keeping it on track, I would like to thank the whole project team, including my editor, Jessica Burdg; cover designer, Michael Nagin; project managers, strategy lead, quality assurance team, layout team, and the marketing crews.

Finally, for bringing me into this world, being my role models, and filling me with overwhelming unconditional love, I owe the greatest debt that I can never repay to my mom and dad. Thank you for bringing me into this wonderful world and making me the woman I am today.

ABOUT THE AUTHOR

LIBO CAO MEYERS is an accomplished engineering executive who has been with Apple since 2011. With a passion for enriching people's lives, she serves on multiple boards and is dedicated to creating innovative products and meaningful services that help individuals reach their full potential.

Despite being diagnosed with polio as an infant while growing up in rural parts of Northern China, Libo Cao Meyers refused to let her disability hold her back. At the age of twenty-four, she immigrated alone to the United States and achieved an incredible feat by completing her MS and PhD simultaneously in two different engineering fields from Ohio University within four years. Her tech profession began in Silicon Valley in early 2004, where she has thrived in the culture of innovation ever since.

Libo's determination to push through limitations extends beyond her academic and professional life. She completed a one-hundred-mile bike ride, battling wind for eleven and a half hours, and is pursuing a black belt in Karate to lead her young sons by example. Additionally, she is learning to use an exoskeleton to play various sports with polio, demonstrating her commitment to defying physical limitations.

Of all Libo has accomplished, she is most proud of her family, including the deep roots of the Cao family from China with 3,000 years of history. Libo lives in California with her husband and their two sons. For more information, please visit her website at www.libomeyers.com.

CPSIA information can be obtained
at www.ICGtesting.com
Printed in the USA
LVHW042054190723
752484LV00011B/454/J